Silver Empowerment

Fostering Strengths and Connections for an Age-Friendly Society

SILVER EMPOWERMENT

Fostering Strengths and Connections
for an Age-Friendly Society

Edited by
Jasper De Witte & Tine Van Regenmortel

LEUVEN UNIVERSITY PRESS

The publication of this work was supported by
HIVA – KU Leuven, be.Source and the KU Leuven Fund for Fair Open Access.

KU LEUVEN HIVA

RESEARCH INSTITUTE FOR
WORK AND SOCIETY

be.Source
A SOURCE OF SOLIDARITY

Published in 2023 by Leuven University Press/Presses Universitaires de Louvain/Universi-
taire Pers Leuven. Minderbroedersstraat 4, B-3000 Leuven (Belgium).

CC BY NC ND

ISBN 978 94 6270 364 3 (Paperback)
ISBN 978 94 6166 507 2 (ePDF)
ISBN 978 94 6166 508 9 (ePUB)
https://doi.org/10.11116/9789461665072
D/2023/1869/10
NUR: 741

Cover design: Anton Lecock
Layout: Crius Group

GPRC
Guaranteed
Peer Reviewed
Content
www.gprc.be

TABLE OF CONTENTS

PREFACE

Brussels, 6 November 2022

In recent years, the theme of ageing has increasingly gained attention in the public debate. Politicians and economists have become particularly aware of the increasing number of older persons in the world.

On the International Day of Older Persons, 1 October 2022, the Secretary-General of the United Nations António Guterres mentioned in his message the following:

> On this International Day of Older Persons, we focus attention on the resilience of the more than one billion older women and men in a changing world. The past years have witnessed dramatic upheavals – and older people often found themselves at the epicenter of crises. They are particularly vulnerable to a range of challenges, including the COVID-19 pandemic, the worsening climate crisis, proliferating conflicts, and growing poverty. Yet in the face of these threats, older people have inspired us with their remarkable resilience. By 2030, 1.4 billion people will be at least 60 years old. Our task as societies and as the global community is to address the challenges of longevity – and unleash its potential. We must promote the social, economic, and political inclusion of all people at all ages. This pledge is enshrined in the Sustainable Development Goals. Lifelong learning, strong social protection, accessible quality long-term health care, bridging the digital divide, intergenerational support, dignity and respect are essential. Older persons are a tremendous source of knowledge and experience. We must strive to ensure their active engagement, full participation, and essential contributions to our societies. Together, let us build more inclusive and age-friendly societies and a more resilient world (Guterres, 1 October 2022).

More than a decade ago, be.Source, a private foundation, took the initiative to promote the quality of life of vulnerable senior citizens by helping them to access a certain art of living and fostering their empowerment to enable them to enhance their participation in the community in which they live. Improving their quality of life by focusing on the social aspects helps maintain their dignity. This is the main goal of the be.Source foundation.

be.Source supports local initiatives in Belgium that aim to improve the living conditions of underprivileged senior citizens. The be.Source private foundation notably created a 'hub', gathering thirteen partner non-profit associations – active in fields such as culture, socialising, mobility and recreation – that all strive to enhance the dignity of underprivileged older persons.

The be.Source foundation hub is a crossroads and meeting point to develop synergies and cooperation among the partner associations providing leverage for their individual achievements. The foundation focuses on underprivileged older persons along five strategic lines of action:
- mobility,
- recreational activities,
- cognitive decline,
- loneliness and
- intergenerational interactions.

We wish to change the way some people view older persons. They are repositories of knowledge and a source of family and social pride.

To enrich the hub with proper scientific standards, a university chair named *Empowerment of Underprivileged Elderly* was commissioned in 2017 by the be.Source foundation at the KU Leuven under the direction of Professor Tine Van Regenmortel with the cooperation of Dr Jasper De Witte. The HIVA (Research Institute for Work and Society) at KU Leuven was determined to be a suitable partner to conduct these studies in cooperation with our hub.

This publication is the result of their research realised in complete independence. The basic assumption of the research was that older persons themselves are the best experts to define their own needs and concerns – in short, they deserve their own empowerment.

We hope that the investigations published in this monograph under the title *Silver Empowerment: Fostering Strengths and Connections for an Age-Friendly Society* will benefit all actors in the sector of caregiving to vulnerable older persons. The research offers a multidisciplinary approach based on the joint reflections of several eminent scientists.

We wish you pleasant and inspiring reading.

Prince Henri d'Arenberg
Founder and President of be.Source   Daniel van Steenberghe
a private foundation under Belgian law   Vice President

References

Guterres, A. (1 October 2022). *Secretar-General's message on the International Day of Older Persons.* United Nations. https://www.un.org/sg/en/content/sg/statement/2022-10-01/secretary-generals-message-the-international-day-of-older-persons-scroll-down-for-french-version

AN INTRODUCTION TO SILVER EMPOWERMENT

Jasper De Witte & Tine Van Regenmortel

The concept 'Silver Empowerment'

With the introduction of the concept 'Silver Empowerment', we would like to express our vision on older people. In the psychology of colours, silver represents reflection and illumination, opening new doors, a change of direction for the future. Silver is also associated with characteristics such as calmness, sensitivity and looking for the best in others (Scott-Kemmis, n.d.). 'Silver Empowerment' aims to counteract the dominant image of ageing, which is all too often one of decline, loss, dependency and vulnerability. This 'ageism' image is problematic because the way we think about ageing influences the way we deal and socialise with older persons. When we consider older persons as unproductive members of society who are unable to participate, we also consciously – or not – exclude them from participating. With a fresh silver image, we want to move away from the dominant grey image of older persons as dependent, passive citizens.

'Silver Empowerment' strives to provide opportunities for each person to grow old with dignity and meaning, warmly connected to a society that invites them to participate. In contrast to the World Health Organization's concept of 'active ageing', which justly emphasises society's responsibility to provide opportunities for older persons to participate in social, political and economic activities (Foster & Walker, 2015), Silver Empowerment does not overlook realities of social inequality, vulnerability and disadvantage, nor does it impose a singular ideal of how older people should live. Instead, Silver Empowerment seeks to expand meaningful choices through which older people can maximally gain mastery over their own lives.

Unfortunately, to this day too much is done *for* older persons, and too little is done *by* and *with* older persons. Therefore, Silver Empowerment emphasises the need to appeal more to the strengths and capacities of older persons, without neglecting their vulnerabilities. According to the empowerment paradigm, people gain strength and grow through connections, and inversely strength results in more connections. Indeed, research has repeatedly shown that social relations and connectedness to others reinforces the resilience of older persons (De Witte & Van Regenmortel, 2019a; Burholt et al., 2020) by giving them information and instrumental support, encouraging coping behaviour and enhancing self-esteem. Resilience in turn contributes to a general sense of mastery and enables older people to overcome adversities and safeguard their well-being (Janssen et al., 2012). Indeed, people need sufficient strength and resilience, for example in the form of social capacities and skills, to form steady social relations and feel connected to others. In this respect, a sense of connectedness and the fulfilment of social needs (i.e. the basic human need for love, acceptance and belonging) strongly relate to the well-being of older persons (Ten Bruggencate et al., 2018), and when those needs are not fulfilled, feelings of loneliness may arise. Through this central duality of *strength* and *connection*, empowerment strives to improve the quality of life for older persons. The overall goal of empowerment is not to realise maximal independence. Instead, interdependence and relational empower-ment are core concepts in the lexicon of empowerment (Van Regenmortel, 2011). Indeed, a balance between individual independence, on the one hand, and connectedness with others, on the other, enables people to fully enjoy individual freedom but at the same time feel safe in the face of limitations and adversity, with which older people are more often confronted (De Witte & Van Regenmortel, 2020a). Together with others, older people can redirect their lives without losing their dignity and integrity (Abma & Bendien, 2019).

Further, what empowerment means in old age requires an in-depth inquiry of older people, their situation and biography, enriched by theoretical insights and professional knowledge. Therefore, we need to include the perspectives of older persons more in practice, policy and research. By including 'the insider perspective' of older persons, the so-called outsiders can gain more understanding of the lifeworld of older persons, which results in more com-prehension and a more positive image of the latter. Moreover, acknowledging the value of experiential knowledge of older persons forms an important source of strength for this group and is a key element of the empowerment paradigm. Practices and policy should not be developed for older persons, but together with them. No empowerment can exist without participation, without considering what is meaningful for older people. To accomplish this, we must create spaces for respectful dialogue and reciprocity that enables the empowerment of older persons. We call these spaces 'enabling niches'.

These enabling niches refer to 'safe havens', social spaces that offer resources and opportunities through which older persons can develop their skills and undertake meaningful interactions with others. Such spaces avoid stigma and define (older) persons as individuals who each have specific wishes, goals and characteristics. That way, older persons feel recognised and appreciated, and can grow by appealing to their strengths (Boone et al., 2020).

As a multilevel concept, empowerment upholds a relational picture of society where factors on the individual, organisational and community level are inherently interconnected. From this follows that the mechanisms of exclusion can also be found on all these levels, and that there is a *shared responsibility* for exclusion which needs to consider various domains such as social participation, housing, health and social care. That way, empowerment clearly contains a political component and moves away from the narrative of blaming the victim (and blaming the system). Indeed, individuals, organisations and the system all have agency within certain boundaries, and thus form part of the solution with respect to mechanisms of exclusion. Therefore, all stakeholders in society should contribute and counteract exclusion and ageism: older persons themselves, professionals, social organisations, academics and policymakers.

Silver Empowerment does not frame ageing and the ageing population as a problem, but rather sees it as a challenge opening new opportunities. By focusing on the strengths and connections of older persons, Silver Empowerment strives to realise an inclusive, warm and age-friendly society that gives older people a voice and influence. Too often this is not realised in practice. This book offers a different philosophy, a drastic shift in the way we look at the health and social care system for older persons and in how we look at ageing in general.

be.Source and HIVA – KU Leuven

be.Source, a private foundation that aims to improve the living conditions of vulnerable senior citizens, and the Research Institute for Work and Society (hereafter HIVA – KU Leuven), found each other in this vision of Silver Empowerment and the joint mission to stimulate a more positive image of older persons and to enhance solidarity in our society. Silver Empowerment focuses on a psychosocial strengthening process of older persons and shows that vulnerability and mastery can go hand in hand. Furthermore, it underlines the importance of solidarity between different generations to stimulate empowerment among older persons.

The private foundation be.Source commissioned the KU Leuven Chair Empowerment of Underprivileged Elderly to promote research about (vulnerable) older persons, and more specifically about psychosocial aspects affecting older persons (e.g. loneliness). The main research question of this university chair is as follows: how can we strengthen older people living in precarious circumstances and improve their connection to their surroundings and society so that they can experience a higher quality of life? Jasper De Witte and Tine Van Regenmortel (holder of the chair) conducted research about, with and for vulnerable older persons. In this respect, we participate with and give voice to professionals and the so-called silenced voices, vulnerable older persons themselves. Along with several research reports (De Witte & Van Regenmortel, 2019a, 2019b, 2020a, 2020b) and workshops, this book, *Silver Empowerment*, is part of this KU Leuven chair.

Structure of the book

This book discusses various ways to stimulate the empowerment of older persons in practice. We give the floor to eminent academics from a variety of backgrounds (among others psychology, sociology and economy), who each have specific expertise about social care and policy for older persons. Hereby, the authors focus on individual, social and structural processes of empowerment, while covering a wide range of subjects such as resilience, loneliness, the possibilities of neighbourhood-oriented care for empowerment, the interplay between formal and informal care, and the inclusion of older persons in research and care. Besides discussing the most recent scientific insights, the authors also explore the practical and policy implications of these insights and formulate – where possible – specific policy recommendations to stimulate empowerment.

We will now zoom in on the different contributions of this book. In the first chapter, Tine Van Regenmortel and Jasper De Witte describe the empowerment framework and discuss its implications for the older population. They emphasise that empowerment – with its focus on strengths, connections and resilience – is a useful way to counteract ageism and to stimulate participation. Indeed, just like any other age group, older persons can acquire a feeling of mastery and control, despite age-related vulnerabilities. In this regard, the authors point to the shared responsibility of all stakeholders to create *enabling niches* in which older persons can deploy themselves and realise empowerment. By appealing to the strengths of older persons and stimulating meaningful connections with their surroundings, the general resilience and quality of life of older persons will improve. This can be done by reinforcing their sources of strength on the individual, relational and structural level. The authors propose, for example, to stimulate *the power of giving* because doing things for other people (e.g. through volunteering, taking care of grandchildren) makes older persons feel better, useful and proud of themselves. Moreover, this often also has positive effects on their social network and society as a whole. Further, the authors underline the importance of strengthening community care and community building, and removing the structural barriers that impede older persons from participating, for example, by increasing access to healthcare, social services (e.g. psychological support) and public and individual transportation.

In the second chapter, Jozef Pacolet, Rodríguez Cabrero Gregorio and Simón Sosvilla Rovera discuss the *economic cost of loneliness* for older persons in Spain and Belgium. In this respect, they not only consider the direct cost of loneliness (e.g. on health expenditure such as hospital admissions) but also its indirect cost (e.g. a loss of economic activity, the need for more social support). Based on an extrapolation of the results from a Dutch study about the financial cost of loneliness on additional healthcare expenditures, the authors suggest that the additional cost of loneliness for healthcare for the total Belgian population could be approximately 3.2 billion euros, which is about 0.7 per cent of the gross domestic product. They also point to additional costs with regard to long-term care, the indirect costs of increased mortality rates and other cost dimensions (e.g. the dangers of providing informal care, for older persons with dementia). They estimate that the indirect cost of loneliness is roughly between 2 and 10 billion euros, depending on the monetary value that is given to life. In line with the empowerment paradigm, the authors stress that loneliness is a *shared responsibility* of individuals, public health and preventive policy, and the professional care sector and civil society.

In the third chapter, Jasper De Witte and Tine Van Regenmortel discuss the state of the art about one of the most important indicators for well-being of older persons – namely, feelings of loneliness. The relevance of this subject is not only demonstrated by the detrimental effects of loneliness on quality of life but also by the prevalence of loneliness, which increased significantly during the Covid-19 pandemic. Based on statistical data analyses, the authors first detect various groups of older persons that are disproportionately affected by feelings of loneliness and on which loneliness interventions could focus (e.g. women, people with a migration background, the *older* old). Subsequently, the authors discuss various factors that *explain* feelings of loneliness on the individual (e.g. health), relational (e.g. social network characteristics) and structural levels (e.g. culture). Based on these analyses, they conclude that loneliness is a complex phenomenon which comes in multiple forms, for which one-size-fits-all interventions do not exist. They stress the importance of creating a wide range of interventions that are tailored around the unique needs of the individual. The authors argue that empowerment is an effective framework that can guide the development of interventions that aim to prevent and alleviate feelings of loneliness among older persons. Indeed, empowerment's central focus on strength and connection is crucial for loneliness interventions because it enhances older persons' resilience and their possibilities to create a satisfying social network.

In the fourth chapter, Leen Heylen considers the potential and pitfalls of the policy concept *neighbourhood-oriented care* to enhance the well-being and empowerment of vulnerable older persons. Neighbourhood-oriented care puts the neighbourhood forward as the field of action for care and support, and it considers the community and civil society as key players. In line with the empowerment paradigm, it upholds a holistic, integrated and inclusive approach whereby the person is put central regardless of age. According to Heylen, a first opportunity of neighbourhood-oriented care is that it stresses that the place where people live matters for their well-being (e.g. proximity of services, green) and gives policymakers additional tools to empower older persons. Second, its inclusive approach (which focuses on people of all ages) counteracts ageism because it moves beyond the simplistic and stereotypical view of dependency in old age: it views older persons as in need of care but at the same time also as persons with control who can support other people in their neighbourhood. Third, this concept implicitly acknowledges the importance of so-called *weak ties*, the social cohesion between neighbours (e.g. regular contacts, a chat with a shopkeeper). Last, its transversal policy view adds to the well-being of older persons. However, Heylen also discusses various pitfalls, such as the fact that not all neighbourhoods are good environments to *age in place* and that nostalgia can be a misleading driver for putting policy into practice (because mutual support among neighbours has its limits). In addition, neighbourhood-oriented care can potentially reinforce inequalities among neighbours because the implicit focus on social networks and neighbours risks excluding those who lack these contacts. These pitfalls form the stepping stone for tackling many of the challenges associated with an ageing population and have the potential to contribute to the empowerment of older persons.

In the fifth chapter, Benedicte De Koker, Leen Heylen, Dimitri Mortelmans and Anja Declercq stress that the sustainability of the long-term care system requires adequately supporting informal caregivers by creating a strengthening environment and enhancing their resources so that they can be resilient and realise empowerment. Although formal support is one of the crucial elements for this, the *support paradox* shows that formal support does not always work. In this respect, the authors point to the importance of having a good connection and trust, recognising and valuing everyone's role in the 'care triad', and home-care policies sufficiently supporting and empowering informal caregivers. Further, the authors consider neighbourly support and citizen initiatives, two new forms that are (re)gaining importance as sources of informal care. Although these forms of care are worthwhile and have predominantly positive outcomes, there are also risks involved when they are relied on too much. Indeed, expectations must be realistic and feasible for those actors to have an empowering experience. We must also be aware of the risk of social exclusion because these types of care are generally more reserved for people who are well off. Further, the authors emphasise that their *bottom-up approach* does not match the top-down logic of formal care. Indeed, policymakers and professionals should not take over these bottom-up initiatives and try to professionalise them by adapting them into traditional structures, but rather respect their informal and often organic nature.

In the sixth chapter, Elena Bendien, Susan Woelders and Tineke Abma discuss some critical moments of (dis)empowerment during participatory action research with older persons as co-researchers. Participatory action research is based on an equal partnership among experts, researchers and end users in the process of creating knowledge, and it aims to strengthen the empowerment of the people involved in the research process. In this respect, the facilitator tries to create a *communicative space* in which all stakeholders feel encouraged, respected and supported to give their perspectives in order to generate knowledge. Based on an example of a participatory action research project with older volunteers in the Netherlands, the authors describe several *critical moments* in which the perspectives and underlying values of the people involved were conflicting, creating an impasse. If not dealt with correctly, those moments could have resulted in disempowerment and may have undermined the entire project. To avoid this, the authors conclude that researchers have a moral responsibility for *ethics work*, in which they act as reflexive practitioners who recognise ethically salient aspects by paying attention to emotions and relationships, and who work out the right course of action together with critical friends. That way, the *co-creation* of knowledge is empowering for everybody involved in this process.

In the seventh chapter, Meriam Janssen, Katrien Luijkx, Aukelien Scheffelaar and Annerieke Stoop emphasise that *person-centred care* requires that older persons are put at the centre of their own care and support. To realise this, the authors argue that older persons must be sufficiently included *in research*, as equivalent partners of researchers and care professionals. Indeed, it is crucial to gather sufficient data about the lifeworlds of older persons, as the most important and primary source. In this contribution, the authors give several examples of how the Academic Collaborative Center (ACC), a long-term and structural collaboration between science and practice at Tilburg University, contributes to person-centred care by giving a voice to older persons in research, and by gaining insight into their experiences, preferences and capabilities. Based on qualitative research methods, the ACC, for example, shows that although nursing home residents still value sexuality and intimacy as important in their lives, they deem that this cannot be satisfactorily experienced in the context of a nursing home because of various practical, emotional and communicational issues. Moreover, staff often experience and label sexual behaviour as a problem and do not feel equipped to empower residents in this life domain. By giving a voice to these nursing home residents, the ACC not only stimulates empowerment but also aims to improve the care. Further, this centre also structurally involves older persons as co-creators of new studies by stimulating them to think along and create a joint vision on their own roles and tasks within the research. It is not only the democratic right of older persons to be involved, but this also results in higher quality research and a better fit and usefulness of services.

In the eighth and final chapter, Katrien Steenssens, Tine Van Regenmortel and Jasper De Witte present the core guiding principles to develop, implement and evaluate empowering policies, practice and research. Apart from the central principle of strength in and through connection, these principles are termed *a positive stance, inclusiveness, participation* and *an integral perspective*. Using these interrelated guiding principles as touchstones during the process of development and implementation offers feedback about the extent to which this process can actually lead to empowerment. The discussion of the principles makes it clear that good intentions alone will not suffice to accomplish the intended empowering process of Silver Empowerment. One has to be willing to go the extra mile to maximally reach and involve all older people, pay attention to and develop all their strengths, and stimulate their mutual connections.

References

Abma, T., & Bendien, L. (2019). Autonomy in old age. *Family & Law*. https://doi.org/10.5553/FenR/.000040

Boone, K., Roets, G., & Roose, R. (2020). Enabling the recognition of people in poverty through social work practice. From being on a par to participating on a par. *European Journal of Social Work*, 23(5), 755–766. https://doi.org/10.1080/13691457.2019.1639626

Burholt, V., Winter, B., Aartsen, M., Constantinou, C., Dahlberg, L., Feliciano, V., De Jong Gierveld, J., Van Regenmortel, S., & Waldegrave, C. (2020). A critical review and development of a conceptual model of exclusion from social relations for older people. *European Journal of Ageing*, 17(1), 3–19. https://doi.org/10.1007/s10433-019-00506-0

De Witte, J., & Van Regenmortel, T. (2019a). *Silver Empowerment. Resilience of vulnerable elderly. A narrative research approach*. HIVA – KU Leuven. https://hiva.kuleuven.be/nl/nieuws/docs/tvr-18-tse-lssrc1-o2010-resilience-of-vulnerable.pdf

De Witte, J., & Van Regenmortel, T. (2019b). *Silver Empowerment. Loneliness and social isolation among elderly. An empowerment perspective*. HIVA – KU Leuven. https://hiva.kuleuven.be/nl/nieuws/docs/tvr-18-tse-lssrc1-o2010-loneliness-and-social.pdf

De Witte, J., & Van Regenmortel, T. (2020a). *Silver Empowerment. A quantitative picture of loneliness among elderly in Belgium and Europe*. HIVA – KU Leuven. https://hiva.kuleuven.be/nl/nieuws/docs/tvr-18-tse-lssrc1-o2010-loneliness-of-people-with.pdf

De Witte, J., & Van Regenmortel, T. (2020b). *Silver Empowerment. Family care for community-dwelling older seniors in times of corona: the power of giving and/or a burden of care?* HIVA – KU Leuven. https://hiva.kuleuven.be/nl/nieuws/docs/tvr-18-tse-lssrc1-o2010-informal-care.pdf

Foster, L., & Walker, A. (2015). Active and successful aging: A European policy perspective. *The Gerontologist*, 55(1), 83–90. https://doi.org/10.1093/geront/gnu028

Janssen, B. M., Abma, T. A., & Van Regenmortel, T. (2012). Maintaining mastery despite age related losses. The resilience narratives of two older women in need of long-term community care. *Journal of Aging Studies*, 26(3), 343–354. https://doi.org/10.1016/j.jaging.2012.03.003

Scott-Kemmis, J. (n.d.). *The Color Silver. The collor of illumination and reflection*. Empowered by color. https://www.empower-yourself-with-color-psychology.com/color-silver.html

Ten Bruggencate, T., Luijkx, K. G., & Sturm, J. (2018). Social needs of older people: a systematic literature review. *Ageing & Society*, 38(9), 1745–1770. https://doi.org/10.1017/S0144686X17000150

Van Regenmortel, T. (2011). Lexicon van empowerment. Marie Kamphuis-lezing [Lexicon of empowerment. Marie Kamphuis Lecture], Marie Kamphuis Stichting.

CHAPTER 1
AN EMPOWERMENT PERSPECTIVE ON OLDER PERSONS: THE POWER OF RESILIENCE

Tine Van Regenmortel & Jasper De Witte

Old age is all too often associated with dependency, passivity, unproductivity. These stereotypes influence how we feel about and deal with older persons. This 'ageism' can erode solidarity between generations and reduces the quality of life of older persons. In reality, older persons provide important social and economic contributions to society (such as looking after children or people who are ill). The World Health Organization (WHO) responded to this with its 'active ageing' concept: 'active ageing is the process of optimizing opportunities for health, participation and security in order to enhance quality of life as people age' (WHO, 2002, p. 12). In this respect, the WHO emphasises society's responsibility to provide these opportunities, for example by promoting a culture of lifelong learning for older persons. The WHO maintains that, through the regular involvement of older persons in social, political and economic activities, 'active ageing' can counteract social isolation and enhance an older person's quality of life. In response to the 2002 WHO strategy, scientific discussions on active ageing started to boom at the beginning of the 2000s (Pfaller & Schweda, 2019).

Active ageing is often criticised for idealising 'active' and 'successful' ageing, which is not feasible for all older persons and may be accompanied by adverse side effects. It is also criticised for overemphasising physical activity and a productive model of active ageing, and for not sufficiently taking into account the heterogeneity of the older population. Indeed, it is important to provide sufficient room for alternative lifestyles for older persons (Foster & Walker, 2015) and to deviate from a singular ideal of how older people should live (see Chapter 8 in this volume).

Besides objections regarding theoretical and empirical shortcomings, the most prominent line of critique focuses on moral and political concerns about exclusion at the intersection of age and social inequality. There are severe structural differences in the distribution of resources for successful and active ageing due to dimensions of social inequality (especially gender, ethnicity, class and sexuality). The effects of this social inequality unfold over the course of a person's life and culminate in old age. Moreover, with advancing age, older people are also increasingly exposed to ageism and age discrimination. Thus, already existing discrimination is further aggravated (Katz & Calasanti, 2015). Against this backdrop, Ranzijn criticises active ageing as 'another way to oppress marginalized and disadvantaged elders' (Ranzijn, 2010, p. 716), as the concept devalues their life experiences. He advocates alternative conceptions of ageing that are more sensitive to the cultural diversity of ageing and that promote social inclusion (Ranzijn, 2010, p. 716). The active ageing discourse takes for granted that older persons are willing and able to become active. As a result, the active ageing approach tends to neglect frailty and limitations. Empirical research conducted by Jensen and Skjøtt-Larsen (2021) shows that inequality in ageing is conditioned by factors such as class and wealth, in other words, factors rooted in the social life biography. In this sense, active ageing is idealistic and unrealistic, and the concept ignores the life situation of large segments of older persons since active ageing opportunities are conditioned by factors such as one's health and position in the social structure.

According to critical gerontology, the emphasis on personal responsibility functions as a mere alibi for dismantling the welfare state and shifting risks and costs to the individual. As a consequence, the attribution of responsibility is not accompanied by more agency (Emirbayer & Mische, 1998) and empowerment but only by the burden of negative consequences.

Therefore, we introduce the framework of empowerment for older persons, which takes into account these bottlenecks of the concept 'active ageing'. The empowerment framework focuses on the strengths and potential of older persons, without neglecting their vulnerabilities and experiences of loss in the process. In fact, it is precisely out of a fundamental recognition of this vulnerability and the resulting state of mental suffering that empowerment arises and a person's resilience can be appealed to. Hereby, empowerment recognises older people who are ill, frail and vulnerable, and stands up for their rights to receive care and security and for being heard in society. But of course, nothing should be done about them without them. Empowerment also promotes social inclusion and is sensitive to cultural diversity. Last but not least, empowerment focuses on structural barriers of exclusion. In this chapter, we first explain the empowerment framework, discuss its relation to vulnerability and resilience, and apply this framework specifically to older people.

Next, we zoom in on a key aspect for empowerment – namely, the concept of resilience. After defining this concept and describing its building stones, we give voice to the older persons themselves through resilient narratives. We conclude this chapter by discussing some implications for practice and policy.

1. The empowerment framework

Against the background of various social evolutions like deinstitutionalisation, person-centred care, 'positive health', and the emphasis on social inclusion and active citizenship, empowerment comes to the foreground as a useful framework. The framework of empowerment entails a different philosophy, a drastic shift in the way we look at vulnerability and the health and social care system. Empowerment is value driven and assumes values of social justice, solidarity and inclusion, and it strives for full citizenship and a high quality of life for everyone, especially for society's most vulnerable groups. In the following, we describe the most important theoretical features of the framework of empowerment.

1.1 Theoretical features of empowerment

A central feature of empowerment is the focus on the strengths of individuals, the *strengths perspective*. A precondition of a strength-based approach is the recognition of both possibilities and vulnerabilities of individuals (Saleebey, 1996; Boumans, 2012). It is not just positive thinking, naive reframing of deficits and misery, or ignoring or downplaying real problems (Janssen, 2013). Empowerment focuses on the strengths and capabilities of persons and groups, without neglecting their vulnerabilities. In fact, it is precisely out of a fundamental recognition of this vulnerability and the resulting state of mental suffering that empowerment arises. Strength and connection form the duality of empowerment. It brings together the 'male' (e.g. control, power, influence) and 'female' (e.g. cooperation, togetherness, alliances) sides of empowerment.

Empowerment supposes a *relational* picture of society, a second important characteristic. Empowerment does not try to realise maximal independency, but rather emphasises that vulnerability can go hand in hand with mastery over one's life. Striving towards mastery, authenticity and identity can only be achieved in cooperation and connectedness with others. We speak about 'interdependency' in the lexicon of empowerment. According to the empowerment framework, people gain strength and grow through connections with others and their surroundings (informal and formal social supporting ties) and, inversely, strength results in increased connectedness. To express the importance of this relational aspect of empowerment, different authors use the concept of 'relational empowerment' (Christens, 2011; Baur & Abma, 2012; Vanderplaat, 1999; Van Regenmortel, 2011).

Although most empirical work on empowerment has been on the individual/psychological level (Peterson & Zimmerman, 2004), the *ecological* nature of empowerment implies giving attention to the broader context within a community. Only focusing on individual empowerment could result in neglecting important social, structural and physical factors in the environment and the organisation (Maertens et al., 2015). This could create bias and a tendency to reduce problems to the individual dynamic whereby individuals are blamed and stigmatised, and interventions are mainly directed towards individual behaviour change (Peterson & Zimmerman, 2004). Empowerment always studies persons or groups in relation with their environment. Therefore, both individual and collective empowerment are essential. Another related and main theoretical characteristic of empowerment is its *multilevel* character, always involving micro (individual, psychological), meso (organisational, neighbourhood) and macro (society, policy) levels. These different levels are interconnected. We will explain these levels in more detail.

Zimmerman, one of the founders of psychological empowerment, distinguishes three components of empowerment on the individual (or psychological) level: the intrapersonal, the interpersonal and the behavioural dimension. The intrapersonal, cognitive component refers to

> *how people think about themselves and includes domain-specific perceived control and self-efficacy, motivation to control, perceived competence, and mastery.* (Zimmerman, 1995, p. 588)

It refers to the perceived control, the belief in one's ability to influence a situation and environment (self-perception), and the motivation to exert influence. The interpersonal (or interactional) component involves critical awareness of societal norms and possibilities as well as the mobilisation of resources and the skills to use them. The behavioural dimension refers to involvement in the community, participation in society and organisations, and constructive behaviour (e.g. resilience, coping, assertiveness, solving) (Zimmerman, 1995).

On the organisational level, empowerment refers to

> *organizational efforts that generate psychological empowerment among members and organizational effectiveness needed for goal achievement.* (Peterson & Zimmerman, 2004, p. 130)

It concerns

> *processes that ensure that individuals get greater control within the organization, but on the other hand also that organizations, for their part, can also influence the policies and decisions of the wider community.* (Maertens et al., 2015)

In this respect, a distinction is made between empowering organisations, which are 'those that produce psychological empowerment for individual members as part of their organizational process' and empowered organisations, which are 'those that influence the larger system of which they are a part' (Peterson & Zimmerman, 2004, p. 130). Empowering organisations need to give professionals sufficient discretionary space and support them in their process of self-empowerment (e.g. through education, stimulating critical reflection and vision) (Van Regenmortel, 2011; Janssen, 2010). The intra-organisational component on the organisational level refers to

> *the ways organizations are structured and function as members who engage in activities that contribute to individual psychological empowerment and organizational effectiveness needed for goal achievement.* (Peterson & Zimmerman, 2004, p. 135)

It assumes connections between employees within the same organisation by stimulating collaboration between teams and groups (Janssen, 2010): 'a good intra organizational structure should include good connections between internal units, leadership, a group-based belief system and have resolved ideological conflicts' (Janssen et al., 2015, p. 6). The internal structure of a team can, for example, stimulate better coordination of care and reflection on ethical questions by supporting collective deliberation.

Further, mutual trust (between professionals, between professionals and management) and clear working routines are also empowering organisational features (Janssen et al., 2015). The interorganisational component 'provides the infrastructure for members to engage in proactive behaviors necessary for goal achievement' (Peterson & Zimmerman, 2004, p. 131). It involves exchanging information between organisations and the coordination of services between organisations (e.g. implementing networks that have a signal function for isolated older persons, multidisciplinary teams) (Janssen, 2010). Important empowering features on this level include improved linkages between participating organisations and gaining more insight into each other's tasks (Janssen et al., 2015). The extra-organisational component refers to 'actions taken by organizations to affect the larger environments of which they are part', such as policy change, creating alternative services or successful advocacy (Peterson & Zimmerman, 2004, p. 131). It involves the relation of the organisation with the broader environment and the way influence is exerted upon that environment (Janssen, 2010).

On the community level, empowerment includes 'efforts to deter community threats, improve quality of life, and facilitate citizen participation' (Peterson & Zimmerman, 2004, p. 130). An empowering community is 'one in which individuals and organizations can use their skills to address their respective needs' (Maertens et al., 2015). Empowerment on the community level refers to policy stimulating (or hindering) empowerment by employing the strengths of individuals, organisations and communities (Van Regenmortel, 2011, p. 29); policymakers should ensure people can participate in society by emphasising their strengths (Janssen, 2010). In this respect, first, a sense of community is important, which refers to a sense of belonging/connectedness. This is a subjective interpretation of identity where people share the same values, norms, needs, objectives and expectations. Important here is that communal needs and goals are recognised. Second, the social quality dimension refers to the quality and quantity of informal and formal interactions within the community that make sure that strengths are linked together and developed into human capital. Third, combined capacity refers to revealing and connecting the resources of people, groups and organisations, since the whole is more than the sum of its parts. Fourth, collective action means individuals use their combined strength to exert influence on community life and on social decision-making processes (Steenssens & Van Regenmortel, 2007). This community dimension is related to the power to institute social change: benefits, accessibility of resources and provisions, a better quality of care, influencing law and decision-making, among others (Van Regenmortel, 2011). Empowerment fights against stigmatisation and exclusion, stimulates a more positive image of vulnerable people, and encourages social solidarity in society.

Finally, empowerment is also an *open-ended* construct. Everyone can always continue to grow in their process of empowerment. Indeed, every person can continuously gain strength during the life course (Van Regenmortel, 2007), which is an important premise of a strength-based approach (Kisthardt, 1997). This means that empowerment is a continuous variable, not a dichotomous variable. It is not a question of having empowerment or not; there are gradations. The concrete empowering process is context determined, dependent on time (the trajectory should not be linear) and the specific population and differentiated according to life domains. Moreover, this process takes times and has peaks and vallies throughout life. These empowering processes are central in the empowerment framework, and empowerment outcomes are the results of these processes.

1.2 'Enabling niches' and definition of empowerment

One cannot receive empowerment; empowerment cannot be given. This is the so-called *paradox of empowerment.* Everyone has to acquire it oneself because power that is given is actually a subtle form of control, of the 'giver' over the 'receiver' (Macaulay et al., 1998, p. 10 in Janssen, 2013, p.22). Power concerns a personal as well a collective aspect. Jacobs distinguishes between three different levels of power: on the individual level, she refers to 'the power from within'; on the collective or interactional level, she refers to 'the power with'; and on the broader political-societal level, she describes the 'power to' (Jacobs et al., 2005). The environment, like professionals, can support and facilitate the individual empowerment process by creating enabling conditions.

These 'enabling niches' (as opposed to 'entrapping niches') are safe and warm places in which people are respected (not stigmatised) and encouraged to grow (Boone et al., 2020). Main characteristics of enabling niches are (Taylor, 1997, pp. 222–223):
– 'People in enabling niches are not stigmatized, not treated as outcasts.
– People in enabling niches will tend to turn to "their own kind" for as-sociation, support, and self-validation. But the enabling niche gives them access to others who bring different perspectives, so that their social world becomes less restricted.
– People in enabling niches are not totally defined by their social category; they are accepted as having valid aspirations and attributes apart from that category. The person is not "just" a "bag lady", a "junkie", an "ex-con", a "crazy".
– In the enabling niche, there are clear, earned gradations of reward and status. People can work up to better positions. Thus there are strong expectations of change or personal progress within such niches.
– In the enabling niche, there are many incentives to set realistic longerterm goals for oneself and to work towards such goals.
– In the enabling niche, there is good reality feedback; that is, there are many natural processes that lead people to recognize and correct unrealistic perceptions or interpretations.
– The enabling niche provides opportunities to learn the skills and expecta-tions that would aid movement to other niches. This is especially true when the enabling niche pushes toward reasonable work habits and reasonable self-discipline and expects that the use of time will be clearly structured.
– In the enabling niche, economic resources are adequate, and competence and quality are rewarded. This reduces economic stress and creates strong motives for avoiding institutionalization.'

A strengthening environment and sufficient resources are vital for the process of empowerment of individuals, families and groups. *Shared responsibility* is a keyword in the lexicon of empowerment. Social problems such as poverty are said to emerge because of a combination of factors on the micro, meso and macro levels. Indeed, empowerment supposes a circular causality that breaks through the classical linear cause-and-effect thinking and consequently avoids 'blaming the victim' and 'blaming the system'. It implies a fundamental shift in the way social problems and their solutions are viewed (Van Regenmortel, 2011). Indeed, individuals, organisations and the system all have agency within certain boundaries and thus form part of the solution with respect to mechanisms of exclusion.

The overall aim of empowerment is to provide social inclusion and full citizenship for each individual by supporting people in their searching process to gain mastery over the determinants of their quality of life (Janssen, 2013; Van Regenmortel, 2013; Steenssens & Van Regenmortel, 2007). Central to this empowerment framework is gaining mastery over one's own situation and environment by gaining more control and insight into a situation and environment and by participation and influencing (Van Regenmortel, 2011). We use the following definition of empowerment, which is based on the theory from Julian Rappaport and Marc Zimmerman (Van Regenmortel, 2011, p. 12):

> *empowerment is a strengthening process whereby individuals, organizations and communities gain mastery over their own situation and their environment through the process of gaining control, sharpening the critical awareness and stimulating participation.*

Mastery is said to positively influence various determinants of quality of life, such as physical, material and emotional well-being, and is itself operationalised by gaining control, sharpening critical awareness and stimulating participation.

> *Control refers to perceived or actual capacity to influence decisions. Critical awareness refers to understanding how power structures operate, decisions are made, causal agents are influenced and resources are mobilized [...]. Participation refers to taking action to make things happen for the desired outcomes.* (Janssen, 2013, p. 20)

1.3 Empowerment and vulnerability

Whereas the active ageing approach tends to neglect vulnerability, empowerment certainly does not. However, from an empowerment perspective, we formulate a different perspective, one that contrasts with mainstream bioethical discourse which starts from the fully functioning, independent and autonomous individual. We do not see old age as a deficient and deviant mode of human existence. As human beings, we are embodied, interdependent persons, and we all share the fundamental experience of vulnerability, albeit to varying degrees depending on our specific situation. Following Bozzaro et al. (2018), we argue that old age should not be used as a marker of vulnerability, since ageing is a process that can develop in a variety of ways and is not always associated with particular experiences of vulnerability.

Bozzaro et al. (2018) make a distinction between 'broad' and 'restrictive' conceptions of vulnerability. As a broad concept, vulnerability describes a basic aspect of the human condition. In this sense, being vulnerable is a universal, inevitable feature of humanity. By contrast, restrictive concepts consider vulnerability as a specific context-dependent susceptibility to harm and exploitation as well as a limited capacity for autonomy. Restrictive concepts refer to particular persons or groups who – due to social injustice, dependencies or impaired capabilities – are presumed to be less able to protect themselves. There is a risk that persons or groups will be labelled 'helpless' without taking into account differences or changes within the identified group. Moreover, restrictive concepts can promote widespread paternalism in an attempt to prevent others from harm and meet their needs. This may lead to a systemic stigmatisation of and discrimination against certain groups that can ultimately even reinforce vulnerability. From an empowerment perspective, we define vulnerability not in terms of a failure to attain or retain full autonomous agency, whereby autonomy is defined as the individual's capacity of rational self-determination, and the person is seen as an isolated, rational agent without any embeddedness in social relationships.

If we exclude special age-associated syndromes, such as frailty or dementia, and we do not define ageing itself as a disease but just as a normal biological process, the assumption that the elderly are per se vulnerable is simply no longer self-evident. Instead, the common categorization of the elderly as vulnerable rather seems to result from widespread deficit models and negative stereotypes of ageing and old age in terms of being miserable, helpless, and dependent. Labeling older people as vulnerable could thus further promote this kind of unwarranted ageism and ultimately lead to ethically problematic effects. For

example, empirical studies suggest that long-term care institutions with a
paternalistic approach have a tendency to increase elderly people's helplessness
and need of care. (Bozzaro et al., 2018, p. 236)

Vulnerability has become an increasingly useful field of research for addressing
risk reduction and the mediation of economic and social impacts. Moro et al.
(2021) state that in the social sciences, vulnerability is associated with the
risk of harm in the face of a possible eventuality and the ability to avoid or
cope with a harmful outcome. Many definitions are available. The current
debate shows that vulnerability captures various thematic dimensions, such
as physical, economic, social and institutional aspects. Moro et al. (2021)
propose a multidimensional approach to vulnerability and incorporate a
personal dimension of vulnerability.

Schröder-Butterfill and Marianti (2006) developed a framework relevant
to the study of ageing. This framework disaggregates vulnerability into its
constituent domains – namely, exposure, threats, coping capacities and
outcomes. Among those in later life, it is impossible to distinguish those
who are vulnerable from those who are secure by examining only exposure
factors or common threats, because vulnerability arises from interactions
between advantages and disadvantages accumulated over the life course
and the experience of threats in later life. Whether this interaction results in
a better or worse outcome depends on the adequacy of the person's coping
resources. The study of vulnerability therefore requires attention not only
to the ways in which exposure factors are created and distributed over time
but also to the ways in which individuals manage or fail to mobilise social,
material and public resources to protect themselves from bad outcomes.

Although a literature review has shown that there is no clear definition
of vulnerability or vulnerable people, common denominators can be found
in the literature about vulnerability and vulnerable populations. Usually,
the use of vulnerability concerns people who do not enjoy full physical,
psychological and social well-being and, as a result, they are at risk of falling
behind in society or becoming socially isolated. Numans et al. (2021) argue
that the concepts of self-reliance and social participation, promoted by social
policy, are linked to the concept of vulnerability. People who do not meet these
standards are labelled 'vulnerable people'. This label is based on an outsider's
perspective. In line with empowerment, the authors explore an insider's
perspective; they question how persons who are classified as vulnerable
perceive this definition. The data also reveals that the expressed feelings of
powerlessness and lack of self-determination are linked to the feeling of being
patronised. Moreover, by emphasising their competencies, respondents see

more potential in themselves to contribute to society: they count in society and must be taken seriously, despite their limitations and shortcomings due to illness and disease. In short, they accept being vulnerable, but they do not accept being of no value to society, as findings prove that the respondents are socially active in several life domains.

A prevailing misconception is that empowerment and vulnerability are opposed to each other, when in fact they are inherently intertwined. Moreover, it is precisely because of and in spite of the vulnerability that strengths are addressed (Van Regenmortel, 2010). It is the challenge to make these strengths visible and to connect them with the strengths of others, the environment and society. In this way, older persons can bear their vulnerabilities and a meaningful role in society can be taken up by the person involved. Paradoxically, strengths and vulnerabilities are thus at stake in empowerment. Empowerment gives broad recognition to the individual vulnerability, but does not individualise it so that the person or group involved is not culpabilised. There is attention for individual as well as for social and societal vulnerability. The psychological dimension, the relational dimension and the structural dimension of vulnerability are always in the spotlight. The paradoxical nature of empowerment also lies in the fact that it is about gaining control as much as it is about receiving support. A plea for more autonomy also goes hand in hand with a stronger sense of community and connectedness in society and care (social cohesion).

1.4   Empowerment in old age

No matter how old we are, we can still play our part in society and enjoy a better quality of life. The challenge is to make the most of the enormous potential that we harbor even at a more advanced age. (European Commission, 2018)

From an empowerment view, ageing is not a problem, but a global challenge today and even more for generations to come. Both Europe and Belgium are characterised by an ageing population, of which the two main causes are the low birth rate and increasing life expectancy (Börsch-Supan et al., 2013). In 2060, about 30 per cent of the total European population will consist of people sixty-five years or older, and 12 per cent will consist of people eighty years and older (Niedzwiedz et al., 2016). Figure 1.1 shows a similar trend for Belgium: while in 2020 there are about 2.2 million older persons of sixty-five years or older and 330,000 older persons of eighty-five years and older, this increases to respectively 3.3 million and 830,000 in 2070. In line with this trend, not only the absolute number but also the proportion of older persons in the total population increases.

Figure 1.1: Prognoses of the older population in Belgium (2010–2071)

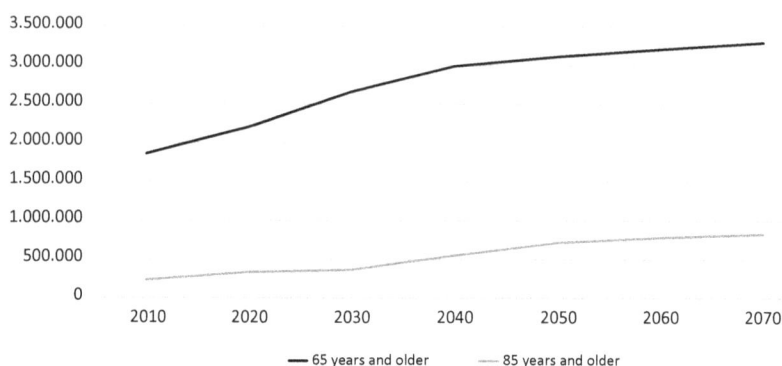

Source: De Witte & Van Regenmortel (2020)

The ageing of our society implies that more people will be dependent on 'the active population', which could pose challenges for health and welfare systems across Europe. Over the last few decades, a number of social trends – like rising health and social care costs, budget cuts, workforce issues in the healthcare sector, increasing chronic illnesses and the wish of older persons to live as long as possible in their own house – have led to the belief that the health and social care system for older people needs to be restructured and improved by developing an alternate philosophy or paradigm (Janssen, 2013).

> *The societal response to population ageing will require a transformation of health systems that moves away from disease-based curative models and towards the provision of older-person-centered and integrated care.* [...] *It will require a coordinated response from many other sectors and multiple levels of government.* [...] *Although these actions will inevitably require resources, they are likely to be a sound investment in society's future: a future that gives older people the freedom to live lives that previous generations could never have imagined* (WHO, 2015, p. 223).

The contemporary organisation of the health and social care system is still directed towards one-sided practical support to remedy problems in functioning that threaten self-reliance. In this respect, the current policy vision sees vulnerability mostly from a medical point of view where the accent lies on physical vulnerability, whereas psychological and societal functioning are not included (Machielse, 2016). This is problematic in the light of increasingly ubiquitous concepts in the health and social care sector, such as quality of life, positive health and frailty. All those concepts emphasise the importance of the interconnectedness of various life domains (physical, social, economic, psychological) when assessing health and healthcare, and they thus surpass the one-sided focus on the physical domain. In short, a restructuration of the health and social care system and a shift in paradigm, in which more attention is paid to vulnerability with respect to the physical, psychological and social domain, seems necessary (Gobbens, 2017).

In addition, the informal resources of older persons are important for improving and maintaining their quality of life. Research has made clear how the process of individualisation negatively affects the available informal support for older persons: family structures evolve, people live farther from each other, networks become smaller and less diverse, and family and neighbourhood relationships are less evident (Machielse, 2016, 2015). Furthermore, changes in social structures (e.g. the increased labour participation of women) also led to a decrease in the availability of informal support (De Koker et al., 2007). In this respect, research shows that the social network of older persons has become less diverse and that older persons increasingly have mostly vertical contacts due to a strong focus on the nuclear family (Cantillon et al., 2007). These modifications in the social network of older persons make it more complicated for them to sustain a supportive social network, which is already difficult given numerous age-related adversities such as deteriorating health. Maintaining supportive social capital is important because everyone, not least older persons, needs social capital to realise goals that give meaning to life.

A positive environment is vital for empowering processes and empowerment outcomes of older persons. The degree to which older persons are enabled to feel in control of their lives, solve their own problems and make choices for themselves seems likely to promote happiness and a feeling of well-being, which is reflected in both health and longevity (Buie, 1988 in Lloyd, 1991). Much depends on the way in which older persons experience the provision of services and care. Older persons need to be encouraged to manage their own health and life within their home environment – of course supported by family, neighbours, friends and professionals. A shift is taking place

from cure to a balance between cure and care by strengthening the sense of mastery of older people and to support them to activate and/or enlarge their social network. Professionals are, in other words, expected to support care recipients in making the right choices that is in accordance with their wishes and expectations and on overcoming paradoxes that are inherent to human life. (Janssen, 2013, p. 15)

As mentioned before, empowerment assumes values such as social justice, solidarity and equality, and it strives for full, relational citizenship and a high quality of life. Consequently, the primary focus of empowerment is on society's most vulnerable groups, the so-called silenced voices. Considering this, extra attention ought to be given to the underprivileged and impoverished older persons. To address social problems (e.g. poverty), it is important to pay attention to the psychological dimension of living in adverse circumstances and to provide care and support to underprivileged older people that is in line with their coping strategies and contributes to the development or strengthening of their sense of mastery. Of course, in addition to the individual-psychological level, there is always a more structural, societal-political level in the concept of empowerment.

Empowerment as a positive concept emphasises society's responsibility to use the strengths and capacities of vulnerable older persons more. Community building and community care come to the foreground (see also Chapter 4). It denotes not only care *in* the community but also care *by* the community. The key components of community care should be to respond flexibly to individual needs, to give consumers a range of options, to foster independence (with no more intervention than is necessary) and to concentrate on those with the greatest needs (Lloyd, 1991). Similar to the proverb 'it takes a village to raise a child', we argue that it takes a whole community to support the empowerment processes of older persons. In this respect, the concept of age-friendly communities seems appropriate. The WHO's movement of 'age-friendly communities' aims to develop infrastructure and facilities that support and value older persons as well as promote their active participation (Gobbens, 2017). The WHO defines 'age-friendly cities and communities' as

> *a good place to grow old. Age-friendly cities and communities foster healthy and active ageing and, thus, enable well-being throughout life. They help people to remain independent for as long as possible, and provide care and protection when they are needed, respecting older people's autonomy and dignity.* (WHO, 2015, p. 161)

Finally, the empowerment framework encompasses a shift from the problem of ageing into positive ageing. Many models have already tried to discover the variables that result in successful ageing. These studies emphasise individually modifiable health promotion behaviour, excluding many older people, especially those with disabilities and impairments. From an empowerment perspective, we consider a more holistic concept of ageing well, including, for example, a spiritual component and taking into account the value of wisdom, a total life history perspective and, last but not least, the limiting social, structural and cultural context. Empowerment, and more specifically the resilience framework, covers these aspects and does not marginalise vulnerable older persons.

As Janssen et al. argue, resilience is positively related to empowerment:

the outcomes of these resilience processes may ultimately contribute to the stabilization or the improvement of a (general) sense of mastery and that those with a greater sense of mastery are able to show resilience in times of crisis and hardships. (Janssen et al., 2012, p. 344)

Resilience helps us understand the processes and mechanisms through which individuals strive to maintain or regain mastery over the determinants of the quality of their lives (Janssen et al., 2012).

1.5   Empowerment and resilience

Empowerment and resilience are widely employed concepts in community psychology and other social sciences. Both are potent processes for responding to adversity and oppression. They both take a strengths-based approach that recognises, respects and promotes local capacity by attending to resources that are inherent or able to be developed within an individual and community (Brodsky & Cattaneo, 2013; Buckingham & Brodsky, 2021). Empowerment and resilience have the potential to facilitate each other. They have been conceptualised and operationalised in various, often overlapping ways. Both concepts have been critiqued for lacking clear consensus regarding definition, operationalisation and measurement (Luthar et al., 2000).

Brodsky and Cattaneo (2013) developed a transtheoretical (or transconceptual) model of empowerment and resilience. This transtheoretical model shows shared outcomes (maintenance, self-efficacy, knowledge, community resources, skills) and processes (awareness and goal setting, action, reflection) and then lays out differences between resilience and empowerment. The aims of empowerment and resilience differ.

Resilience refers to 'successful adaptation despite risk and adversity' (Masten, 1994, p. 3) and is operationalised as 'more than the absence of pathology, as exemplified by not only surviving, but thriving, sometimes even with enhanced functioning, and as a dynamic process rather than a stable trait'. Persons can adapt to and withstand adversity and oppression through resilience processes. Empowerment spurs external change, a meaningful shift in the experience of power attained through interaction in the social world. Power refers to influence at any level of interaction, including in personal relationships, settings and systems, and the broader society. Resilience in the absence of empowerment may uphold oppressive power structures. Resilience always occurs within a context of fundamental risk endemic to the context in which an individual is situated, while empowerment may or may not. Resilience is focused on internally focused goals – adapting, withstanding, resisting – while empowerment is aimed at power-oriented, external change. Empowerment is a bridge between the intrapersonal and social realms. Articulating this dynamic bridging aspect of empowerment is very important.

> *Unless we understand that empowerment is not only experienced internally but also enacted socially, requiring a response from the social world, we risk laying the blame for disempowerment at the feet of marginalized communities.* (Brodsky & Cattaneo, 2013, p. 337)

The ultimate goal of empowerment is second-order change which influences the status quo by shifting power dynamics and imbalances between the target individual or community and the larger system. Brodsky and Cattaneo (2013) note that the differentiation between the transformative, external focus of empowerment and the adaptive, internal focus of resilience is in no way a criticism of resilience. The ability to cope with the situation as it is can be a pivotal step towards gaining the strength, consciousness and resources necessary to ultimately work towards empowerment goals that will change the status quo. Empowerment builds on resilience to provide the bridge that connects individual power to social power.

2. Resilience: The (hidden) capital of older persons

> *The true quest as we age should not be for successful aging, but our goal should be for resilience, an undervalued and not fully examined concept in aging.* (Harris, 2008, p. 43)

2.1 Framework and definition of resilience

Since the 1990s, there has been broad attention for resilience. Research about resilience is rooted in positive psychology (Seligman & Csikszentmihaly, 2000) and was originally developed in the domain of developmental psychology dealing with childhood and adolescence (Garmezy, 1991; Werner & Smith, 1982; Rutter, 1987). Today, resilience has been extended to other periods of the lifespan including old age (Ryff et al., 1998; Masten & Wright, 2009). Resilience research can be situated within the broad shift from the 'damage' to the 'challenge' model where the focus is shifting from the damage of adversity to how people positively overcome adversity (Van Regenmortel, 2006, 2002). Resilience originally comes from the discipline of ecology and can be defined as 'an ecosystem's ability to absorb and recover from the occurrence of a hazardous event' (Akter & Mallick, 2013, p. 114).

Resilience research (Janssen et al., 2011) focuses on ways to improve well-being and stimulate health (Van Regenmortel, 2009). The belief in the potency and strengths of people, even among the most vulnerable, is an important aspect of resilience. However, resilience is not a synonym for invulnerability (Werner & Smith, 1982; Rutter, 1993). People can be vulnerable and hurt even though they are able to manage challenging circumstances – in short, they are 'vulnerable but invincible' (Werner & Smith, 1982; Van Regenmortel, 2002).

Resilience not only relates to empowerment; it is also essential with respect to the newer concept of 'positive health', which was introduced by Machtelt Huber. 'Positive health' emphasises 'the resilience or capacity to cope and maintain and restore one's integrity, equilibrium, and sense of wellbeing' (Huber et al., 2011, p. 344), with respect to the physical, mental and social domains. Huber regards health as a dynamic balance between opportunities and limitations, which are affected by external conditions (Huber et al., 2011). Therefore, not surprisingly, high levels of resilience in later life correlate with reduced vulnerability to depressive symptomatology and mortality risks, better self-perceptions of successful ageing, and increased levels of mental health, well-being and quality of life (Gerino et al., 2017).

Resilience research holds on to a holistic view in which attention is directed to the complex interplay between adversities, sources of strength and adaptation processes, and the variations of this according to individual, familial and contextual factors (Van Regenmortel, 2006). While coping refers to the abilities to handle certain circumstances, resilience serves as a framework for understanding healthy development in the face of risk (Janssen, 2013). It refers to the ability to maintain a stable and good way of psychological and physical functioning during difficult circumstances and even to become stronger by learning from adversities (Geraerts, 2013). On a conceptual level, resilience is considered the bridge between coping and development (Greve & Staudinger, 2006; Leipold & Greve, 2009).

Resilience is often defined as 'patterns and processes of positive adaptation and development in the context of significant threats to an individual's life or function' (Janssen, 2013, p. 21). Two coexisting concepts are central to resilience: first, the presence of a significant (developmental) threat or risk to a given person's well-being; second, the evidence of a positive adaptation in this individual despite the adversity encountered (Fraser et al., 1999; Luthar et al., 2000; Van Regenmortel, 2002).

Although old age is often accompanied by feelings of loss (e.g. the death of partner or friends, divorce) and other developmental stressors (e.g. physical or cognitive impairments, functional limitations, changing residence, health problems), many older persons are capable of moderating the impact of these distresses (Hardy et al., 2002, 2004). The 'life course theory' states that older persons are faced with adversities that can be both cumulative, lifelong (e.g. poverty) and age-specific (Fuller-Iglesias et al., 2008, p. 182). People make use of their 'sources of strength' or 'protective factors' to deal with adversity (Earvolino-Ramirez, 2007). Besides personal attributes (e.g. positive self-concept, self-efficacy beliefs, internal locus of control, optimism), external factors like families, communities and wider contextual circumstances influence people's reactions to stressful situations (Neimeyer, 1997). This means that protective factors are context-specific, and both the amount and type of resources may differ at different times across the lifespan (Hochhalter et al. in Resnick et al., 2011). Moreover, they can lead to different outcomes for different individuals. Every individual experiences challenges through a particular lens, which is formed and framed by personal history and specific individual, social, cultural and environmental characteristics. Moreover, in dealing with adversity, people can age successfully and be resilient in some domains (emotional, spiritual, social, cognitive and physical), but not in others (Hochhalter et al. in Resnick et al., 2011). Therefore, it is essential to understand life stories and how previous adversity was dealt with and incorporated in recent experience. Consequently, a narrative research approach is valuable for investigating resilience processes.

In common with empowerment, resilience encompasses a positive and appreciative perspective on human functioning.

Resilient individuals have a sense of active and meaningful engagement with the world. Their positive and energetic approach to life is grounded in confident, autonomous, and competent functioning and a sense of mastery within a wide range of life-domains. (Greve & Staudinger, 2006, p. 812)

In addition, resilience is a relational and dynamic concept, in which persons are studied in a complex interplay with their environment (Van Regenmortel, 2006). The (social and societal) environment has an important role to play in supporting the resilience of older people. In this respect, it is important to acknowledge both internal and external sources of strength, and thus also a shared responsibility of both older persons and their social environment with respect to their resilience (Janssen et al., 2012). Indeed, resilient people do not take on a subordinate position or see themselves solely as a victim, nor do they seek to internalise adversities. It is important not to put adversities each time out of the personal responsibility because this could result in alienation and a lack of bonding. On the other hand, acknowledgment of contextual factors can allow social actions to emerge, and people can protect themselves from negative self-evaluation. Hence, it is appropriate to regain grip on one's own life without feelings of self-reproach and without neglecting structural causes (Van Regenmortel, 2013).

Our emphasis is on understanding and researching resources and mechanism that allow older persons (also organisations and communities) to grow and to develop in a positive way.

In this chapter, we focus on individual resilience, not on resilient families (see Paddock, 2001) or resilient communities (see Atlantic Health Promotion Research Centre, 1999).

2.2. Building stones of resilience

We state that resilience is not a fixed personality trait, but a social construct which results from a dynamic, non-deterministic, context-related (multi-layered) process of development (Van Regenmortel, 2006; Peeters, 2012). Many factors contribute to personal resilience, which is in part based on bonding and engagement with significant others and an informal social network, as presented in the casita or 'house of resilience' (Peeters, 2012). In the literature, we find a number of global building blocks for resilience, such as secure attachment, internal locus of control, meaningfulness and humour.

From the scientific literature, we find that the sources of strength that give rise to resilience are situated in the individual, interactional and contextual domain and that they are all inherently linked to each other (Van Regenmortel, 2013). Indeed, an optimal climate for development and resilience requires that these three domains interact favourably. Specifically for older persons, based on narrative research, the following sources of strength give rise to resilience among older persons (Janssen et al., 2011).

Sources of strength on the individual domain

The individual domain refers to

> the qualities within older people and comprises of three subdomains, namely beliefs about one's competence, efforts to exert control and the capacity to analyze and understand ones situation. (Janssen et al., 2011, p. 145)

Sources of strength in this domain include the following (De Witte & Van Regenmortel, 2019):
- beliefs about one's competence:
  - pride about one's personality: having an easy-going or down-to-earth, for example, character which results in people not being embittered or that they blame others;
  - acceptance and openness about one's vulnerability: this takes time and is difficult but is said to result in people not being too susceptive to others' negative views of their limitations.
- efforts to exert control:
  - anticipation of future losses: taking action to influence outcomes of their situation, e.g. moving to a neighbourhood with shops close by, in appropriate housing;
  - mastery by practising skills: staying active and practicing knowledge and skills;
  - acceptance of help and support: this takes time and is difficult (e.g. using a wheelchair).
- capacity to analyse and understand one's situation:
  - having a balanced view on life: this helps to put things in perspective;
  - not taking on the role of a victim: emphasising strengths instead of vulnerabilities;
  - having the perspective of wanting to seize the day.

Older persons more frequently display positive, low-arousal emotions and fewer negative emotions of either high or low arousal, which suggests that older persons regulate their emotions better than younger people do. This allows them to better adapt to negative life events. In addition, older persons do not demonstrate a diminished sense of control:

> they display strengths such as more nuanced understanding of emotion, better ability to regulate that emotion, and are more likely to accept circumstances as being out of their personal control. (Mlinac et al., 2011, p. 71)

Older persons behave more in accordance with their feelings than with social expectations. Although in later life people are perhaps more dependent on external resources (Greve & Staudinger, 2006), some research finds that resilience and a sense of coherence is more present among the oldest old than the younger old (Clark et al., 2011).

Sources of strength on the interactional domain

The interactional domain is defined as 'the way older people cooperate and interact with others to achieve their personal goals' (Janssen et al., 2011, p. 145). It concerns how people interact with significant others like relatives and friends, neighbours and professionals to achieve goals and to endow meaning to their lives (Mlinac et al., 2011). Sources of strength in this respect are as follows (De Witte & Van Regenmortel, 2019):
-   empowering informal relationships with family: this helps older persons to make sense of their situation, offers practical and emotional support, and contributes to their feeling of agency.
-   empowering formal relationships with professionals: commitment, reliability and interest are important characteristics of these relationships.
-   the power of giving ('reciprocity').
-   societal responses: society acknowledging and valuing older persons.

Both the quantity and quality of social relations are important with respect to resilience.

> *Optimally, as the needs and circumstances of individuals change, and when confronted with stressful life events, social relations in the form of social networks and high-quality relationships, facilitate their ability to meet the challenges they face.* (Fuller-Iglesias et al., 2008, p. 184)

Having close, affectional relationships within the family, broader family and external environment is an important protective factor that stimulates resilience in later life because these conditions make it easier to receive help and guidance (Van Regenmortel, 2006). People receive information through social relations, which also encourages coping behaviour and enhances self-esteem and instrumental support (Fuller-Iglesias et al., 2008). Hence, integration into the community – having friendly neighbours, people looking out for each other, a good community spirit and a good mix of people – is important.

Figure 1.2: Sources of strength that give rise to resilience in old age (Janssen et al., 2011, p. 49)

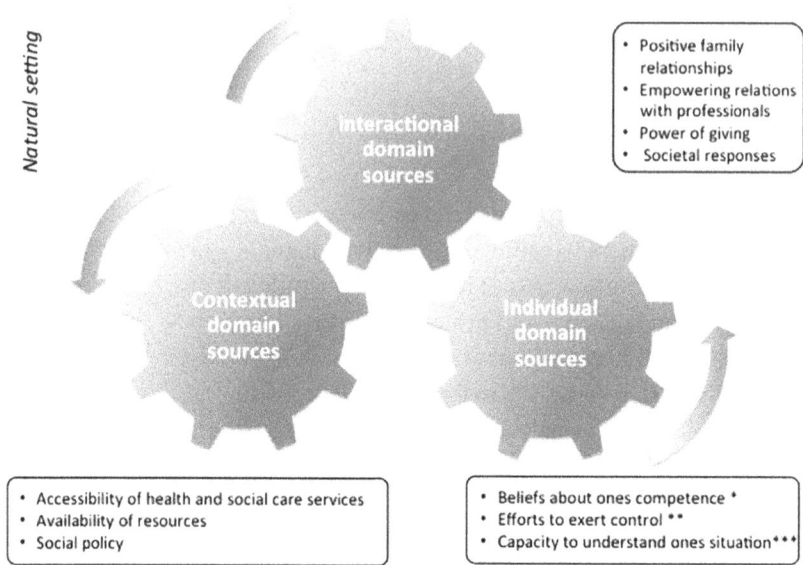

This community integration is strengthened by paid work, voluntary work and community organisations (Clark et al., 2011).

> *We found that there were differences depending on the personal characteristics of the individual* (i.e. *age, gender, and race), and social relations* (i.e. *network size and spousal relationship quality), in the presence of resilience in old age.* [...] *Our findings indicate that a larger social network and a higher quality of relationships with spouse predicted fewer depressive symptoms and greater life satisfaction despite experiencing a significant number of adversities.* (Fuller-Iglesias et al., 2008, p. 190)

Sources of strength on the contextual domain

The contextual domain refers to 'a broader political-societal level including the efforts on this domain to deter community threats, improve quality of life and facilitate citizen participation' (Janssen et al., 2011, p. 149). From this, it is clear that the environment plays a significant role in gaining resilience, by offering possibilities and by stimulating collective and individual participation

(Van Regenmortel, 2013). The contextual domain includes the following sources of strength (De Witte & Van Regenmortel, 2019):

- accessibility of health and social care,
- availability of social and material resources (e.g. mutual self-help groups) and
- social policy (e.g. the possibility to go to a nursing home, income) (Janssen et al., 2011).

In sum, various environmental factors (e.g. care delivery) which are not in direct control of older persons also determine their resilience (Van Kessel, 2013). The different domains are interrelated; for example, openness about one's vulnerability is closely linked to accepting help, which may stimulate interaction with the social environment, and participation, which may in turn result in acquiring more resources and skills. Accepting help and support is not always easy for older persons because it can be in conflict with feelings of 'wanting to take care of yourself' (Janssen, 2013). Ideally, the individual, interactional and contextual domains interact favourably, as a gearwheel.

2.3   Resilient narratives

Using this Janssen's framework (2013), we conducted narrative interviews with fifteen vulnerable community-dwelling older persons in Belgium who were selected through a 'purposive sampling' strategy between May and July 2019 (De Witte & Van Regenmortel, 2019). In narrative research, stories of experience are created in a dialogue with the respondent. Although researchers may use a topic-based schedule (as we did), they are not governed by it. Interviewers take on an informal and friendly stance to create a climate of trust; the interviewer is non-judgemental and takes the time to 'really listen' (Fraser, 2004; Moen, 2006). We contacted various organisations in Belgium who work with Dutch-speaking older persons (55 years or older) with limited financial means or other vulnerabilities that affect their well-being and who are able to give informed consent. A relatively diverse group of respondents – with respect to gender, age, household status and migration background – was selected with the aid of three organisations. The interviews were recorded and transcribed verbatim, and thematic content was analysed. We used 'sensitizing concepts' from the literature, especially from the Janssen's framework (2013).

This research is based on a limited number of narratives of vulnerable community-dwelling older persons in Flanders who are all active in at least one organisation. As a result, the research results cannot simply be transposed to contexts other than the one described here.

However, our findings correspond closely with the results of scientific research conducted in other countries (e.g. Janssen, 2013). Our narratives show that various life domains and sources of strength are indeed strongly interconnected and need to interact favourably in order to create an optimal climate for resilience and empowerment.

Various respondents are proud of their personality (e.g. being honest and courageous, having a good heart and meaning well), the activities they undertake (e.g. editing a book, meeting politicians to discuss social issues, helping others, counteracting injustices) and their knowledge (Respondent 4, 5, 6, 9, 13, 14). Respondent 5 says that although it is important to talk about specific problems (e.g. cancer, death of partner) with friends or family, it is essential not to complain too much (Respondent 3, 11, 15).

> *People don't always sympathize [with someone's health problems]. They themselves also have their issues, so they don't always want to hear from other people what's wrong with them.* (Respondent 11)

The narrative of Respondent 15 shows the detrimental influence of stigmatisation, the blaming-the-victim mechanism and the lack of basic resources (e.g. decent income). On the other hand, we observe the empowering force of participation. Respondent 15 lived in poverty for a long time because his invalidity made him unable to work and led to high medical costs. This negative spiral made him feel angry and even resulted in social withdrawal. By engaging in social organisations and being asked to come back, he regained pride in himself and a sense of self-worth:

> *that is more for a human being than you would think. That is how I started again. [...] At the time, they [people from that poverty organization] asked me to come back. During those five years [when his financial difficulties were very high], nobody has asked me that. I was so little approachable that nobody was waiting for me. So that was pleasant, and I went back. That's something: from time to time they ask you something, and people take into account what you say. That is very different from when you always need to talk about those debts and when they say it's your own fault all the time.* (Respondent 15)

From our narratives, it becomes apparent that acceptance of one's own limitations – which is a process that takes time – is an important source of strength which helps older persons to deal with adversities. Indeed, accepting one's own vulnerabilities makes it easier to accept support from others. However, various respondents do not seem to accept their limitations and are sometimes even ashamed of their situation, which negatively affects their resilience. For example, Respondent 12 states 'that would be a big step for me to give things out hand. Even groceries I still want to do myself'. Respondents describe how they try to preserve their mastery over their situation by practising their skills. Respondent 13, for example, states that he performs physical exercises during his morning ritual in order to maintain a good physique.

Various respondents also seem to have a balanced view on life, which helps them put negative encounters into perspective. They talk about both the positive and negative things they encountered during their lives.

> *I think that I already had the best behind me. And I am grateful, because I had a beautiful time. […] I think that I am very realistic. […] My mother taught me not to look up to all those who have more. Look down to all those who have less. That is something that still works [to be positive].* (Respondent 5)

Various respondents who have a rather optimistic view on life also do not adopt the role of a victim. In this respect, Respondent 9, for example, always tried to counteract injustices, which clearly gives her a sense of self-worth and general courage. On the other hand, we find that Respondent 15 explicitly blames 'the system' for the long period he lived in poverty. Taking the role of a victim allows him not to feel guilty for his situation and to be able to feel well again.

Most respondents indicate that they don't know what tomorrow will bring; through this sentiment, they do not anticipate much on future losses, try not to worry a lot and live in the moment and enjoy as much as possible (Respondent 1, 4, 6, 11, 12), as exemplified by Respondent 6:

> *I think every day has its value. I am very aware that time will never return. […] That's is a sort of philosophy of life I try to follow since long. […] I try to live in the present. […] I life day by day. I know from experience that when things come closer, that they are often easier to solve than when you think of them in advance. That is my experience in life.*

On the other hand, the awareness that every day can be one's last can also have negative implications with respect to future life projects. Most respondents find it important to continuously realise certain (small or big) goals, despite difficulties such as health problems and pain (Respondent 3, 5, 6, 7, 9, 12, 13): performing certain household tasks such as cleaning and doing groceries, giving this interview, writing a book, doing physical exercises every day and going outside are all included in these goals.

Based on these fifteen narratives, we find that people with a lot of interests and activities have a more positive outlook on life and seem to be more resilient. As Respondent 13 says, 'If you go sit down, it's over'. Various respondents indicate they never get bored and have various interests and activities such as engagement in organisations, volunteering, maintaining a household, communication with friends and family, reading, cooking, walking dogs, and participating in culture, food, alternative medicine, painting or gardening (Respondent 1, 4, 5, 6, 8, 9, 11, 12, 13, 14, 15). These activities not only give them energy and courage and help them to maintain a good physique, but the social aspect is also very important.

Respondents explain that positive relations with family and friends are a source of strength which helps them to maintain mastery over the determinants of their lives (Respondent 4, 5, 6, 7, 8, 11, 12, 13, 15): 'I get my energy from other people. […] I need that; I need people' (Respondent 5). Although positive relations offer both practical and emotional support, which reduces stress levels, the respondents state that they are somewhat hesitant to appeal to their family and friends because they do not want to burden them too much. Further, it is important that those family members and friends live nearby so that they are able to help them with small practical problems.

An intimate relationship with a partner is especially important because it can create a feeling of love and belonging. A lack of close relations is associated with feelings of (emotional) loneliness. Indeed, respondents who explicitly indicate that they do not feel lonely often still have a partner, contact with various family members or friends (Respondent 5, 6, 8), and people who feel lonely foremost lack an intimate relationship with someone, and some of them live a socially withdrawn life (Respondent 2, 3, 7, 10). Respondents give various reasons why they do not succeed in having a new intimate relationship, despite feeling lonely. One respondent explains that he does not want to start a new relationship because of the love and affection for his deceased partner: 'I still hold dear to her. That was the best woman in the world' (Respondent 13). Another respondent states that his psychological problems make him afraid of being rejected by others and make him think that nobody wants him: 'nobody wants me anymore. […] I don't know. Maybe I am too fat [laughs], or not attractive enough' (Respondent 10).

Some narratives demonstrate the important role professionals can play in the respondents' lives with respect to practical, emotional and relational issues (e.g. trust). A respondent states that thanks to the support of a specific professional and her psychologist, she has found the courage to take up contact with her grandchildren again (Respondent 3).

Some respondents mention the impact of how society perceives them on their well-being. One respondent states that he no longer has a professional identity since his retirement:

> you have the awareness that you no longer count as before. In the past, I had to gather legislation and vulgarise it and speak about it and handle that, I am a jurist, and now that is all a lot less. (Respondent 7)

We find that numerous useful services exist: social housing, service flats, recreational activities, debt mediation, social restaurants, transport, and so on. Nevertheless, the cost of and lack of access to some of these services prevent respondents from receiving the desired and needed support. Most of our respondents cannot afford a taxi. This is problematic because their health makes it difficult to get by on public transportation. As a result, they go out less than they would like to (Respondent 3, 5, 15). In addition, various respondents indicate that they would like to have some professional psychological support (e.g. to deal with grief or traumatic experiences), but they no longer make use of it because of the financial cost (Respondent 2, 3). Nevertheless, some respondents seek support by participating in group discussions of the organisations in which they are active, which offers them perspective and lets them know they are not alone with their problems (Respondent 2, 10).

Our respondents use various primary and secondary control processes to deal with adversities they encounter in life. Primary control is considered to be a constant and universal motive (Janssen et al., 2012), whereby people use their resources to influence outcomes in the environment and to realise personal goals (e.g. constructing a large social network) (Janssen, 2013). An example is an older person who actively engages in a social organisation in order to meet people and create new relations. Secondary control processes come to the foreground when people are unable to realise certain goals (e.g. enlarging their social network). At that moment, they apply psychological processes (e.g. adjusting goals, expectations and preferences) to bring themselves in line with their specific context (Janssen, 2013; van Tilburg, 2005):

> adaptations of the system of personal values and preferences, reinterpretations of stressful problem situations, changes in perspective and deliberate (downwards) comparisons are typical examples of processes that contribute to resolving the actual/ought discrepancy. (Greve & Staudinger, 2006, p. 818)

That way, older persons can disengage from goals that are no longer attainable and select goals that are more realistic to achieve (Greve & Staudinger, 2006). An example is older persons who learn to accept that their contact possibilities decrease because of severe mobility limitations.

To counter memory problems, some of our respondents write things down in a notebook as reminder. Physical health problems affect their daily life. When they go out, they think carefully about which routes and busses they can take (so as to walk as little as possible) and where there are benches on which they can rest (Respondent 7, 12, 13, 15).

Older persons are sometimes compelled to use secondary control processes through which they adapt goals and accept their vulnerabilities. Financial limitations force them to live economically, for example by not eating a warm meal every day (Respondent 1, 4, 6, 10). Furthermore, the respondents try to accept these limitations and focus on what they can still do, as Respondent 1 describes, for example:

> *I find that I have a luxurious life. People always want so much more and more, and sometimes I think: but we already have a luxurious life where we can do what we want, eat what we want. [...] I live well I think, and for example in the winter I put the heat on 18 degrees: for a lot of people that is very low, but I put on a big sweater. So in that way, I think that I live economic but I find that I live well.*

3. Implications for practice and policy

By thoroughly depicting the resilience processes of vulnerable older persons, we are able to make a number of relevant observations and formulate recommendations for practice and policy.

First, a global observation is that resilience is a process that takes time, not in the least because older persons themselves need to understand and be able to express their problems.

> *Accepting one's vulnerability or accepting the use of medical devices is not something that the majority of the older people easily deal with. Often, a period of having doubts, being insecure and considering one's options precedes such a more or less stable situation.* (Janssen, 2013, p. 62)

Although some problems can be dealt with relatively quickly, numerous (age-related) difficulties take a significant amount of time to deal with. This is especially the case when it concerns changes in social networks (e.g. due to divorce, death of a partner) or when it concerns emotions (e.g. feelings of loneliness) which require psychological adjustments. Therefore, we think that both professionals and the social network of older persons should try to enhance older persons' sources of strength and bear in mind that older persons often go through various stages when dealing with their problems, which takes time. Further, many respondents indicate that they find it difficult to accept certain vulnerabilities that cannot be overcome (e.g. health problems, memory problems), and often continue to struggle with them. In this respect, we are of the opinion that many older persons could benefit from some psychological help to learn to accept vulnerabilities that cannot be overcome. In general, much more attention should be given to the mental health of older persons. This was especially the case in the current Covid-19 pandemic, when many older persons indicated that they were lonelier (De Witte & Van Regenmortel, 2020). In accordance with other scientific literature (Plantinga, 2019), it is essential that older persons who live in poverty are supported not only materially but also emotionally and socially. Policy and practice should guarantee accessible, affordable and tailored psychological services for older persons.

Second, since older persons are more aware that they are in their last life phase, they seem to anticipate less specific problems they might face in the future. Although this awareness makes them enjoy the moment more (carpe diem), it can also pose difficulties when those problems do occur. Hence, it seems that older persons should at least already think about possible problems they might face in the future and how they would deal with them. That way, older persons would be mentally and emotionally better prepared the day they are faced with those problems. In the same vein, it is essential that the social network, professionals and society in general detect various hinge moments in the lives of older persons such as the death or divorce of a partner, retirement or severe health problems such as cancer. The detection of those junctures at the moment they present themselves is essential, since they are often accompanied by severe stressors that threaten the quality of life of older persons.

Last but not least, our narratives demonstrate that the power of giving has enormous beneficial effects on both older persons and society in general. In line with other research (Janssen et al., 2011), we find that doing things for other people (individually or through volunteering, practical or moral support) and looking to be meaningful to others is a crucial source of strength. Moreover, it has numerous positive effects on the quality of life of older persons; it results in increased feelings of self-worth and self-esteem, and it makes older persons feel good, useful, needed, valued and proud of themselves. Since the power of giving often includes social contact, other benefits can be constructing a social network, coming out of one's own comfort zone and having a challenge and engaging activities which distract from the own sorrows. Stimulating reciprocity and participation in daily life and in care are fruitful pathways for the resilience of older persons. How society, family, friends and professionals can trigger the give-take balance and tailor-made forms of participation is an important aspect in facilitating processes of resilience and empowerment. At present, it seems like the strengths of older persons are not fully made use of. For instance, by offering the necessary and personalised support (e.g. moving to more suitable home, psychological support, practical aid to stimulate mobility), escalation of those problems and their side effects (such as loneliness and social withdrawal) can be prevented. To this end, a more positive image of old age, exploring the numerous sources of older persons' strengths through authentic listening to the older persons themselves and embedding their experiential knowledge in practice and policy are of utmost importance.

In sum, it is essential that society invests more in seeking how older persons can contribute to and participate in society, by helping them find out what they can do. Furthermore, it is equally important that policymakers take away the contextual, structural barriers that impede older persons from participating to society by increasing their mobility and access to health and social services, for example. By creating 'enabling niches' in which older persons can further develop themselves and are no longer stigmatised and by investing in warm, empowering, reciprocal formal and informal relations, resilience in old age is strengthened.

4. Conclusion

The paradigm of empowerment focuses on the strengths of older persons without neglecting their vulnerabilities. It recognises older people who are ill, frail and vulnerable, and stands up for their rights to receive care and security and for being heard in society. Empowerment takes into account the pitfalls of 'active ageing', promotes social inclusion and focuses on structural barriers of exclusion. A strengthening environment (e.g. by creating enabling niches) is necessary to realise empowerment. If meaningful relations are stimulated, the resilience of older persons will improve. Rooted in positive psychology, resilience focuses on how people can positively overcome adversity and vulnerabilities and how they can manage challenging circumstances. Our resilient narratives of older persons show that various sources of strength on the individual, interactional and contextual domains are interconnected. For an optimal climate for resilience, these resources need to interact favourably. The importance of the power of giving, warm and positive relationships, strengthening community care and community building, and increasing access to health and social services are important ways to facilitate resilience and empowerment.

Older persons are full citizens and, in line with empowerment, co-creation seems to be the positive approach for policy, practice and research for cooperating with them. This benefits both older persons and society as a whole, and brings us another step closer in realising Silver Empowerment.

References

Akter, S., & Mallick, B. (2013). The poverty-vulnerability-resilience nexus: Evidence from Bangladesh. *Ecological Economics, 6*, 114–124. https://doi.org/10.1016/j.ecolecon.2013.10.008

Atlantic Health Promotion Research Centre (1999). *A study of resiliency in communities.* Health Canady. https://publications.gc.ca/collections/Collection/H39-470-1999E.pdf

Baur, V., & Abma, T. (2012). 'The Taste Buddies': participation and empowerment in a residential home for older people. *Ageing and Society, 32*(6), 1055–1078. https://doi.org/10.1017/S0144686X11000766

Boone, K., Roets, G., & Roose, R. (2020). Enabling the recognition of people in poverty through social work practice. From being on a par to participating on a par. *European Journal of Social Work, 23*(5), 755–766. https://doi.org/10.1080/13691457.2019.1639626

Börsch-Supan, A., Brandt, M., Hunkler, C., Kneip, T., Korbmacher, J., Malter, F., & Zuber, S. (2013). Data resource profile: the Survey of Health, Ageing and Retirement in Europe (SHARE). *International Journal of Epidemiology, 42*(4), 992–1001. https://doi.org/10.1093/ije/dyt088

Boumans, J. (2012). *Naar het hart van empowerment. Deel 1. Een onderzoek naar de grondslagen van empowerment van kwetsbare groepen* [To the heart of empowerment. Part 1. An examination of the foundations of empowerment of vulnerable groups]. Movisie.

Bozzaro, C., Boldt, J., & Schweda, M. (2018). Are older people a vulnerable group? Philosophical and bioethical perspectives on ageing and vulnerability. *Bioethics, 32*(4), 233–239. https://doi.org/10.1111/bioe.12440

Brodsky, A. E., & Cattaneo, L. B. (2013). A transconceptual model of empowerment and resilience: Divergence, convergence and interactions in kindred community concepts. *American Journal of Community Psychology, 52*(3), 333–346. https://doi.org/10.1007/s10464-013-9599-x

Buckingham, S. L., & Brodsky, A. E. (2021). Relative privilege, risk and sense of community: understanding Latinx immigrants' empowerment and resilience processes across the United States. *American Journal of Community Psychology, 67*(3–4), 364–379. https://doi.org/10.1002/ajcp.12486

Cantillon, B., Van den Bosch, K., & Lefebure, S. (2007). *Ouderen in Vlaanderen 1975–2005: Een terugblik in de toekomst* [Older people in Flanders 1975–2005: A look back into the future]. Acco.

Christens, B. D. (2011). Toward relational empowerment. *American Journal of Community Psychology, 50*(1), 114–128. https://doi.org/10.1007/s10464-011-9483-5

Clark, P. G., Burbank, P. M., Greene, G., & Riebe, D. (2011). What do we know about resilience in older adults? An exploration of some facts, factors, and facets. In B. Resnick, L. P. Gwyther & K. A. Roberto (Eds.), *Resilience in aging. Concepts, research, and outcomes* (pp. 51–66). Springer.

De Koker, B., Jacobs, T., Lodewijckx, E., & Vanderleyden, L. (2007). Recente ontwikkelingen in gezinnen en families: implicaties voor de ouderenzorg [Recent developments in families: implications for elderly care]. In B. Cantillon, K. Van den Bosch & S. Lefebure, *Ouderen in Vlaanderen 1975–2005. Een terugblik in de toekomst* [Older people in Flanders 1975–2005: A looking back into the future] (pp.79–107). Acco.

De Witte, J., & Van Regenmortel, T. (2019). *Silver Empowerment. Resilience of vulnerable elderly. A narrative research approach*. HIVA – KU Leuven. https://hiva.kuleuven.be/nl/nieuws/docs/tvr-18-tse-lssrc1-o2010-resilience-of-vulnerable.pdf

De Witte, J., & Van Regenmortel, T. (2020). *Silver Empowerment. A quantitative picture of loneliness among elderly in Belgium and Europe*. HIVA – KU Leuven. https://hiva.kuleuven.be/nl/nieuws/docs/tvr-18-tse-lssrc1-o2010-loneliness-of-people-with.pdf

Driessens, K., & Van Regenmortel, T. (2006). *Bind-Kracht in armoede. Leefwereld en hulpverlening. Boek 1* [The strength of ties in poverty. Lifeworld and social care. Book 1]. LannooCampus.

Earvolino-Ramirez, M. (2007). Resilience: A concept analysis. *Nursing Forum, 42*(2), 73–82. https://doi.org/10.1111/j.1744-6198.2007.00070.x

Emirbayer, M., & Mische, A. (1998). What is agency? *American Journal of Sociology, 103*(4), 962–1023. https://doi.org/10.1086/231294

European Commission, *European Year for Active Ageing and Solidarity between Generations*, consulted on 5 December 2018, http://europa.eu/ey2012/ey2012main.jsp?catId=971&langId=en.

Foster, L., & Walker, A. (2015). Active and successful aging: A European policy perspective. *The Gerontologist, 55*(1), 83–90. https://doi.org/10.1093/geront/gnu028

Fraser, H. (2004). Doing narrative research: Analysing personal stories line by line. *Qualitative Social Work, 3*(2), 179–201. https://doi.org/10.1177/1473325004043383

Fraser, M. W., Richman, J. M., & Galinsky, M. J. (1999). Risk, production and resilience: toward a conceptual framework for social work practice. *Social Work Research, 23*(3), 131–143. https://doi.org/10.1093/swr/23.3.131

Fuller-Iglesias, H., Sellars, B., & Antonucci, T. C. (2008). Resilience in old age: Social relations as a protective factor. *Research in Human Development, 5*(3), 181–193. https://doi.org/10.1080/15427600802274043

Garmezy, N. (1991). Resilience and vulnerability to adverse developmental outcomes associated with poverty. *American Behavioral Scientist, 34*(4), 416–430. https://www.proquest.com/scholarly-journals/resiliency-vulnerability-adverse-developmentel/docview/1306757830/se-2?accountid=17215

Geraerts, E. (2013). Van Marshmallows tot Veerkracht: Empowerment van Mens en Maatschappij [From Marshmallows to Resilience: Empowering People and Society]. *Christen-Democratische Reflecties, 2*(1), 7–12. CEDER Studiecentrum van de Vlaamse Christendemocraten.

Gerino, E., Rollè, L., Sechi, C., & Brustia, P. (2017). Loneliness, resilience, mental health, and quality of life in old age: A structural equation model. *Frontiers in Psychology, 8*, 2003. https://doi.org/10.3389/fpsyg.2017.02003.

Gobbens, R. (2017). *Health and well-being of frail elderly. Towards interventions that really count!* Inholland.

Greve, B., & Staudinger, U. M. (2006). Resilience in later adulthood and old age. Resources and potentials for successful aging. In D. Cichetti & D. Cohen (Eds.), *Developmental psychopathology* (Vol. 2, pp. 796–840). Wiley.

Hardy, S., Concato, J., & Gill, T. M. (2002). Stressful life events among community-living older persons. *Journal of General Internal Medicine, 17*(11), 841–847. https://doi.org/10.1046/j.1525-1497.2002.20105.x

Hardy, S., Concato, J., & Gill, T. M. (2004). Resilience of community dwelling older persons. *Journal of the American Geriatrics Society, 52*(2), 257–262. https://doi.org/10.1111/j.1532-5415.2004.52065.x

Harris, P. B. (2008). Another wrinkle in the debate about successful aging: The undervalued concept of resilience and the lived experience of dementia. *International Journal of Aging and Human Development, 67*(1), 43–61. https://doi.org/10.2190/AG.67.1.c

Hochhalter, A. K., Smith, M. L., & Ory, M. G. (2011). Successful Aging and Resilience: Applications for Public Health and Health Care. In B. Resnick, L. P. Gwyther & K. A. Roberto (Eds.), *Resilience in Aging. Concepts, Research, and Outcomes* (pp. 15-29). Springer.

Huber, M., Knottnerus, J. A., Green, L., van der Horst, H., Jadad, A. R., Kromhout, D., & Schnabel, P. (2011). How should we define health?. *British Medical Journal, 343.* https://doi.org/10.1136/bmj.d4163

Jacobs, G., Braakman, M., & Houweling, J. (2005). Op eigen kracht naar gezond leven. Empowerment in de gezondheidsbevordering: concepten, werkwijzen en onderzoeksmethoden [Self Stimulation to a Healthy Life. Empowerment in the Health Care Promotion: Concepts, Procedures and Research Methods]. Universiteit voor Humanistiek.

Janssen, B. M. (2010). Professionele ondersteuning vanuit het perspectief van kwetsbare ouderen. Het gevoel er niet meer bij te horen is moeilijk [Professional support from the perspective of vulnerable older people. The feeling of no longer belonging is difficult]. In T. Van Regenmortel (Ed.), *Empowerment en participatie van kwetsbare burgers. Ervaringskennis als kracht* [Empowerment and participation of vulnerable citizens. Expertise by experience as strength] (pp. 205–226). SWP Publishers.

Janssen, B. M. (2013). *Resilience and old age: Community care from an insider and empowerment perspective* [Doctoral dissertation, Vrije Universiteit Amsterdam].

Janssen, B. M., Van Regenmortel, T., & Abma, T. A. (2011). Identifying sources of strength: resilience from the perspective of older people receiving long-term community care. *European journal of ageing, 8*(3), 145–156. https://doi.org/10.1007/s10433-011-0190-8

Janssen, B. M., Abma, T. A., & Van Regenmortel, T. (2012). Maintaining mastery despite age related losses. The resilience narratives of two older women in need of long-term community care. *Journal of Aging Studies, 26*(3), 343–354. https://doi.org/10.1016/j.jaging.2012.03.003

Janssen, B. M., Snoeren, M. W., Van Regenmortel, T., & Abma, T. A. (2015). Working towards integrated community care for older people: Empowering organisational features from a professional perspective. *Health Policy, 119*(1), 1–8. https://doi.org/10.1016/j.healthpol.2014.09.016

Jensen, P.H., & Skjøtt-Larsen, J. (2021). Theoretical challenges and social inequalities in Active Ageing. *International Journal of Environmental Research and Public Health, 18*(17), 9156. https://doi.org/10.3390/ijerph18179156

Katz, S., & Calasanti, T. (2015). Critical perspectives on successful aging: Does it 'appeal more than it illuminates'? *The Gerontologist, 55*(1), 26–33. https://doi.org/10.1093/geront/gnu027

Kisthardt, W. (1997). The strengths model of case management: Principles and helping functions. In D. Saleebey (Ed.), *The strengths perspective in social work practice* (pp. 97–113).

Leipold, B., & Greve, W. (2009). Resilience. A conceptual bridge between coping and development. *European Psychologist, 14*(1), 40–50. https://doi.org/10.1027/1016-9040.14.1.40

Lloyd, P. (1991). The empowerment of elderly people. *Journal of Aging Studies, 5*(2), 125–135. https://doi.org/10.1016/0890-4065(91)90001-9

Luthar, S. S., Cicchetti, D., & Becker, B. (2000). The construct of resilience: a critical evaluation and guidelines for future work. *Child Development, 71*(3), 543–562. https://www.jstor.org/stable/1132374

Macaulay, A. C., Commanda, L. E., Freeman, W. L., Gibson, N., McCabe, M. L., Robbins, C. M., & Twohig, P. L. (1998). Responsible research with communities: Participatory research in primary care. Policy statement on participatory research at NAPCRG Annual Membership Meeting. https://www.napcrg.org/media/1271/1999pr.pdf

Machielse, A. (2015). The heterogeneity of socially isolated older adults: A social isolation typology. *Journal of Gerontological Social Work, 58*(4), 338–356. https://doi.org/10.1080/01634372.2015.1007258

Machielse, A. (2016). *Afgezonderd of ingesloten? Over sociale kwetsbaarheid van ouderen* [Secluded or enclosed? On the social vulnerability of older people]). Universiteit voor Humanistiek.

Maertens, M., Desmet, B., & Defrenne, C. (2015). *Report: empowerment vision and theoretical foundation*. Centrum Empowerment in Ouderenzorg.

Masten, A. S. (1994). Resilience in individual development: Successful adaptation despite risk and adversity. In M. Wang & E. Gordon (Eds), *Risk and resilience in inner city America: Challenges and prospects* (pp. 3–25). Erlbaum.

Masten, A. S., & Wright, M. O. (2009). Resilience over the lifespan: development perspectives on resistance, recovery, and transformation. In J. W. Reich (Ed.) *Handbook of adult resilience* (pp. 213–237). Guilford Publications.

Mlinac, M. E., Sheeran, T. H., Blissmer, B., Lees, F., & Martins, D. (2011). Psychological Resilience. In B. Resnick, L. P. Gwyther & K. A. Roberto (Eds.), *Resilience in Aging. Concepts, Research, and Outcomes* (pp. 67-87). Springer.

Moen, T. (2006). Reflections on the narrative research approach. *International Journal of Qualitative Methods, 5*(4), 56–69. https://doi.org/10.1177/160940690600500405

Moro, Á., Maiztegui-Oñate, C., & Solabarrieta, J. (2021). Vulnerability among European youth: A proposal for a multidimensional approach (2013–2017). *Sustainability, 13*(16), 9252. https://www.mdpi.com/2071-1050/13/16/9252

Neimeyer, R. (1997). Meaning construction and the experience of chronic loss. In K. J. Doka (Ed.), *Living with grief: when illness is prolonged* (pp. 223–237). Taylor and Francis.

Niedzwiedz, C. L., Richardson, E. A., Tunstall, H., Shortt, N. K., Mitchell, R. J., & Pearce, J. R. (2016). The relationship between wealth and loneliness among older people across Europe: Is social participation protective? *Preventive Medicine, 91*, 24–31. https://doi.org/10.1016/j.ypmed.2016.07.016

Numans, W., Van Regenmortel, T., Schalk, R., & Boog, J. (2021). Vulnerable persons in society: an insider's perspective. *International Journal of Qualitative Studies on Health and Well-being, 16*(1), 1863598. https://doi.org/10.1080/17482631.2020.1863598

Paddock, D. (2001). *Bent but not broken: Building resilient adoptive families.* https://adopting.org/.

Peeters, J. (2012). Social work and sustainable development: Towards a social-ecological practice model. *Journal of Social Intervention: Theory and Practice, 21*(3), 5–26. https://doi.org/10.18352/jsi.316

Peterson, N. A., & Zimmerman, M. A. (2004). Beyond the individual: Toward a nomological network of organizational empowerment. *American Journal of Community Psychology, 34*(1–2), 129–145. https://doi.org/10.1023/B:AJCP.0000040151.77047.58

Pfaller, L., & Schweda, M. (2019). Excluded from the good life? An ethical approach to conceptions of Active Ageing. *Social Inclusion, 7*(3), 44–53. https://doi.org/10.17645/si.v7i3.1918

Plantinga, A. (2019). *Poor psychology: Poverty, shame, and decision making* [Doctoral dissertation, Tilburg University].

Ranzijn, R. (2010). Active ageing: Another way to oppress marginalized and disadvantaged elders? Aboriginal elders as a case study. *Journal of Health Psychology, 15*(5), 716–723. https://doi.org/10.1177/1359105310368181

Rutter, M. (1987) Psychosocial resilience and protective mechanisms. *American Journal of Orthopsychiatry, 57*(3), 316–331. https://doi.org/10.1111/j.1939–0025.1987.tb03541.x

Rutter, M. (1993). Resilience: some conceptual considerations. *Journal of Adolescent Health, 14*(8), 626–631. https://doi.org/10.1016/1054–139X(93)90196-V

Ryff, C. D., Singer, B., & Love, G. D. (1998). Resilience in adulthood and later life: defining features and dynamic processes. In J. Lomranz (Ed.), *Handbook of aging and mental health: an integrative approach* (pp. 69–96). Plenum Press.

Saleebey, D. (1996). The strengths perspective in social work practice: extensions and cautions, *Social Work, 41*(3), 296–305. https://doi.org/10.1093/sw/41.3.296

Schröder-Butterfill, E., & Marianti, R. (2006). A framework for understanding old-age vulnerabilities, *Ageing & Society, 26*(1), 9–35. https://doi.org/10.1017/S0144686X05004423

Seligman, M., & Csikszentmihaly, M. (2000). Positive psychology: an introduction. *American Psychologist, 55*(1), 5–14. https://psycnet.apa.org/doi/10.1037/0003–066X.55.1.5

Steenssens, K., & Van Regenmortel, T. (2007). *Empowerment Barometer. Process evaluation of empowerment in neighbourhood-based activation projects. Equal project: Labour for neighbour 2005–2007.* HIVA – KU Leuven.

Taylor, J. B. (1997). Niches and practice: Extending the ecological perspective. In D. Saleebey (Ed.), *The Strengths Perspective in Social Work Practice (second edition)* (pp. 217–227). Longman.

Vanderplaat, M. (1999). Locating the feminist scholar: relational empowerment and social activism. *Qualitative Health Research, 9*(6), 773–785. https://doi.org/10.1177/104973299129122270

Van Kessel, G. (2013). The ability of older people to overcome adversity: a review of the resilience concept. *Geriatric Nursing, 34*(2), 122–127. https://doi.org/10.1016/j.gerinurse.2012.12.011

Van Regenmortel, T. (2002). *Empowerment en maatzorg. Een krachtgerichte, psychologische kijk op armoede* [Empowerment and tailored care. A strength-oriented psychological view on poverty]. Acco.

Van Regenmortel, T. (2006). Veerkracht [Resilience]. In K. Driessens & T. Van Regenmortel (Eds.), *Bind-kracht in armoede. Leefwereld en hulpverlening. Boek 1* [The strength of ties in poverty. Lifeworld and social care. Book 1] (pp. 113–140). Acco.

Van Regenmortel T. (2007). Empowerment in de zorg. Krachten en kwetsbaarheden [Empowerment in care. Strengths and vulnerabilities]. In P. Develtere, I. Nicaise, J. Pacolet & L. Sannen (Eds.), *Werk & Wereld in de Weegschaal. Confronterende visies op onderzoek en samenleving.* [Work & world in the balance. Confronting visions on research and society] (pp. 261–280) Lannoocampus.

Van Regenmortel, T. (2009). Empowerment als uitdagend kader voor sociale inclusie en moderne zorg [Empowerment as a challenging framework for social inclusion and modern care]. *Journal of Social Intervention. Theory and Practice, 18*(4), 22–42. https://doi.org/10.18352/jsi.186

Van Regenmortel, T. (2010). Empowerment en maatschappelijke kwetsbaarheid [Empowerment and societal vulnerability]. In *PRVMZ. De gezondheidsagenda voor de Toekomst.* [The health agenda for the future] (pp. 130–143). Fontys.

Van Regenmortel, T. (2011). Lexicon van empowerment. Marie Kamphuis-lezing [Lexicon of empowerment. Marie Kamphuis Lecture], Marie Kamphuis Stichting.

Van Regenmortel, T. (2013). Empowerment Times. Een uitdagend en hoopvol kader voor de bestrijding van armoede en uitsluiting [Empowerment Times. A challenging and hopeful framework for combating poverty and exclusion]. In *Christen-Democratische Reflecties, 2*(1), 17–30. CEDER Studiecentrum van de Vlaamse Christendemocraten.

van Tilburg, T. (2005). *Gesloten uitbreiding. Sociaal kapitaal in de derde en vierde levensfase* [Closed expansion. Social capital in the third and fourth stages of life]. https://home.fsw.vu.nl/tg.van.tilburg/2005%20oratie.pdf

Werner, E. E., & Smith, R. S. (1982). *Vulnerable but invincible: a longitudinal study of resilient children and youth.* McGraw-Hill.

WHO (2002). *Active Ageing. A policy framework.* WHO.

WHO (2015). *World report on ageing and health.* WHO.

Zimmerman, M. A. (1995). Psychological empowerment: issues and illustrations, *American Journal of Community Psychology, 23*(5), 581–599. https://doi.org/10.1007/BF02506983

CHAPTER 2
THE ECONOMIC COST OF THE LONELINESS OF OLDER PERSONS

Jozef Pacolet, Gregorio Rodríguez Cabrero,
Simón Sosvilla-Rivero

1.   Introduction

Although until recently, loneliness and social isolation were often taboo and received little attention, loneliness is increasingly recognised as an important social risk. From being a strictly private problem, loneliness and social isolation are increasingly considered social problems. This transition has been progressive and favoured by phenomena such as ageing, the importance of mental health and increased attention for quality of life. The restrictive measures implemented to deal with the Covid-19 pandemic have further increased attention for loneliness and social isolation among older persons and other age groups (see e.g. O'Sullivan et al., 2021). The increasing awareness of this subject has triggered academic researchers to estimate its costs and to discern effective loneliness policies.

This chapter contributes to the literature by comparing the experiences of Spain and Belgium, two countries with different welfare states and care models but with similar levels of loneliness. The following section presents a theoretical framework to evaluate the economic cost of loneliness of older persons. The two subsequent sections successively analyse the case studies of Spain and Belgium, including several comparisons. Finally, we provide some concluding remarks and policy implications.

2. Theoretical dimensions of the economic cost of loneliness of older persons: A literature review

Loneliness is a fundamental part of the human condition and can be described as 'the unpleasant experience that occurs when a person's network of social relations is deficient in some important way, either quantitatively or qualitatively' (Perlman & Peplau, 1981, p. 31). It is a significant societal challenge, and although it is not only a problem for older persons, they appear to have relatively high loneliness rates (Dykstra, 2009). In the section that follows, we offer a review of the measurement of loneliness and social isolation, the identification of the financial costs of loneliness and its quantification.

2.1 Measuring loneliness and social isolation

Loneliness is measured directly by asking people about their subjective feelings of loneliness. In this respect, two main measurement scales have been extensively used in empirical research, which are particularly suitable for large surveys. The first is the revised UCLA Loneliness Scale (Russell, 1996), which consists of twenty items designed to measure feelings of loneliness, and its shorter version, the three-item UCLA Loneliness Scale (Hughes et al., 2004). The second scale was developed by De Jong Gierveld and collaborators (De Jong Gierveld & Kamphuis, 1985); it consists of eleven items, and there is also a shorter six-item version (De Jong-Gierveld & van Tilburg, 2006). Further, loneliness can also be measured indirectly by measuring important determinants of loneliness, such as household type (see Chapter 3 in this volume) or social isolation. The latter refers to the lack or almost complete absence of relations with other people and can be measured by the number of contacts or contact frequency. For the measurement of social isolation, the Lubben social network scale (Lubben & Gironda, 2003) is usually used, providing information about a person's social contacts with family, close friends and acquaintances.

2.2 Identifying the cost of loneliness

The cost of loneliness of older persons can be estimated using the financial costs for persons who feel lonely and for their family and friends, as well as for the health system, the community and the economy in general.

Concerning the socio-health costs of loneliness, there have been hundreds of published papers on the detrimental effects of loneliness on health and quality of life (Nyqvist et al., 2019). In this regard, it is important to consider both the costs of medical care and social assistance according to different socio-economic groups and types of loneliness (because the costs depend on specific loneliness characteristics). Medically, different studies have linked loneliness to multiple chronic conditions, heart disease, lung disease, cardiovascular disease, hypertension, atherosclerosis, stroke and metabolic disorders, such as obesity and metabolic disease (Adam et al., 2006; Vander Weele et al., 2011; Cacioppo et al., 2014; Cacioppo et al., 2015; Valtorta et al., 2016). Indeed, there is consensus on the link between loneliness and morbidity and mortality, especially in the older population (Hawkley & Cacioppo, 2010). Psychologically, loneliness is also associated with various problems such as depression, psychological stress and anxiety (Lauder et al., 2006; Cacioppo et al., 2006), cognitive decline and the progression of Alzheimer's disease (Wilson et al., 2007). Further, loneliness has a significant impact on lifestyle such as diabesity, smoking, less physical activity, high cholesterol (Richard et al., 2016) and sleep dysfunction (Cacioppo et al., 2002).[1] Based on these insights, we conclude that loneliness has a considerable impact on the increasing healthcare costs of Western countries (WHO, 2018) because it results in a higher need and utilisation of healthcare, especially among older persons who suffer disproportionally from multiple conditions (Andersen & Newman, 2005). Moreover, loneliness can also create additional burdens on health services. Indeed, it is associated with more general practitioner consultations, regardless of health status, because people who feel lonely may seek medical assistance to satisfy their need for social interaction (Ellaway et al., 1999).[2] In this respect, Gerst-Emerson and Jayawardhana (2015) stress that successful loneliness interventions for older persons may result in a significant decrease in physician visits and healthcare costs.

As for the indirect costs for society, loneliness has wider societal implications because persons with mental health problems require more social support from families and communities, and there is a loss of economic activity when individuals are unable to work due to health problems. In sum, there are substantial costs to individuals, families, the public purse and society related to loneliness, and some of these costs can potentially be avoided.

2.3 Quantification of the cost of loneliness

Despite the considerable impact of loneliness on the health system in most Western countries (WHO, 2018), economic research on the financial costs of loneliness is scarce. A recent review by Mihalopoulos et al. (2020) concludes that there is a lack of evidence about the economic costs of loneliness and cost-effective loneliness interventions. This study highlights the importance of understanding the economic burden of loneliness or social isolation and is one of the first to evaluate the cost-effectiveness of interventions targeting loneliness or social isolation.

McDaid et al. (2016) present the most detailed and comprehensive study to date, estimating some economic benefits associated with a reduction in loneliness in the United Kingdom. To that end, the authors calculate total costs representing the net value of current and future costs due to new cases of loneliness in a given year. They use a decision analytical model that takes on an incidence-based approach to costing, whereby they identify all new loneliness cases for a specific geographical population in a given year and subsequently estimate the costs associated with treating them, as well as other direct and indirect financial and non-financial costs over ten years. They contend that effective action to avoid loneliness in a general population cohort, some of whom will already be lonely, could avoid a net value of more than £1,700 (values from 2015) per person spread over ten years. Their model suggests that the majority of these savings (59 per cent) are due to avoiding unplanned hospital admissions, followed by avoiding excess general practitioner consultations (16 per cent) and the delay in the use of dementia services for most of the remaining averted costs (20 per cent). Moreover, McDaid et al. (2016) claim that the avoidable costs for older persons who are severely lonely may increase to £6,000 over ten years.

3. A southern or family-oriented welfare state regime: Spain

Loneliness is a social problem in Western countries (Cacioppo & Cacioppo, 2018). In Spain, the scientific and political debate on loneliness is relatively recent (Bermejo, 2003; Pinazo & Donio-Bellegarde, 2018; Yanguas, Pinazo-Hernandis et al., 2018; Yanguas, Cilveti et al., 2020, among others): it is only since 2000 that loneliness has been considered as a social problem and has been increasingly incorporated into regional and local social policies. Covid-19 has given a new push to the debate to promote a national agenda to combat loneliness, which does not yet exist in Spain.

In this section, we tentatively answer three questions: (1) Does the incidence of loneliness vary between different welfare regimes, with a specific focus on Spain? (2) Which social policies that aim to combat loneliness and social isolation of older persons are put in place? (3) Which social policies are necessary to stimulate the social inclusion of older people?

3.1   Panoramic view of loneliness and social isolation in Spain

Our analysis of loneliness and social isolation in Spain is based on European and national numbers that allow us to present a panoramic view of the phenomenon. According to the European Quality of Life Survey 2016 (EQLS), 5 per cent of Spanish older persons (65 years or older) feel lonely all the time or much of the time, which is about 6 per cent of the Spanish adult population (eighteen years or older). Further, the percentage of older persons in Spain who feel lonely is lower than that in other countries of the Mediterranean welfare regime (9 per cent in Portugal, 13 per cent in Italy and 14 per cent in Greece) and even in certain countries with a Continental welfare regime (such as in Germany, Austria, Belgium and France). However, it is higher than several Nordic welfare regime countries, which have rates of about 2 per cent (in Denmark and Sweden). In this respect, d'Hombres et al. (2018) observe that loneliness is unevenly distributed among the countries of the European Union, with the type of welfare regime being a fundamental explanatory factor (see e.g. European Commission, 2019a, 2019b; Nyqvist et al., 2019; Sundström et al., 2009).

With respect to social isolation, the vast majority of older persons in Spain (sixty-five years or older) are not socially isolated: they maintain networks of social contacts in the area where they live (84 per cent), and they have personal contact with relatives (82 per cent), friends or neighbours who do not live at home (93 per cent), as well as with relatives over the telephone and internet (86 per cent). Social isolation – defined as a lack of social contacts and having few people to interact with regularly – affects approximately one out of seven older persons in Spain. The importance of personal and family contacts (i.e. interaction with extended family members and friends) is, in general, greater in Mediterranean welfare regime countries (85 per cent of them have regular contact with their family and friends) than in the Nordic welfare regime countries and Continental regime countries. However, the differences between the EU countries are not significant concerning social isolation.

In sum, the European indicators for loneliness and social isolation among older persons provide a moderately higher integration profile in Spain than in Mediterranean welfare regime countries and several Continental welfare regime countries, but lower than the Nordic countries. While Mediterranean welfare regime countries have relatively more positive indicators of neighbourhood and family relations, their loneliness levels are also higher than those of the Nordic and Anglo-Saxon countries. Although the Mediterranean welfare regime is a model oriented towards family, neighbours and friends, social participation indicators (which are associated with lower loneliness levels) is lower than in countries of the Continental and Nordic regime. Only 12 per cent of the Spanish population over sixty-five years old participates in associations, clubs or different types of civil society organisations, which is higher than in other Mediterranean countries such as Greece (4 per cent), Portugal (8 per cent) and Italy (11 per cent). Moreover, this participation of older persons in Spain is less than half than that of the Continental countries and three times lower than in Nordic and Anglo-Saxon countries, where it lies between 34 per cent and 42 per cent. Similar conclusions can be drawn regarding participation rates of older persons as volunteers in social and community service activities. In Spain, the volunteer rate is 5 per cent, which is half of Continental regime countries and one third the participation found in Nordic and Anglo-Saxon countries.

The pioneering research about loneliness and social isolation by Díez Nicolás and Morenos Páez (2015) highlights that 20 per cent of the Spanish adult population in 2016 lived alone; 41 per cent of this group lived alone because they had no choice. People over sixty-five years who live alone represent 32 per cent of this group (2,792,390), of which 18 per cent (1,615,367 people) feel lonely in some way. Almost half of the Spanish population (49.5 per cent) believes that the group that suffers the most from loneliness is people over sixty-five years. The difference with the EQLS is that this indicator refers to persons who experience loneliness all the time or almost all the time, while the Spanish survey refers to loneliness regardless of its intensity. Using different methodologies and samples, other studies (see e.g. FEM-CET, 2018; Yanguas et al., 2019) demonstrate a growing incidence of loneliness among the population over sixty-five years old in Spain.

3.2 Spanish social policies to address loneliness

What is the nature of the social policies that aim to prevent or alleviate loneliness and social isolation in Spain? This question has an ambivalent answer. On the one hand, the public opinion finds that loneliness should be an object of interest of public institutions (64.6 per cent), followed by individuals (27.8 per cent), non-governmental organisations (NGOs, 3.7 per cent) and private institutions (2.4 per cent) (Díez & Morenos, 2015). Hence, loneliness is already part of the institutional logic of social policies in Spain, where loneliness and social isolation are increasingly recognised as social problems. However, people who feel lonely indicate that the answer to loneliness must first be investigated within the family (86.6 per cent), followed by social services (4.2 per cent) and volunteering (1.1 per cent). In other words, the problem of loneliness is increasingly visible, but social inertia makes it so that the answer resides mainly in the intimate family environment and secondarily in public institutions and private organisations.

Is a national strategy needed to combat loneliness in Spain? In this respect, the need for a national strategy has made its way in Spain as a consequence of trends in the EU, the demand for professional organisations and NGOs, and the growing development of regional and municipal programmes for the prevention and fight against loneliness.[3] Programmes aimed at promoting the well-being of older persons in autonomous communities and local corporations are increasingly taking into account loneliness and isolation.[4] The scientific debate on loneliness underlies these public programmes and most private initiatives against loneliness and social isolation. Finally, in December 2018, Spain joined the growing trend of social policies in the Member States of the European Union to promote national strategies and action plans that address social visibility, institutional commitment and operational guidance for loneliness policies (CEOMA, 2018).

Thus, the activities of municipal and regional public initiatives are increasing, in which pioneering initiatives stand out.[56] The municipal elections in April 2019 have given institutional visibility to the policies against the loneliness in the programmes of the political parties and to the initiatives of the municipalities to create local councils to combat loneliness. Meanwhile, organised civil society initiatives are numerous and the good practices in the fight against loneliness and social isolation are being consolidated.[7]

A common denominator of public and private initiatives is the need to consolidate public-private collaboration programmes and projects (Pinazo & Donio-Bellegarde, 2018) that consider the complexity of organising a comprehensive response to the problem; have the leading role of people who experience loneliness and social isolation; and, finally, develop preventive actions that reinforce the social capital of people and the social environments in which they live.

Finally, it is necessary to highlight that Spain has recently joined the current EU welfare states, which put loneliness on the political agenda. In 2018, the Spanish Parliament approved the 'non-legislative proposal relating to the promotion of measures to combat chronic loneliness' (see Boletín Oficial de las Cortes Generales, 2018). This proposal urges the Government of Spain, in collaboration with the autonomous communities, to promote awareness in society and improve knowledge about loneliness, with special reference to older persons, as well as to approve a national strategy to tackle loneliness in relation to the National Elderly Strategy for Active Ageing 2018–2021. Following this, compliance with the non-legislative proposal regarding the creation of a State Volunteering Platform to accompany older persons who feel lonely, approved by the Equality Commission of the Parliament in September 2018.

3.3   Policies to stimulate social inclusion

Based on the growing social awareness of loneliness, social research has developed relevant advances in the understanding of the phenomenon in Spain. Almost two decades have passed during which progress was made to increase social awareness of the problem and in the parliamentary initiative to design a national strategy against loneliness. Beyond the characterisation of the event as an epidemic or disease by the media, the empirical evidence indicates that we are indeed facing an important social phenomenon, which is not a disease that can be the object of medicalisation, but a multidimensional reality that demands the joint response of the public sector and organised civil society. Several studies (see e.g. Bermejo, 2003; Pinazo & Donio-Bellegarde, 2018; Sancho Castiello, 2019; Yanguas et al., 2018) highlight the importance of the problem, differentiating between its different dimensions, its particular prevalence in older age groups and the need to develop a comprehensive answer whose fundamental core must revolve around the construction of community environments compatible with the personal autonomy of people (see the Flemish policy initiative of 'caring neighbourhoods', Chapter 4). Prevention stands out as a central objective of policies against loneliness.

Experts consider policies to combat loneliness and social isolation as an investment in social cohesion and social inclusion. Although the risk group that stands out in several studies is that of people over sixty-five years of age, the importance of this subject is confirmed for all ages. The acceleration of the increasing longevity of the population, the persistent fall in fertility rates and changes in the social structure of households in Spain (Abellán García et al., 2020) do not imply a loss of the role of the family in the fight against loneliness, but a new configuration of its role within national, regional and local strategies in which the fight against loneliness and isolation are transversal to all ages (Martínez & Celdrán, 2019). Family support is solid in Spain, but relational social capital (social participation and volunteering) is still weak compared to the countries of the Continental, Anglo-Saxon and Nordic welfare regimes. The strengthening of civil society in Spain is also decisive to stimulate the empowerment of older people (De Witte & Van Regenmortel, 2019). Policy programmes to combat loneliness in Spain will have to combine individual support, which today is reduced to the family environment, with greater development of community activities, active ageing, volunteering and the extension of intergenerational programmes in the framework of programmes for age-friendly cities.

4. A Bismarckian oriented welfare state regime: Belgium

Well-developed welfare states that provide adequate income support and health and social care services support older persons to cope with the risks of life. In this section, we first situate the risk of older persons in Belgium living alone, being socially isolated or feeling lonely. Second, we provide some tentative estimates of the increased cost of illness due to loneliness. Even when the risk of loneliness concerns people of all ages, the cost of reduced health is situated mostly in later life. In this respect, advanced welfare states have a huge responsibility in absorbing and preventing the negative impact of loneliness. Third, we discuss some policy initiatives to prevent and alleviate loneliness in Belgium.

4.1 Panoramic view of loneliness and social isolation in Belgium

In what follows, we discuss some indicators for social isolation (e.g. living alone or not, having regular contacts or not) and loneliness of older persons in Belgium and from an international perspective. We not only compare Belgium with Spain but also with the Netherlands because hereafter we will use evidence from the Netherlands to estimate healthcare costs.

Table 2.1 shows that older persons in Belgium largely live alone (31 per cent), with even 43 per cent in the Brussels Region living alone. On top of that, about 6 per cent live in a residential care setting, which implies that in this so-called collective household, they are most of the time living alone. Those at home can benefit from a high level of home care, but this is not the case in the Brussels Region. Table 2.2 demonstrates that the share of older persons living alone in Belgium is higher than the European average, but that compared to the Netherlands, we have more mixed-household situations, in addition to the situation of living with a partner. These mixed-household situations are, however, much more frequent in Spain. Table 2.2 illustrates also that this situation is completely different between men and women. These two tables give some insight into certain dimensions of loneliness – namely, the objective household situation, the urban role of the capital region, the gender dimension, the availability of home care that might alleviate feelings of loneliness, and the share of older persons living in a residential care setting, which might solve or create new problems of isolation.

Table 2.1: Living and care situation of older persons in Belgium (65+), in absolute numbers (in thousands) and as percentage of the total number of older persons (65+) (2018).

	Persons of 65+	Persons of 65+ living alone	Persons of 65+ staying in retire-ment homes	Persons of 65+ with no district nursing or other related services	Persons of 65+ using district nursing	Persons of 65+ in other tem-porary services	Persons of 65+ staying in hospital	Total popula-tion
Number of persons (in thousands)								
Brussels Region	168	72	13	149	6	0	3	1,199
Flanders	1,376	395	73	1,182	117	4	24	6,553
Wallonia	725	242	44	631	49	1	13	3,624
Belgium	2,275	710	130	1,968	173	6	41	11,376
In % of population 65+								
Brussels Region		42.9	7.6	88.5	3.7	0.1	2.1	
Flanders		28.7	5.3*	85.9	8.5	0.3	1.7	
Wallonia		33.4	6.1	87	6.7	0.2	1.8	
Belgium		31.2	5.7	86.5	7.6	0.3	1.8	

* This percentage increased in Flanders even further if we look at available places (some 6.2 per cent of persons above 65) and should be added with the service flats (some 2.4 per cent of persons above 65), individual flats, mostly built near retirement homes.Source InterMutualistisch Agentschap and Agentschap Zorg en Gezondheid

Table 2.2: Distribution of population aged 65 and over by the type of household in Belgium and from an international perspective, 2019 (in %)

Household type	One adult 65 years or older	Couple without children and without other persons	Couple living with other persons	Other household
		Total		
European Union – 27 countries	32.6	47.1	10.7	9.6
Belgium	33.8	53.2	6.2	6.7
Spain	24.4	40.3	18.9	16.3
Netherlands	30.8	64.8	2.7	1.7
		Men		
European Union – 27 countries	22.6	57.3	15.3	4.9
Belgium	24.2	63.4	8.7	3.7
Spain	17.2	49.3	25.2	8.3
Netherlands	19.7	75.2	4.0	1.1
		Women		
European Union – 27 countries	40.5	39.2	7.3	13.1
Belgium	41.7	44.9	4.2	9.2
Spain	30.1	33.3	14.1	22.5
Netherlands	40.6	55.7	1.5	2.3

* The Survey on Income and Living Conditions data implies that persons in institutional care are not included. The percentage of a population living in those settings could be added to the share of persons living on their own. Source Eurostat, based on EU-SILC survey [ilc_lvps30]

In Table 2.3, we summarise some evidence of loneliness and social isolation among older persons in Belgium. Based on the Survey of Health, Ageing and Retirement in Europe (SHARE), De Witte and Van Regenmortel (2021) show that 24 per cent of older persons felt lonely in 2015. This is somewhat higher than in the other 'northern' countries (19 per cent) and central European countries (21 per cent), in which Belgium is included, but lower than in eastern and southern Europe (36 per cent), where Spain is included. Despite the higher level of older persons living alone in Belgium and the Netherlands compared to Spain, the subjective feeling of loneliness is similar or even lower. De Witte and Van Regenmortel (2021) show how feelings of loneliness are higher in single households or in older persons without a partner, so the fact that the overall feeling of loneliness in Belgium is not much different from Spain is surprising. This might be related to the lower levels of social participation of older persons in Spain in comparison to Belgium. Further research is needed to study whether loneliness levels are mitigated by the support received from welfare state provisions, professional care and income support. Welfare state provisions allow older persons to live in a residential care setting. Although this could remedy feelings of loneliness, at the same time, it could also reinforce those feelings (or at least not succeed to mitigate these feelings). Many of the population surveys that are in use, such as SILC, SHARE and European Health Interview Survey (EHIS), limit themselves to persons living at home or under-represent those living in institutions. This makes it difficult to assess the situation of older persons living in residential care institutions. Although based on a small sample in SHARE, the different loneliness levels between those interviewed at home or in an institution are substantial (see Table 2.3). While in 2015 about 24 per cent of the persons who lived in a private household felt lonely in Belgium, almost 38 per cent of persons who live in a nursing home felt lonely (in 2013 it was even 44 per cent; see Table 2.3). If we apply those percentages to the total older population and those living in a retirement home, one out of ten older persons feeling lonely lived in a retirement home.[8] There is probably a selection bias, as those living alone or who have problems of social isolation or loneliness tend to go to a residential care setting sooner than those who have more social support.

Van Regenmortel et al. (2021) combined information on loneliness with in-formation on social exclusion. About 71 per cent of the older persons in Belgium had a low risk of social isolation or had a relatively large social network. But the other 29 per cent had a severe level of social isolation or exclusion. The research by Vandenbroucke et al. (2012) provides further information on the combined prevalence of loneliness and having a small or large social network. Again, a relatively large group (23 per cent) felt lonely and had a small social network.

Table 2.3: Loneliness and social participation of older persons in Belgium and from an international perspective

Categories of old-age social exclusion, Flanders and Brussels, N=20,275 (rural and urban) (a)	%
Low risk of social exclusion	45.7
Non-participating financially excluded but with high levels of social relations	25.5
Environmentally excluded, excluded from social relations	12.5
Severely excluded in all dimensions of old-age exclusion	16.2

Categories of loneliness among older persons 2011, 1,500 Belgians above 65 (b)	%
The lonely, feel lonely and have a broad social network	23.0
The socially isolated, feel lonely and have a small social network	23.0
The socially resistant, do not feel lonely and have a broad network	45.0
The contact poor, do not feel lonely and have a small social network	9.0

Prevalence of loneliness based on SHARE, population 65+ (private households) (c)

	2013		2015	
	N	% of older persons who feel lonely	N	% of older persons who feel lonely
Belgium				
Interview conducted in private household	2,661	24.0	2,823	24.3
Interview conducted in nursing home	83	43.7	89	37.6
Total Europe	26,134	25.8	24,696	26.5
Northern Europe	4,849	17.5	4,602	18.9
Central Europe	11,871	21.0	11,134	20.9
Eastern and southern Europe	9,415	34.0	8,963	36.1
Spain	3,679	23.7	3,144	26.1
The Netherlands	2,208	15.4		

* For the analysis on the SHARE survey, Belgium was included in central Europe, Spain in eastern and southern Europe.
Source
a) Van Regenmortel (2017).
b) Vandenbroucke et al. (2012).
c) De Witte & Van Regenmortel (2021).

In a recent study by the Joint Research Centre (JRC) of the European Commission, information about the prevalence of social isolation and severe loneliness is analysed (D'Hombres et al., 2018). Belgium and Spain are situated in the second-lowest quintile for social isolation (meeting friends and family at most once a month) with a percentage between 12 and 15 per cent. For loneliness ('frequently feeling lonely'), both countries are situated in the middle quintile with a prevalence of 7–9 per cent. The analysis is made for the total population and based on the European Social Survey of 2010, 2012 and 2014. Correcting for other determinants, adults aged sixty-four and older have 9 percentage points fewer social contacts compared to the twenty-six to forty-five age group, but the feeling of frequent loneliness is slightly lower for persons of sixty-five years and older compared to the twenty-six to forty-five age group. Those other determinants help explain this unexpected result. Bad health has a negative influence on both social isolation and feeling of loneliness, but living without a partner and being widowed especially increase feelings of loneliness. Further, the negative impact of the economic situation, the income situation and unemployment add to feelings of loneliness. An update to this study shows that favourable economic circumstances protect against loneliness and social isolation and that living alone and poor health are important risk factors for loneliness (D'Hombres et al., 2021).

In table 2.3, there seems to be a lower level of feelings of loneliness in the Netherlands compared to Belgium. This seems to be confirmed by the evidence in the JRC report where the level of feeling lonely and the level of social isolation is lower in the Netherlands compared to Belgium. In the following section, we will make a stylised translation of the burden of loneliness in economic costs in Belgium. We start from the Dutch study that assessed the acute healthcare cost in a large sample of the population. The report reports that 33.5 per cent of the sample felt somewhat lonely, 5.4 per cent considered themselves severely lonely, and 2.9 per cent very severely lonely. The percentage of severe loneliness lay around 8.3 per cent what we will use hereafter as some 10 per cent of prevalence for Belgium, what probably is a conservative estimate to calculate the cost of loneliness for Belgium since the evidence above suggest that the feeling of loneliness is less prevalent in the Netherlands. We start with a transfer of the acute healthcare cost estimated in the Netherlands to the situation in Belgium (and also Spain). It is probably a conservative estimate.

THE ECONOMIC COST OF THE LONELINESS OF OLDER PERSONS

4.2   An estimate of the societal and healthcare cost of loneliness and social isolation

In an interview at his retirement (Andries, 2021), head of the Belgian health insurance Jo De Cock quoted a study estimating the cost of loneliness in the Netherlands at around 2 billion euros (Meisters et al., 2021). He discussed it in the broader context of lifestyle causes of ill health, such as nutrition, alcohol use and obesity. He pointed also to the fact that this study of the Netherlands situated the cost as well in the younger age group. Hereafter, we use this study to estimate the potential impact of loneliness in more detail.

The impact of lifestyle, living and health conditions on the economy are assessed via health-economic analysis (as described in paragraphs 2.2 and 2.3). For Belgium, no original estimates are made of the economic cost of loneliness or social isolation. By using the evidence available in other countries, we could, however, point to some interesting although partial and tentative results – tentative because it is not always clear how to distinguish between loneliness, lack of social relations or even the simple situation of living alone. There is, however, growing international evidence of the detrimental effect of all those situations on health and even mortality. The analysis remains partial because comprehensive studies that include all the elements of a full-blown societal cost of illness analysis remain scarce, including direct healthcare costs but also social care, lost productivity, loss of lives and the translation of it in economic terms. This is surprising since the impact of loneliness on mortality has been documented already for much longer, and the impact is qualified by some (see further) as a 'major public health' problem.

The additional cost of curative healthcare

We use the total healthcare expenditures of the Eurostat System of Health Accounts (SHA) for Belgium, the Netherlands and Spain, to put the estimates for the Netherlands (Meisters et al., 2021) in perspective. Expenditures for pharmaceuticals are separately mentioned. Figures for general practitioners or mental healthcare are not easily accessible. Nevertheless, similar figures for Flanders, including information on expenditures for general practitioners, are available. According to Meisters et al. (2021), the cost of curative care to deal with loneliness without considering covariates is about 8 per cent of total expenditures. It is even higher for pharmaceuticals and especially for mental care. It remains high for general practitioner and mental care, even when covariates are considered. We extrapolate this share of additional expenditures to some aggregated figures for health expenditures in Belgium,

Table 2.4: Estimate of some direct healthcare costs because of loneliness for the total population, based on estimates for the Netherlands

	Flanders 2016	Belgium 2019	Netherlands 2019	Spain 2019
GDP, in billions of euros	273	476	810	1 245
Total expenditures, public and private, in billions of euros				
Total health expenditures	30.57	50.76	82.37	113.67
Total healthcare minus LTC	22.54	39.56	58.79	105.66
General practitioner	1.25			
Pharmaceuticals	3.71	5.66	6.01	16.80
*Estimated share of health cost because of loneliness. based on estimated impact in the Netherlands**				
in billions of euros				
Total healthcare minus LTC	1.83	3.20	4.76	8.56
General practitioner	0.09			
Pharmaceuticals	0.40	0.61	0,65	1,81
as % of GDP				
Total healthcare minus LTC	0.67	0.67	0.59	0.69
General practitioner	0.03			
Pharmaceuticals	0.15	0.13	0.08	0.15

* Impact of loneliness on healthcare cost estimated in the Netherlands, in Meisters et. al. (2021): for total healthcare minus long-term care (LTC): 8.1 per cent; for general practitioner: 7.3 per cent; for pharmaceuticals: 10.8 per cent.
Source: own calculations based on Eurostat, SHA; De Smedt et al. (2021); Meisters et al. (2021)

Flanders, Spain and the Netherlands.[9] This leads to the total of the considered healthcare expenditures related to loneliness to about 3.2 billion euros for Belgium yearly or about 0.7 per cent of the gross domestic product (GDP). It could be a first and direct cost of loneliness. The estimate for Spain is of the same magnitude. This is because healthcare spending as a share of GDP, net of long-term care spending, is in Spain on the same level as in Belgium. It is long-term care spending that is less developed (see Pacolet et al., 2021).

The prevalence of more severe feelings of loneliness (severe and very severe loneliness) in the Dutch study is around 8 per cent for the younger age groups (between nineteen and sixty-five years), also for the younger 'old' (between sixty-five and eighty years), but around 12 per cent for people eighty-one years and older. The estimates hereafter are for the total population.

The additional cost of long-term care

The Meisters et al.'s study (2021) analyses the impact of loneliness on acute healthcare. Long-term care becomes important, particularly for older persons.

An example is how socially isolated older persons in a study in the United States (Shaw et al., 2017) were confronted with higher healthcare costs, especially hospitalisation, but also nursing home care. Despite this higher healthcare cost, they also had a 30 per cent greater risk of death. The study was based on a group of 5,270 older persons with an average age of seventy-four years. A minority, 13.7 per cent, was at risk of social isolation, and 55.3 per cent reported feeling lonely. For the more limited group of socially isolated persons, especially the impact of greater use of nursing facilities was obvious, while the higher risk of increased mortality remained. The study on the older persons in the United States mentions also that 17 per cent of the American older adult population lives alone. This is substantially higher in Belgium, through which the risk of isolation can be higher. However, it depends on the profile of the older person's social network and the availability of professional care, as provided by a generous welfare state. Even when this international evidence is informative for assessing the impact in Belgium, there is a need for original estimates in Belgium by either a detailed health survey, including all information of care received, or by a detailed translation of international evidence of the additional cost for all types of diseases.

When it comes to the direct care cost, not only the healthcare costs are relevant for the population of sixty-five years and older, but also the long-term care costs. In Belgium, long-term care expenditures are about 2.2 per cent of GDP, of which 1.35 per cent is residential long-term care (LTC) and 0.86 per cent for home LTC (in Flanders, LTC costs are estimated at 2.95 per cent of the total GDP, with 2.05 per cent for residential care and 0.89 per cent for home care) (De Smedt et al., 2021, p. 180).

The European Health Interview Survey provides some information on the use of home care, as part of LTC, according to household type. For almost all age groups in Belgium, Spain and the Netherlands, the uptake of home care (self-reported use of home care, district nursing but also other home care) is higher for persons living in a single household, illustrating how professional

Table 2.5: Self-reported use of home-care services by age, household type and level of difficulty with personal care or household activities, 2019, as percentage of total reference group

Level of difficulty	Moderate			Limited			Severe			None		
	Total	Single	Other	Total	Single	Other	Total	Single	Other	Total	Single	Other
European Union – 27 countries												
55–64	4.3	9.1	2.5	8.4	15.6	5.6	15.3	26.4	10.8	1.1	1.4	1.1
65–74	3.8	4.9	3.3	9.5	14.1	7.5	17.5	26.7	13.5	1.9	2.2	1.8
≥75	9.8	13.2	7.0	24.2	29.8	19.4	33.3	40.1	27.4	4.1	5.7	3.1
Belgium												
55–64	17.6	22.5	15.9	28.0	39.8	22.6	39.0	53.5	30.9	5.9	11.3	4.7
65–74	16.1	13.4	16.8	31.8	40.8	28.4	47.6	57.3	42.4	8.7	8.7	8.7
≥75	23.3	30.9	18.0	46.4	54.9	37.8	56.2	62.6	48.6	14.2	25.0	9.4
Spain												
55–64	2.9	2.4	3.0	8.0	8.4	8.0	11.9	13.8	11.7	0.6	0.9	0.6
65–74	2.7	6.0	2.1	10.2	13.1	9.8	16.5	19.5	16.1	1.6	1.5	1.6
≥75	10.7	13.8	9.6	26.9	32.7	25.0	33.3	40.5	31.0	4.1	5.9	3.6
Netherlands												
55–64	2.6	8.2	1.0	8.5	18.6	4.8	18.0	28.4	12.1	0.9	0.7	0.9
65–74	3.5	4.6	3.2	14.1	28.1	8.4	33.4	58.3	19.5	1.0	2.9	0.4
≥75	20.3	34.2	10.1	43.6	56.3	30.7	61.9	69.2	52.3	5.3	7.0	4.5

* Based on the EHIS European Health Interview Survey; some of the cells in table 2.5 are flagged by Eurostat as statistically unreliable, but we provide them nevertheless to have a complete overview.

Source Eurostat, Self-reported use of home care services by age, household type and level of difficulty with personal care or household activities [HLTH_EHIS_AM7TH__custom_1205258]

care likely replaces for the single household the care that in another household would be provided by an informal caregiver. Further, this professional home care provides not only care but also contacts and social relations, which could reduce the risk of social isolation and loneliness. The use of professional home care is higher in Belgium and the Netherlands than in Spain. Belgium is also remarkable with regard to another aspect. Even with no difficulties with personal care or household activities, older persons – even at a younger age or when people not living alone – have a higher uptake of home care. This is the case in comparison with the Netherlands, which is known as a country with a high level of home care, and certainly compared to Spain. This illustrates the generosity of the home-care system in Belgium.

Could it be that home care also compensates for the need for care because of social isolation that is not provided if only the use of professional care to persons dependent for activities of daily living (ADL) and instrumental activities of daily living (IADL) are targeted? It could illustrate the additional cost, but a care cost that is standing for the responsiveness to an enlarged definition of needs. Meisters et al. (2021) observe also an increased visit to easily accessible and free-of-charge general practitioners by lonely individuals in search of social interactions. Their study concludes further that the incremental healthcare costs because of loneliness are more important for younger age groups. In addition, Gerst-Emerson and Jayawardhana (2015) highlight that chronically lonely persons might more frequently turn to professionals.

The same goes for residential care. In the past, we observed in Belgium that going to a nursing home was triggered already by the need for IADL. This trend implies that people need to go to a care home sooner: when they become single, for example, or because of the limited possibilities to receive informal care. Allowing residents to go to a care home could be a consequence of more people living alone or feeling lonely. A residential care system that is responsive to this increased need will be encountering increasing costs that add further to the additional cost of loneliness. This seems to be confirmed by the final report of McDaid et al. (2021, p. 28); they illustrate that the prevented cost due to an intervention related to loneliness includes not only acute care but also many additional costs due to the increased risk of dementia and a substantial avoided cost of residential care. For an intervention programme of £376,000 reducing loneliness, the cost savings due to reduced loneliness were estimated at £417,339, of which £242,482 or 58 per cent was prevented residential long-term care. And that still does not include the value of reduced mortality, as we calculate hereafter.

The indirect cost of increased mortality

Observing the meta-analysis of the impact of loneliness on health and mortality, we see a lack of transparency for practitioners as well as policymakers to grasp the real impact. Although increased risk ratios should be telling enough, it could help to translate them into real numbers of deaths and life years lost, and put a value on it.

In a societal cost-benefit analysis of alcohol use and misuse in Belgium, one of us estimated the total cost in 1999 at about 6 billion euros or 2.5 per cent of the GDP (Degreef et al., 2003).[10] The direct healthcare cost was only 0.5 billion or 0.23 per cent of GDP. For alcohol misuse, specific costs include work (lost productivity or accidents at work) and traffic accidents, including fatal ones. The indirect cost of increased morbidity and mortality was substantial. Based on traditional values of human capital, the cost of increased mortality was estimated at 1 billion or 0.46 per cent of GDP, double the healthcare cost. However, when we applied much higher values to a statistical life, as revealed by the 'willingness to pay' estimates, this cost became seven to sixteen times higher. But what is the value of human life?[11] Hereafter, we similarly calculate the indirect cost of lives lost due to loneliness or social isolation.

An interesting starting point is the study of Holt-Lunstad et al. (2015) on the impact of loneliness, social isolation and living alone as risk factors for mortality. They underline that the three indicators are conceptually different and sometimes – but certainly not always – overlap. When they overlap, the impact can be even worse. However, remarkable in their study is that the quantitative impact for the three indicators is on average around an effect size of an odds ratio of 1.3 in the more complete modelling (Holt-Lunstad, Smith et al., 2015; Holt-Lunstad, Robles et al., 2017).[12]

In Table 2.6, we use this information in a stylised way to translate it into an estimate of the value of lost lives due to loneliness, social isolation or living alone. Since the definitions are not identical, we use the recent estimates of the JRC of either loneliness or social isolation. Since the definitions do not overlap, the impact could be larger (more people concerned). For the situations where they overlap, the impact is perhaps even higher (greater impact on health and mortality). Those are tentative, and probably conservative, estimates.

The recent estimates of the JRC for social isolation and loneliness are for the total population. Using hereafter a stylised figure of 10 per cent for the prevalence of loneliness, we are in between the percentages for Belgium and Spain of 10–12 per cent for social isolation, and 8 per cent for loneliness.[13] We calculate it also for the Netherlands, to put the above-used estimates of the cost of care in perspective, where the percentage is similar for social isolation but lower for loneliness. We finally have to identify the basic risk of death for all causes for those not confronted with loneliness. We take from the WHO Global Health Estimates statistics on leading causes of death and years of life lost (YLL). For Belgium, in 2019, 113,000 people died in a population of eleven million, from all causes of death. We provide also the figures for the age groups sixty to seventy and seventy and above, the focus of our interest here on older persons, showing that the people dying are concentrated in those age groups. The WHO also estimates the YLL because of these premature deaths. We estimated the additional risk of those confronted with loneliness at 1.3 times the risk for those not confronted with loneliness, leading to approximately an odds ratio as concluded by the meta-analysis of Holt-Lunstad et al. (2017). The normal number of deaths for the people at risk of loneliness is estimated at 11,000; the increased number is estimated at 14,300. Comparing the number of deaths at the augmented risk with the average risk of the population gives us an estimate of the incremental number of deaths, 3,300. Those increased numbers of death count for a total number of years lost of 51,500 years, at an average estimate YLL of about 15.6 years. In our estimate of the years lost because of the abuse of alcohol, we came to 93,445 YLL for 3,847 premature deaths.[14] Depending on the value in monetary terms we give to life (per year of life lost), we arrive at an indirect cost for Belgium of mortality between 2 and 10 billion euros. This is respectively 0.4 to 2 per cent of the GDP. We use the same monetary values for YLL for the Netherlands and for Spain, which explains why the share of GDP lost is somewhat lower in the Netherlands and higher in Spain.

Loneliness and social isolation are considered by some authors a major public health risk. Holt-Lunstad et al. (2017) compare the increased mortality because of a lack of social connections with several leading health indicators. The analysis is taken over by the United States' National Academies of Sciences. Engineering. and Medicine (2020, p. 42), comparing the risk for social isolation with the risk of smoking more than fifteen cigarettes per day and almost double the risk of severe drinking (more than six drinks per day). The additional mortality risk of loneliness is less severe and somewhat lower than the risk of hazardous drinking.

Holt-Lunstad (2015) argued that the awareness of the public health impact of loneliness and social isolation is now at the same level of concern as that for the impact of obesity three decades ago. The same goes for the level of exhaustiveness of the cost studies of loneliness, whereby the impact on mortality or increased morbidity is not translated into total cost estimates.

Table 2.6: Estimate of the indirect cost of increased mortality

	Belgium all ages	Belgium age 60–70	Belgium age 70+	Nether- lands all ages	Spain all ages
Population (in thousands)	11,539	1,348	1567	17,097	46,737
Estimated deaths, all causes (in thousands)	113.3	13.9	88.5	153.1	426.7
Estimated YLL. all causes (in thousands)	1,767.3	362.1	932.1	2,463.5	6,270.8
Average estimated YLL, all causes	15.6	26.1	10.5	16.1	14.7
Share of population confronted with loneliness	0.10	0.10	0.10	0.10	0.10
Rest of population	0.90	0.90	0.90	0.90	0.90
Risk of death	0.0098	0.0103	0.0565	0.0090	0.0091
Supposed risk ratio	1.30	1.30	1.30	1.30	1.30
Corrected risk for popula- tion without loneliness	0.0095	0.0100	0.0548	0.0087	0.0089
Corrected risk for popula- tion with loneliness	0.0124	0.0130	0.0713	0.0113	0.0115
Number of deaths for population without loneli- ness (in thousands)	99.0	12.1	77.3	133.7	372.9
Number of deaths for population with loneliness (in thousands)	14.3	1.8	11.2	19.3	53.9
Number of deaths normally (in thousands)	11.0	1.3	8.6	14.9	41.4
Additional deaths because of loneliness (in thousands)	3.3	0.4	2.6	4.5	12.4
Additional YLL (in thousands)	51.5	10.5	27.1	71.8	182.6
Value at 40,000 euro per year (in millions of euros)	2,059	422	1,086	2,870	7,306
Value at 3 million per statistical life (in millions of euros)	9,896	1,212	7,730	13,375	37,289
GDP 2019 (in billions of euros)	476	476	476	810	1245

	Belgium all ages	Belgium age 60–70	Belgium age 70+	Nether-lands all ages	Spain all ages
GDP per capita in euro	41,266	41,266	41,266	47,370	26,640
Value of YLL at 40,000 euro as % of GDP	0.43	0.09	0.23	0.35	0.59
Value of lives lost at 3 million euro as % of GDP	2.08	0.25	1.62	1.65	2.99
Implicit odds ratio	1.304	1.304	1.323	1.303	1.303

Source: own calculations based on WHO statistics

Other cost dimensions

Many of the cost estimates are based on older persons living at home, in a community dwelling. However, when they age, they increasingly stay in residential care settings. The impact of loneliness on their quality of life, their quality of care, their health prospects and life expectancy should be further investigated.

A second specific group at risk are older persons with dementia, both for themselves and for the impact on their caregivers, mostly involving one main carer. In Belgium, there were about 192,926 persons with dementia in 2018, or 1.7 per cent of the total population (Alzheimer Europe, 2019). About 183,307 were sixty-five years or older, which was about 8 per cent of the total population above sixty-five years. Adequate care for those persons, at home or in institutions, needs to take care of the specific problems of isolation and loneliness.

There is a growing concern about the promotion of informal care because this increases the burden on the caregiver, including an increasing incapacity for them to participate in social activities.

De Witte & Van Regenmortel (2021) revealed also a fourth category of persons with specific risks of isolation and loneliness – namely, persons with a migration background.

Those four additional dimensions of loneliness, and their size, confirm the magnitude of the problem and could add to the total cost of loneliness.

Summary

We presented an estimated direct cost of loneliness at about 3.2 billion euros, and an indirect cost of between 2 and 10 billion euros, depending on the value we give to life in monetary terms. This is, respectively, 0.7 and 0.4 to 2 per cent of GDP.[15] Other costs are mentioned but not estimated. The mere size of those figures confirms that the cost of loneliness is a major public health risk.

4.3 Belgian social policies to address loneliness

The responsibility to cope with the burden of loneliness lies in many hands. We indicate four: the individual, the public health (and especially prevention) policy, the professional care sector and civil society.

The risk of loneliness and lack of social contact is in line with other dimensions of lifestyle and puts the responsibility in the hands of older persons themselves (during the complete life course).

Belgium has a strong safety net of social protection, which is widely accessible. We illustrated above that Belgium is, for instance, even an outlier at the European level in that persons with no ADL dependency apply for home care. And in the residential care setting for older persons, even after decades of targeting it more to persons with ADL or IADL needs, there may be other reasons for going to a nursing home.[16] This is in line with other studies (Meisters et al., 2021; Gerst-Emerson & Jayawardhana, 2015). The care system should be more accessible and responsive to problems of loneliness, which of course will increase the cost of loneliness. On the other hand, it could trigger the need for more preventive measures that could preclude loneliness from occuring in the first place. Concern about loneliness starts to be included in a preventive public health policy. Hopefully, preventive policies will continue to become fully engaged.

The Covid-19 crisis triggered a greater awareness of loneliness. Nevertheless, the interest for stronger loneliness interventions was already emerging before the Covid-19 crisis. For instance, in 2019 the Flemish Council for the Elderly recommended a broad range of policies to fight loneliness, ranging from raising awareness and avoiding poverty to improved housing, mobility, digital literacy and participation (Vlaamse Ouderenraad, 2019).

There seems to be a substantial underestimation of the cost of loneliness, especially when it is compared with the cost of interventions to cope with it. In this respect, there is a need for a comprehensive cost-benefit analysis of those interventions. The cost-benefit analysis is often limited to the sphere of the healthcare itself, not translating the indirect benefits into monetary terms. But even then, there is evidence that some of those interventions are not rocket science and seem to be limited in costs. Sometimes loneliness interventions can be as small as an excursion day from a standard organisation for older persons (Pitkala et al., 2009). They result nevertheless in improved self-perceived health and reduced mortality. Those studies (Mihalopoulos, 2020) did not reveal the major public health problem, as suggested by Gerst-Emerson and Jayawardhana (2015). Most of the interventions were oriented to social participation and visiting and were relatively cheap so that most of the time they were cost-effective and sometimes even cost-saving. But even more important than the health, social and economic costs is perhaps the conclusion of Gerst-Emerson and Jayawardhana (2015, p. 1018) that 'some researchers have suggested that loneliness may be more treatable than other determinants of functional decline among elderly, such as chronic conditions'. It should in any case be part of a more fully engaged prevention policy.

Beyond that, the major knowledge gap is to assess what really happens in the care process to see how it copes with the risk of loneliness and social isolation that make frail older persons even more vulnerable. Do they succeed in making isolated persons more autonomous without abandoning them?

Belgium has not only a strong welfare state but also a well-developed network of civil society organisations.[17] For Flanders alone, six out of ten persons are members of such an organisation. On top of the professional care sector, those social movements are an additional antidote against loneliness and social isolation. Most civil society organisations are under pressure because they depend on public financial support from the state. As a lesson of the Covid-19 crisis, their role in avoiding isolation and constructing cohesion will probably be recognised again. At the same time, it should challenge them to increase their reach to those that are at risk of being isolated.

Many of those efforts could be situated within a greater emphasis on prevention. The efforts for prevention are too limited. Already in 2004, one of us quoted the Wanless report in the United Kingdom, advocating the transition in elderly care from a 'healthcare' approach to a 'public health' approach (Wanless, 2002). Half of the increased healthcare costs of ageing could be compensated by a 'fully engaged' policy in prevention and increased efficiency (Wanless report quoted in Pacolet et al., 2004).

Typical for a mature welfare state like Belgium is the large support for professional care but also for civil society. However, despite realising those massive efforts and resources, the size of the loneliness problem is confronting. When estimating tentatively the impact of loneliness, social isolation and living alone at 0.7 per cent of GDP for direct cost and 0.4 to 2 per cent of GDP for the indirect costs, and with many cost components still left out in the tentative estimate, we illustrate that it is also a major public health concern for Belgium. Prevention should be a major point of focus in the public health approach. However, coping with this cost of frailty should also be the major concern of the more than 10 per cent of GDP we spend in Belgium yearly on healthcare and LTC. The professionals active in this 'silver economy of care' and civil society have the competencies but also the responsibility to give more attention to those problems in their day-to-day work. In this respect, the 'empowerment' framework can change their perspectives and ways of working to prevent them from lethargy and provide them with weapons to 'resist'[18] the risk of having too little attention for reaching the lonely. The same goes for the above-mentioned civil society.

5.   Concluding remarks

Loneliness and social isolation, especially among older persons, are at present a social problem with a great impact on European societies. Their impact not only affects the individual well-being of those who suffer from it and the well-being of societies, but it is also accompanied by significant economic costs in terms of health and social services and opportunity costs for families and society. In this chapter, we analyse the economic cost of loneliness for older persons. We stress the importance of measuring its social and economic impact and, therefore, discuss some tentative recommendations regarding the improvement of public policies aimed to combat loneliness. There are several main conclusions that we highlight below.

First, after a review of the literature, we highlighted how the cost of loneliness of older persons can be estimated using the financial costs for people who feel lonely and their family and friends, the community, the health system and the economy in general. The costs associated with loneliness are health-related but also psychosocial. However, there is a lack of evidence concerning the economic costs of loneliness and on cost-effective loneliness interventions.

Second, the problem of loneliness and social isolation has been analysed in two countries: Spain, as an example of the Mediterranean welfare regime, and Belgium, as an example of the Continental welfare regime. The prevalence of loneliness and social isolation in Spain is similar to that of Belgium: around 7–9 per cent of the total population if we consider loneliness and between 12–15 per cent in terms of social isolation. This similarity is remarkable, despite a significant difference in the household structure.

Spain has recently joined the current EU welfare states, which put the social problem of loneliness on the political agenda. On 11 December 2018, the Spanish Parliament approved the 'non-legislative proposal relating to the promotion of measures to combat chronic loneliness (Boletín Oficial de las Cortes, 2018)' – an initiative that reflects the different policies and programmes applied by local and regional governments with the support of civil society. However, such policies are not all-encompassing and lack preventive programmes and programmes that help curb poverty and social exclusion. Further, they also often lack the promotion of active ageing guided by the criteria of empowerment of frail older persons (see Chapter 1). Meanwhile, the social policies against loneliness implemented in Belgium have a robust system of social protection and social services, more developed than in Spain; Belgium's limitations in this regard lie in the policies to prevent the risk of loneliness, which require the participation of various political, professional and institutional actors. As a general conclusion, there is room for new forms of prevention and interventions in both countries, but particularly in Spain.

Finally, two recommendations emerge from this chapter. The first is that it is necessary to deepen the assessment of the direct and indirect costs of loneliness and social isolation as well as the opportunity costs. A cost measure allows us to gain more knowledge about the impact of loneliness and social isolation and consequently to have qualitative information available for the design of effective prevention and social intervention policies. Second, we need to pay more attention to loneliness in public health policy, through prevention and greater involvement of formal care providers and civil society. Public policy alternatives focused on the autonomy of people in friendly social contexts and the empowerment of fragile people constitute a positive approach to reinforcing prevention and social intervention programmes.

Notes

1.   Wang et al. (2020) find that decreased loneliness was also associated with greater social network size and increased neighbourhood social capital.
2.   Kung et al. (2021) provide evidence on the link between loneliness, health and healthcare usage in Australia by age group and gender, illustrating the difference in loneliness by levels of education, household income and local area socio-economic disadvantage.
3.   For example, a pilot project for the prevention of unwanted loneliness was implemented as part of the plan 'Madrid, Ciudad de los Cuidados' ('Madrid, City of Care').
4.   The Spanish territorial system has been normally featured as quasi-federal, comprising three levels of governance: central, regional (autonomous communities) and local (Provinces and Municipalities), conceding a remarkable level of self-government to their substate entities.
5.   The Social Links Program (Vincles BNC) in Barcelona aimed to promote the use of new technologies in the seventy-three neighbourhoods of the capital in collaboration with the

Bloomberg Foundation, channelled through the social services centres) and primary health centres. The campaign against loneliness promoted by the Asturian Federation of Network of Sustainable Town Halls aims to make visible the different ways of coping with and experiencing unwanted loneliness by older people. The programme of care for older people in loneliness, of the Department of Family, Social Affairs and Women of the City Council of Pozuelo de Alarcón (Madrid). The Radars de Barcelona programme, created in 2008, is a neighbourhood network dedicated to the prevention and detection of risk situations for older people who live alone in their neighbourhood.

6. The ombudsman of the Aragon Region's 'Justice Table on elders in non-elected loneliness' is a unique initiative.

7. Some programmes can be highlighted: the programme against the loneliness by the organisation Amics de la Gent Gran in Catalonia; the Great Neighbours programme, promoted by the organisation Grandes Amigos, with a presence in Madrid, Galicia and the Basque Country; the Better in Company programme, from the Pilares Foundation (Madrid); the programme 'Confidants against the loneliness of the elderly'; or the agreement of the Mémora Foundation and the San Juan de Dios Hospital, in Santurce, against the loneliness at the end of life for people with serious illnesses, to name only a few.

8. Share of lonely people in retirement homes (calculations based on Table 2.1 and Table 2.3)

	in thousands	% feeling lonely in 2013	in thousands	as % of total	% feeling lonely in 2015	in thousands	as % of total
Population in retirement home	130	44	57	10	38	49	9
Rest of population 65+	2145	24	515	90	24	515	91
Total			572	100		564	100

9. The figures for the Netherlands are also estimates on SHA figures and for that reason are somewhat different from the original estimates in Meisters et al. (2021).

10. The study also calculated beneficial effects of alcohol use of some 1.5 billion (see Degreef et al., 2003). They are not subtracted from the six billion.

11. In our cost-benefit analysis, we used as a human capital value some 0.5 million euros for the statistical life in 1999, while the willingness-to-pay values available at that time for a statistical life was from 2.7 to 5.5 million euros (Degreef et al., 2003). We reported at that time already that the value of such a statistical life might not change whatever the age of dying, illustrating that there is a greater willingness to pay when people get older. The Nobel Prize winner Paul Krugman quoted in a Twitter message recently (2021) a value of 10 million dollars or 8.5 million euros. The author he quoted was Kip Viscusi. This kind of figure is commonly used in transport economics or environmental economics and recently also to calculate the benefit of avoided deaths during the Covid lockdown and anti-pandemic measures. In a recent contribution, the health economist Eisen (2021) mentioned the average cost of a 'life' as 3 million euros.

12. In the comprehensive design of McDaid et al.'s cost-assessment study (2016; see paragraph 2.3 above), the authors highlight the importance also of the cost of increased mortality, but for reasons of adapting a conservative estimate, they do not put a value on it.

13. To put those figures further in perspective: in Holt- Lunstad et al. (2017, p. 18), the prevalence of loneliness in the adult US population is up to 40 per cent and older persons living alone is somewhat more than 25 per cent.
14. But we used at that time also positive health effects of 'alcohol use', of 2,460 avoided deaths and 25,191 potential gained lives. A lost life can occur at a younger age, for instance, in a road accident, with a high number of years lost, while the potential avoided death can come later in life, with a lower number of gained life years (Degreef et al., 2003).
15. Just another comparison of a well-recognised major public health risk of smoking: a study for DG Sanco estimated the premature mortality in Belgium due to smoking at almost 20,000 and use for a year of life lost in 2009 €52,000. This resulted in a monetary value of premature mortality in Belgium of some 12 billion or 4 per cent of the GDP (GHK, 2012). In this study, the direct healthcare cost was only estimated at 0.25 per cent of Belgium's GDP (see p. 26)
16. This enlargement of needs is confirmed by a recent initiative for defining a new assessment scale for persons with a handicap who are entitled in Belgium to an integration allowance (Teppers et al., 2018). By adding questions about social participation, we revealed that on top of classical ADL and IADL needs, there are clear additional needs related to social participation. Sometimes the need for support was only determined by this dimension.
17. See the website of the federation of those organisations, the united organisations (De verenigde verenigingen): https://www.deverenigdeverenigingen.be/downloads/infographic.
18. As Van Regenmortel invites social workers to do in her inaugural speech as a full professor at Tilburg University, 2020, p. 11

References

Abellán García, A., Ayala García, A., Pérez Díaz, J., & Pujol Rodríguez, R. (2020). *Un perfil de las personas mayores en España, 2019*. Consejo Superior de Investigaciones Científicas.

Adam, E. K., Hawkley, L. C., Kudielka, B. M., & Cacioppo, J. T. (2006). Day-to-day dynamics of experience-cortisol associations in a population-based sample of older adults. *Proceedings of the National Academy of Sciences, 103*(45), 17058–17063. https://doi.org/10.1073/pnas.0605053103

Alzheimer Europe (2019). *Dementia in Europe Yearbook (2019): Estimating the prevalence of dementia in Europe*. Alzheimer Europe.

Andersen, R., & Newman, J. F. (2005). Societal and individual determinants of medical care utilization in the United States. *Milbank Quarterly, 83*(4), 1–28. https://doi.org/10.2307/3349613

Andries, S. (2021, 4 Juli), Interview Jo De Cock: we moeten nu transparantie krijgen in de artsenlonen. *De Standaard*, https://www.standaard.be/cnt/dmf20210702_97772450

Bermejo, J. (2003). La soledad en los mayores. ARS MÉDICA. *Revista de Estudios Médico Humanísiticos, 32*, 126–144. http://dx.doi.org/10.11565/arsmed.v32i2.264

Boletín Oficial de las Cortes Generales (2018). Proposición no de ley 162/000612, 20 December, 7-10.

Cacioppo, J. T., & Cacioppo, S. (2018). The growing problem of loneliness. *The Lancet, 391*(10119), 426. https://doi.org/10.1016/S0140-6736(18)30142-9

Cacioppo, J. T., Hawkley, L. C., Berntson, G. G., Ernst, J. M., Gibbs, A. C., Stickgold, R., & Hobson, J. A. (2002). Do lonely days invade the nights? Potential social modulation of sleep efficiency. *Psychological Science, 13*(4), 384–387. https://doi.org/10.1111/1467-9280.00469

Cacioppo, J. T., Hughes, M. E., Waite, L. J., Hawkley, L. C., & Thisted, R. A. (2006). Loneliness as a specific risk factor for depressive symptoms: Cross-sectional and longitudinal analyses. *Psychology and Aging, 21*(1), 140–151. https://doi.org/10.1037/0882-7974.21.1.140

Cacioppo, S., Capitanio, J. P., & Cacioppo, J. T. (2014). Toward a neurology of loneliness. *Psychological Bulletin, 140*(6), 1464. https://doi.org/10.1037/a0037618

Cacioppo, J. T., Cacioppo, S., Capitanio, J. P., & Cole, S. W. (2015). The neuroendocrinology of social isolation. *Annual Review of Psychology, 66*, 733–767. https://doi.org/10.1146/annurev-psych-010814-015240

CEOMA (2018). La Soledad y el Aislamiento No Deseado en las Personas Mayores. Madrid: Confederación Española de Organizaciones de Mayores.

De Jong Gierveld, J., & Kamphuis, F. (1985). The development of a rasch-type loneliness scale. *Applied Psychological Measurement, 9*(3), 289–299. https://doi.org/10.1177/014662168500900307

De Jong Gierveld, J., & van Tilburg, T. (2006). A 6-item scale for overall, emotional, and social loneliness: confirmatory tests on survey data. *Research on Aging, 28*(5), 582–598. https://doi.org/10.1177/0164027506289723

De Smedt, L., Pacolet, J., Moens, D., & Breda, M. (2021). *Financiering van de Vlaamse social profit. Een nieuwe satellietrekening voor de socialprofitsector in Vlaanderen* [Financing of the Flemish social profit. A new satellite account for the social profit sector in Flanders]. HIVA – KU Leuven.

De Witte, J., & Van Regenmortel, T. (2019). *Silver Empowerment. Loneliness and social isolation among elderly. An empowerment perspective.* HIVA – KU Leuven. https://hiva.kuleuven.be/nl/nieuws/docs/tvr-18-tse-lssrc1-o2010-loneliness-and-social.pdf

De Witte, J., & Van Regenmortel, T. (2021). The relationship between loneliness and migration among Belgian older adults. *Ageing International,* 1–23. https://doi.org/10.1007/s12126-021-09460-8

d'Hombres, B., Schnepf, S., Barjaková, M., & Teixeira Mendonça, F. (2018). *Loneliness: An unequally shared burden in Europe.* European Commission.

d'Hombres, B., Barjaková, M., & Schnepf, S.V. (2021). *Loneliness and Social Isolation: An Unequally Shared Burden in Europe.* Discussion Paper 14245. Institute for Labour Economics.

Degreef, T., Pacolet, J., & Bouten, R. (2003), *Sociale kosten-batenanalyse van alcoholgebruik en -misbruik in België* [Social cost-benefit analysis of alcohol use and abuse in Belgium]. HIVA – KU Leuven.

Díez Nicolás, J., & Morenos Páez, M. (2015). *La soledad en España.* Fundación ONCE.

Dykstra, P. A. (2009). Older adult loneliness: Myths and realities. *European Journal of Ageing, 6*(2), 91–100. https://doi.org/10.1007/s10433-009-0110-3

Eisen, R. (2021). *From financial crisis to Covid-crisis – A radical change in economic Policy?* [Presentation]. Sixth European conference on the State of the Welfare State in the EU, Germany.

Ellaway, A., Wood, S., & Macintyre, S. (1999). Someone to talk to? The role of loneliness as a factor in the frequency of GP consultations. *British Journal of General Practice, 49*(442), 363–367.

European Commission (2019a). Peer Review on Strategies for supporting social inclusion at older age. *Projects, measures and strategies for tackling social isolation, loneliness and social exclusion in older age.* European Commission.

European Commission (2019b). Host country. Discussion Paper – Peer Review on Strategies for supporting social inclusion at older age. Loneliness in Europe. *Projects, measures and strategies for tackling social isolation, loneliness and social exclusion in older age.* European Commission.

FEM-CET (2018). *Soledad y riesgo de aislamiento social en las personas mayores.* Obra Social 'la Caixa'.

Gerst-Emerson, K., & Jayawardhana, J. (2015). Loneliness as a public health issue: The impact of loneliness on health care utilization among older adults. *American Journal of Public Health, 105*(5), 1013–1019. https://doi.org/10.2105/AJPH.2014.302427

GHK (2012). *A study on liability and the health costs of smoking.* GHK.

Hawkley, L. C., & Cacioppo, J. T. (2010). Loneliness matters: a theoretical and empirical review of consequences and mechanisms. *Annals of Behavioral Medicine, 40*(2), 218–227. https://doi.org/10.1007/s12160-010-9210-8

Holt-Lunstad, J., Smith, T. B., Baker, M., Harris, T., & Stephenson., D. (2015). Loneliness and social isolation as risk factors for mortality: A meta-analytic review. *Perspectives on Psychological Science, 10*(2), 227–237. https://doi.org/10.1177/1745691614568352

Holt-Lunstad, J., Robles, T. F., & Sbarra., D. A. (2017). Advancing social connection as a public health priority in the United States. *American Psychologist 72*(6), 517–530. https://doi.org/10.1037/amp0000103

Hughes, M. E., Waite, L. J., Hawkley, L. C., & Cacioppo, J. T. (2004). A short scale for measuring loneliness in large surveys: Results from two population-based studies. *Research on Aging, 26*(6), 655–672. https://doi.org/10.1177/0164027504268574

Kung, C. S. J., Kunz, J. S., & Shields, M. A. (2021). Economic aspects of loneliness in Australia. *Australian Economic Review, 54*(1), 147–163. https://doi.org/10.1111/1467-8462.12414

Lauder, W., Mummery, K., Jones, M., & Caperchione, C. (2006). A comparison of health behaviours in lonely and non-lonely populations. *Psychology, Health and Medicine, 11*(2), 233–245. https://doi.org/10.1080/13548500500266607

Lubben, J., & Gironda, M. (2003). Centrality of social ties to the health and wellbeing of older adults. In B. Berkman and L. Harooytan (Eds.), *Social work and health care in an aging world* (pp. 319–350). Springer.

Martínez, R., & Celdrán, M. (2019). *La soledad no tiene edad. Explorando vivencias multigeneracionales.* Fundación Privada Amics de la Gent Gran.

McDaid, D., Park, A. L., & Fernandez, J. L. (2016). *Reconnections Evaluation Interim Report.* London School of Economics and Political Science.

McDaid, D., Park, A. L., & Fernandez, J. L. (2021). *Reconnections: Impact Evaluation Final Report.* London School of Economics and Political Science.

Meisters, R., Westra, D., Putrik, P., Bosma, H., Ruwaard, D., & Jansen, M. (2021). Does loneliness have a cost? A population-wide study of the association between loneliness and healthcare expenditure. *International Journal of Public Health, 66*, 581286. https://doi.org/10.3389/ijph.2021.581286

Mihalopoulos, C., Le, L., Chatterton, M. L., Bucholc, J., Holt-Lunstad, J., Lim, M. H., & Engel, L. (2020). The economic costs of loneliness: A review of cost-of-illness and economic evaluation studies. *Social Psychiatry and Psychiatric Epidemiology, 55*(7), 823–836. https://doi.org/10.1007/s00127-019-01733-7

National Academies of Sciences, Engineering, and Medicine (2020). *Social Isolation and Loneliness in Older Adults: Opportunities for the Health Care System.* The National Academies Press.

Nyqvist, F., Nygård, M., & Scharf, T. (2019). Loneliness amongst older people in Europe: A comparative study of welfare regimes. *European Journal of Ageing, 16*(2), 133–143. https://doi.org/10.1007/s10433-018-0487-y

O'Sullivan, R., Burns, A., Leavey, G., Leroi, I., Burholt, V., Lubben, J., Holt-Lunstad, J., Victor, C., Lawlor, B., Vilar-Compte, M., Perissinotto, C., Tully, M., Sullivan, P., Rosato, M., McHugh Power, J., Tiilikainen, E., & Prohaska, R. (2021). Impact of the COVID-19 pandemic on loneliness and social isolation: A multi-country study. *International Journal of Environmental Research and Public Health, 18*(19), 9982. https://doi.org/10.3390/ijerph18199982

Pacolet, J., Deliège, D., Artoisenet, C., Cattaert, G., Coudron, V., Leroy, X., Peetermans, A., & Swine, C. (2004). *Vieillissement, aide et soins de santé en Belgique. Working Paper DGSOC 1.* Direction Générale Politique Sociale.

Pacolet, J., Wöss, J., De Smedt, L., & De Wispelaere, F. (2021). *Revisiting EU Social Monitoring: A needs-driven Approach from a Workers' Perspective.* European Trade Union Confederation.

Perlman, D., & Peplau, L. A. (1981). Toward a social psychology of loneliness. In R. Gilmour and S. Duck (Eds.), *Personal relationships in disorder* (pp. 31–56). Academic Press.

Pinazo, S., & Donio-Bellegarde, M. (2018). *La soledad de las personas mayores. Conceptualization, valoración e intervención.* Fundación Pilares.

Pitkala, K.H., Routasalo, P., Kautiainen, H., & Tilvis, R.S. (2009). Effects of psychosocial group rehabilitation on health, use of health care services, and mortality of older persons suffering from loneliness: A randomized controlled trial. *Journal of Gerontology, 64*(7), 792–800. https://doi.org/10.1093/gerona/glp011

Richard, A., Rohrmann, S., Vandeleur, C. L., Schmid, M., & Eichholzer, M. (2016). Loneliness is adversely associated with lifestyle and physical and mental health. *European Psychiatry, 33*(1), S82. https://doi.org/10.1016/j.eurpsy.2016.01.033

Russell, D. W. (1996). UCLA loneliness scale (Version 3): Reliability, validity, and factor structure. *Journal of Personality Assessment, 66*(1), 20–40. https://doi.org/10.1207/s15327752jpa6601_2

Sancho Castiello, M. (2019). *La soledad en España: Dilemas, paradojas.* Universidad Internacional Menendez Pelayo.

Shaw, J. G, Farid, M., Noel-Miller, C., Joseph, N., Houser, A., Asch, S. M., Bhattacharya, J., & Flowers, L. (2017). Social isolation and medicare spending: among older adults, objective isolation increases expenditures while loneliness does not. *Journal of Aging and Health, 29*(7), 1119–1143. https://doi.org/10.1177/0898264317703559

Sundström, G., Fransson, E., Malmberg, B., & Davey, A. (2009). Loneliness among older Europeans. *European Journal Aging, 6*(4), 267–275. https://doi.org/10.1007/s10433-009-0134-8

Teppers, E., Pacolet, J., Falez, F., Godderis, L., Kuppens, S., & Mélot, C. (2018). *Développement d'un instrument pour l'évaluation des besoins de soutien dans les situations de handicap, Volet 2.* HIVA – KU Leuven.

Valtorta, N. K., Kanaan, M., Gilbody, S., Ronzi, S., & Hanratty, B. (2016). Loneliness and social isolation as risk factors for coronary heart disease and stroke: Systematic review and meta-analysis of longitudinal observational studies. *Heart, 102*(13), 1009–1006. http://dx.doi.org/10.1136/heartjnl-2015-308790

Vandenbroucke, S., Lebrun, J.-M., Vermeulen, B., Declercq, A., Maggi, P., Delye, S., & Gosset, C. (2012). *Oud word je niet alleen. Een enquête over eenzaamheid en sociaal isolement bij ouderen in België.* [You don't get old alone. A survey on loneliness and social isolation among older persons in Belgium]. Fondation Roi Baudouin.

VanderWeele, T. J., Hawkley, L. C., Thisted, R. A., & Cacioppo, J. T. (2011). A marginal structural model analysis for loneliness: Implications for intervention trials and clinical practice. *Journal of Clinical and Consulting Psychology, 79*(2), 225–235. https://doi.org/10.1037%2Fa0022610

Van Regenmortel, S. (2017). *Social exclusion in later life (SELL). Measurement and drivers of social exclusion among older adults.* Vrije Universiteit Brussel.

Van Regenmortel, S., Winter, B., Thelin, A., Burholt, V., & De Donder, L. (2021). Exclusion from Social Relations Among Older People in Rural Britain and Belgium: A Cross-National Exploration Taking a Life-Course and Multilevel Perspective. In K. Walsh, T. Scharf, S. Van Regenmortel & A. Wanka (Eds.), *Social Exclusion in Later Life. Interdisciplinary and Policy Perspectives,* International *Perspectives on Ageing* (Vol. 28, pp. 83–98). Springer Nature.

Van Regenmortel, T. (2020). *Bouwen aan een wetenschappelijke basis voor sterk sociaal werk. Onderzoek dat er toe doet!* [Building a scientific foundation for a strong social work. Research that matters!]. Tilburg University. https://www.tilburguniversity.edu/sites/default/files/download/TiU_200173_Oratie%20Tine%20Van%20Regenmortel-digitaal.pdf

Vlaamse Ouderenraad (2019). *Over de aanpak van eenzaamheid bij ouderen. Advies 2019/4* [On tackling loneliness in older persons. Advice 2019/4]. Vlaamse Ouderenraad.

Wang, J., Lloyd-Evans, B., Marston, L., Mann, F., Solmi, F., & Jonhnson, S. (2020). Epidemiology of loneliness in a cohort of UK mental health community crisis service users. Social Psychiatry and Psychiatric Epidemiology, 55(7), 811–822. https://doi.org/10.1007/s00127-019-01734-6

Wanless, D. (2002), Securing Our Future Health: Taking a Long-Term View.

Wilson, R. S., Krueger, K. R., Arnold, S. E., Schneider, J. A., Kelly, J. F., & Bennett, D. A. (2007). Loneliness and risk of Alzheimer disease. *Archives of General Psychiatry*, 64(2), 234–240. https://doi.org/10.1001/archpsyc.64.2.234

WHO (2018). *Public spending on health: a closer look at global trends*. WHO.

Yanguas, J., Pinazo-Henandis, S., & Tarazona-Santabalbina, F. J. (2018). The complexity of loneliness. *Acta Biomededica* 89(2), 302–314. https://doi.org/10.23750%2Fabm.v89i2.7404

Yanguas, J., Cilvetti, A., & Segura, C. (2019). *¿A quiénes afecta la soledad y el aislamiento social?* Observatorio Social de 'la Caixa'.

Yanguas, J., Cilveti, A., & Segura, C. (2020). Loneliness in Old Age. *Encyclopedia of Biomedical Gerontology* (pp. 326–331). Academic Press.

CHAPTER 3
AN EMPOWERMENT PERSPECTIVE ON LONELINESS AMONG OLDER PERSONS

Jasper De Witte & Tine Van Regenmortel

1. Introduction

Research has repeatedly demonstrated that severe feelings of loneliness are related to numerous health problems (e.g. depression, mortality risks) (Holt-Lunstad et al., 2015; Ward et al., 2021), increased health expenditure (Meisters et al., 2021) and negatively impacts the quality of life of older persons (De Witte & Van Regenmortel, 2019b; Ten Bruggencate et al., 2018). The significance of this subject is further demonstrated by its prevalence rates in Belgium and Europe: about 22 per cent of the older Belgians (sixty-five years and older) felt lonely in 2017 (De Witte & Van Regenmortel, 2020a). And while loneliness was already a growing public health concern during the past years (Marquez et al., 2021; Victor et al., 2020), the Covid-19 pandemic put this subject even higher on the policy agenda by showing the importance of social connections and the opportunity to meet others for our general well-being. Indeed, the restrictive measures taken to deal with the pandemic limited possibilities for interaction, which resulted in higher loneliness rates. In Flanders (Belgium), the telephone help service Tele-Onthaal noted, for example, a record number of 139,000 calls in 2020, whereby loneliness was the third most important theme, with an increase of 42 per cent (Tele-Onthaal, 2021).

Unsurprisingly, loneliness is increasingly acknowledged as a public policy issue that asks for theory-driven and evidence-based interventions (Burholt et al., 2017; Victor et al., 2020). However, to this day, there is insufficient evidence about the effectiveness of interventions.

> *The inadequate attention [...] is reflected in insufficient investment in monitoring, investigation of causes and maintenance factors, and evaluation of strategies to reduce the prevalence and impact.* (Smith & Lim, 2020, p. 3)

As a result of this lacking knowledge, 'many of the myriad programs that are being offered to improve social connectedness and wellbeing, though well-intentioned, are of uncertain benefit' (Smith & Lim, 2020, p. 3). Therefore, it is crucial to gain more knowledge about which factors relate to loneliness and which interventions can prevent and alleviate those feelings.

In this chapter, we discuss the current state of loneliness. First, we define loneliness and present a theoretical framework to analyse this phenomenon. Next, we discuss several (intra-individual, inter-individual and societal) factors that are associated with and explain feelings of loneliness among older persons, based on statistical analyses concerning older persons in Belgium and Europe. In the following, we argue that empowerment is an effective framework to develop loneliness interventions. We conclude this chapter by formulating several policy recommendations.

2.   A theoretical framework for loneliness

2.1   The cognitive discrepancy theory of loneliness

According to the cognitive discrepancy theory, loneliness is the result of a cognitive process whereby people subjectively evaluate the quality and quantity of their relations. Based on this evaluation, people can make adjustments to reduce feelings of loneliness, which can be seen as a signal that stresses the importance to preserve social relations (Cacioppo et al., 2015). From this follows that loneliness *as such* is not a problem: everybody feels lonely sometimes. Feelings of loneliness become problematic when they persevere for a longer period. During the Covid-19 crisis, about 59 per cent of all adults in Flanders, Belgium, indicated that they sometimes or often feel lonely, and 36 per cent reported severe loneliness (in February 2021) (Steyaert & Heylen, 2021).

Loneliness can be defined as

> *the unpleasant experience that occurs when a person's network of social rela-*
> *tions is deficient in some important way, either quantitatively or qualitatively.*
> (Perlman & Peplau, 1981, p. 31)

Connectedness, as opposed to loneliness, refers to

> *a positive subjective evaluation of the extent to which one has meaningful*
> *close, and constructive relationships with other individuals, groups, or society.*
> (O'Rourke et al., 2018)

Figure 3.1: Loneliness and social isolation

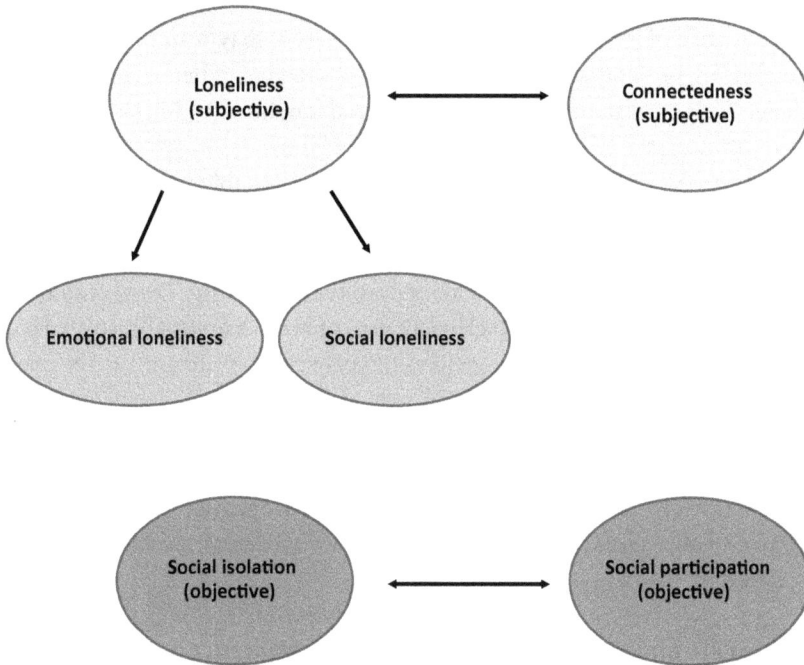

Source: De Witte and Van Regenmortel (2019b).

In sum, loneliness and connectedness both refer to a *subjective* feeling people have when they assess their *objective* social relations. We can further divide loneliness into emotional and social loneliness. Whereas emotional loneliness stems from the absence of a meaningful, intimate and exclusive relationship (e.g. with a partner), social loneliness results from the lack of an adequate, broad social network of friends, neighbours and acquaintances (De Jong Gierveld & van Tilburg, 2006; Weiss, 1973). The distinction between these dimensions is crucial to determine which interventions are effective to counteract specific types of loneliness, since each type of loneliness requires a customised approach (De Witte & Van Regenmortel, 2019b).

In this regard, *objective* social relations can be placed on a continuum from social isolation to social participation, based on objective indicators that deal with the frequency of social contact and the size, structure and functioning of social networks more broadly. While social isolation refers to the lack or almost complete absence of relations with other people, social participation refers to the situation whereby people have many social relations (De Jong Gierveld & van Tilburg, 2008). In this respect, the distinction between emotional and social loneliness implies that both intimate and peripheral relationships are important: whereas intimate relationships are associated with a sense of love and belonging (a lack thereof may result in emotional loneliness), peripheral relationships relate to a feeling of being connected to society (a lack of thereof may result in social loneliness) (Ten Bruggencate et al., 2018).

It is important to bear in mind that although the subjective evaluation of social relations (e.g. loneliness or connectedness) and the objective characteristics of those relations (e.g. social isolation or participation) are strongly related to each other, this is not a one-to-one relationship. People can have many social relations but still feel lonely, or people can live socially isolated but not feel lonely. This is because loneliness is not exclusively determined by one's objective social relations, but also by personal (e.g. character, expectancies) and structural factors (e.g. culture), which explains why people with similar objective social relations do not experience loneliness (or connectedness) to the same extent (Vandenbroucke et al., 2012). Moreover, subjective social needs and objective social relations are not static but change over time (Peplau & Perlman, 1979).

2.2   Resilience: A crucial ingredient to construct a satisfying social network

Older persons need sufficient resilience to prevent or alleviate feelings of loneliness. Indeed, resilience is crucial to surmount various challenges during life and to realise goals, such as constructing a satisfying social network (Wilson et al., 2021). The theoretical link between loneliness and resilience has also been shown to be statistically valid, since Gerino et al. (2017) have demonstrated that the effect of loneliness on quality of life is mediated by resilience. In Chapter 1, resilience is defined as 'patterns and processes of positive adaptation and development in the context of significant threats to an individual's life or function' (Janssen, 2013, p. 21), which matches the Luthar et al.'s definition (2000, pp. 543–562) of resilience as 'a dynamic process resulting in positive adaptation within the context of adversity'. With respect to loneliness, resilience processes consider the adversities, resources and control processes of older persons to construct a satisfying social network and alleviate feelings of loneliness (De Witte & Van Regenmortel, 2019a). Indeed, resilience implies that older persons are able to overcome adversities (e.g. death of partner, mobility limitations) by using their resources (e.g. psychological hardiness, social services) to construct a satisfying social network and reduce feelings of loneliness.

In this respect, we first find that older persons are confronted with various age-related adversities and resources that can be found in the individual (e.g. mobility limitations), relational (e.g. death of partner, shrinking social network) and contextual domains (e.g. ageism). With respect to control processes, the motivational theory of lifespan development distinguishes between primary and secondary control processes that can be used to deal with adversities and construct a satisfying social network (see Chapter 1). An older person who actively engages in an organisation to meet new people is an example of a primary control strategy that is applied to realise a satisfying social network. An older person who learns to accept that his contact possibilities decrease because of severe mobility limitations is an example of a secondary control strategy: this person applies a psychological process to bring himself in line with his specific context. This concurs with the ascertainment of Peplau and Perlman (1979) that there are three ways to alleviate feelings of loneliness. The first way consists of *improving social relations* to the desired level by creating new relations or by ameliorating existing relations (this is an example of primary control). The second and third ways are psychologically based (examples of secondary control): older persons could *lower their standards* by adjusting unrealistic desires about their social relations, or they could *deal with feelings of loneliness* by acceptance, relativisation (e.g. devaluing the importance of social contact), denial (e.g. suppressing emotional reactions) or distraction (e.g. gratifying their needs in different ways) (Fokkema & van Tilburg, 2007). In this respect, older persons are often confronted with increasing adversities (e.g. death of a partner, chronic diseases) and decreasing resources (e.g. a declining social network), through which their possibilities to use primary control strategies decrease, and secondary control processes become more promising (De Witte & Van Regenmortel, 2019a). Last, it is important to take the specific context into account when studying loneliness because resilience processes always take place in a given social, cultural and economic context (Fuller-Iglesias et al., 2008; Siriwardhana et al., 2014; Wilson et al., 2021). Indeed, certain populations (e.g. people with a migration background) often have more adversities and fewer resources (Visser & El Fakiri, 2016), and people's expectations regarding social relations differ according to their specific culture (Pruchno & Carr, 2017).

3.   The focus of loneliness interventions

To know which intervention strategy is most effective to alleviate loneliness in a specific situation, it is important to gain sufficient understanding of what loneliness entails for different groups and to detect specific barriers that impede those groups from participating and from constructing satisfying social networks. Indeed, an intervention strategy is more effective when it fits the specific cause and type of loneliness:

> *there would, for example, be little use in encouraging an old man to go to a men's club if he is in search of a new female partner, if he suffers from social anxiety, if he can barely understand people because he is hard of hearing, or if he is very demanding in terms of the friends he makes.* (Fokkema & van Tilburg, 2007, p. 165)

In this section, we first gain insight into which groups of older persons (sixty-five years or older) in Belgium are most affected by loneliness (Table 3.1), based on the analysis of data of the Survey of Health, Ageing and Retirement in Europe (SHARE). This information is useful to detect target groups on which loneliness interventions could focus. In the following, we discuss the factors that *explain* feelings of loneliness among older persons (sixty-five years or older) in Europe, based on a logistic regression analysis of SHARE data (Table 3.2).

We make use of the sixth wave of the SHARE data, which were collected in 2015.[1] SHARE is a cross-national survey taken among community-dwelling Europeans of fifty years or older, which has been conducted by twenty European countries and Israel on several different occasions since 2004 (Börsch-Supan et al., 2013). The result is a database with microdata about several relevant life domains such as health, socio-economic status and social networks (Dolberg et al., 2016). The data were ex ante harmonised and all aspects (e.g. translation, sampling) followed strict quality standards.[2] In 2019, the individual registration was filled out whereby the authors agreed to the SHARE Conditions of Use, after which they were allowed to use the data.

3.1   The unequal distribution of loneliness

Fokkema and van Tilburg (2007) divide the causes of loneliness into intra-individual, inter-individual and societal causes. *Intra-individual causes* can be found within the personal life sphere of the person (e.g. lack of social capacities). In line with other research, we find that the prevalence of loneliness is higher among the 'older' old (eighty-five years or older), women (Vozikaki et al., 2018), people who live alone, people with a lower education level (De Witte & Van Regenmortel, 2020a; Takagi & Saito, 2015) and people with an immigration background (De Witte & Van Regenmortel, 2021). Further, we observe that French-speaking older Belgians are lonelier than Dutch-speaking older Belgians and that people who live in nursing homes are lonelier than those who live in a private household. With respect to the relation between loneliness and health, we observe that older persons with better health (i.e. self-perceived health, number of mobility limitations, or depression) and a higher level of cognitive functioning are less lonely, which corresponds to other research (Aroonsrimorakot et al., 2019; Van Campen et al., 2018). Also, persons with a higher net household income are less lonely (with the exception of the tenth decile) than those with a lower income, which is in accordance with Vozikaki et al.'s (2018) research. Last, with respect to the link between loneliness and personality traits (e.g. social capacities, self-confidence), older persons are lonelier when they feel that 'what happens is out of their control' and when they have less trust in other people. *Inter-individual causes* of loneliness refer to the contact with other people, and include characteristics such as the network size, contact frequency and diversity of network members (De Witte & Van Regenmortel, 2019a). In this regard, we observe that the prevalence of loneliness is higher among older persons without children, with a smaller social network, with fewer network members that live nearby, with fewer network members with whom they have weekly contact, and older persons who are less 'emotionally close' to their closest network member. The latter is an indication that it is important to have at least one person with whom older persons have a strong bond. In addition, while people who do more activities (e.g. charity or voluntary work) are less lonely, older persons who give help with personal care and practical chores to their own household members feel lonelier than those who do not. In this respect, family caregivers are often confronted with a *burden of care*, which can manifest itself on various domains (such as the social domain). Indeed, we find that the social life of partners of older persons with high care needs can be negatively affected by the care relation, for example, because they would feel guilty when they have fun without their counterpart (De Witte & Van Regenmortel, 2020b). With respect to *the societal causes* (e.g. population changes), the scientific literature shows that the accessibility of healthcare services, negative stereotyping, changes in family and population structures (Fokkema et al., 2012; Fokkema & van Tilburg, 2007) and culture (Vandenbroucke et al., 2012) affect the contact between people and feelings of loneliness.

Based on analyses, we can distinguish various groups of older persons on whom loneliness interventions could focus: the 'older' old (eighty-five years or older), women, people who live alone, those with a migration background, those who live in nursing homes, those with depression or mobility limitations, and those with a low income or a small social network.

Table 3.1: The distribution of loneliness among older persons (65 years and older) in Belgium (2015)

	Loneliness (%)	N
	***	
Loneliness	24.7	2,912
Age groups	***	
65–74	22.0	1,578
75–84	25.8	963
≥ 85	32.0	371
Gender	***	
Men	19.9	1,315
Women	28.5	1,597
Household size	***	
1	39.1	997
≥ 1	17.1	1,915
ISCED-97 (%)	***	
(Pre-)primary	28.2	656
Lower and upper secondary	25.4	1,336
First stage of tertiary	20.9	895
Immigrant generation	**	
Natives	23.5	2,343
Second generation	32.0	197
First generation	29.4	168
Language of questionnaire	***	
French	30.2	1,364
Dutch	20.6	1,548
Interview conducted in household type	***	
Private household	24.3	2,823
Nursing home	37.6	89
Self-perceived health (US scale)	***	
Excellent–very good	13.3	623
Good	21.0	1,390
Fair–poor	38.5	899
Number of mobility limitations	***	
0	16.2	1,079
1	19.5	496
2	25.8	387
≥ 3	36.4	950
Euro depression scale	***	
0–3 (not depressed)	15.0	2,063
4–8	47.8	820
9–12 (very depressed)	75.7	29

	Loneliness (%)	N
Memory test	***	
Excellent–very good	16.9	622
Good	22.4	1,522
Fair–poor	33.2	768
Equivalent income (in deciles)	***	
Decile 1	39.9	286
Decile 2	35.6	296
Decile 3	25.9	293
Decile 4	23.1	289
Decile 5	23.1	287
Decile 6	17.9	249
Decile 7	19.6	300
Decile 8	19.2	305
Decile 9	17.0	314
Decile 10	24.2	293
What happens is out of your control?	***	
Often	49.4	301
Sometimes	33.4	826
Rarely	19.1	935
Never	13.0	815
Trust in other people	***	
0–3 (low)	41.9	75
4–6	24.8	152
7–10 (high)	15.0	140
Number of children	***	
0	32.0	337
1	25.7	586
≥ 2	23.2	1,989
Social network size	***	
0	26.6	95
1	27.5	520
2	26.5	615
3	27.9	541
≥ 4	18.9	798
Number of network members who live within 1km	***	
0	35.4	711
1	21.6	1,130
≥ 2	17.5	536
Number of network members with weekly contact	***	
0	43.8	84
1	27.4	727
2	25.6	694
≥ 3	20.0	966

	Loneliness (%)	N
Emotional closeness with closest network member	***	
Somewhat close	44.7	132
Very close	25.9	893
Extremely close	21.7	1,439
Number of activities	***	
0	36.9	212
1	27.3	613
≥ 2	22.0	1,998
Have you done voluntary or charity work in the last year?	***	
Yes	19.2	741
No	26.0	2,068
Given help with personal care and practical chores to household member(s)?	***	
Yes	28.7	220
No	17.3	1,758

χ^2-test or non-parametric Wilcoxon test: *$p<0.1$; **$p<0.05$; ***$p<0.01$.
Source: De Witte & Van Regenmortel (2020a).

3.2 The causes of loneliness

The previous paragraph shows that feelings of loneliness are distributed unequally among different groups of older persons. Although this is important information that can guide policymakers to set up interventions for specific groups, these characteristics do not necessarily *explain* feelings of loneliness. Are women lonelier than men simply because they are women, or is it rather because of certain gender-related factors (e.g. lower income, more health limitations)?

The theoretical framework about resilience helps us explain the unequal distribution of loneliness among various groups. Indeed, we suppose that those groups are characterised by more adversities and less resources that are needed to construct a satisfying social network and to prevent feelings of loneliness. In Table 3.2, we present the results of a logistic regression analysis that gives us more insight into the factors that explain feelings of loneliness among older persons in Europe (sixty-five years or older).[3] Hereby, we analyse three models that assess the correlation of several variables with loneliness, controlled for all other variables. In the first model, we include socio-demographic characteristics, which we complement with health variables (model 2) and social network variables (model 3). Our final model explains 28 per cent of the variance in loneliness (Pseudo R of Nagelkerke), which is satisfactory.

Based on our final model, we find that most variables are significantly related to feelings of loneliness among older persons in Europe. First, contrary to second-generation immigrants, we observe that first-generation immigrants are lonelier than natives. This concurs with the scientific literature which finds that people with a migration background have higher loneliness levels than people without a migration background (De Witte & Van Regenmortel, 2021), and that this is not only attributable to demographic, socio-economic and health factors (Wu & Penning, 2015). Indeed, higher loneliness levels of first-generation immigrants can be explained by migration-related factors that play into loneliness and general resilience: leaving former relationships behind, experiencing difficulties integrating into a new culture (Van Campen et al., 2018), cultural dislocation, acculturative processes (e.g. learning a new language) and loss of social status (Keung Wong et al., 2007). Moreover, people with a migration background often have more social and economic difficulties and health problems (van Tilburg & Fokkema, 2021). Second, citizens in central Europe are less lonely than those in northern and eastern and southern Europe, with the citizens in eastern and southern Europe being the loneliest.[4] This is contrary to our simplified views of anomie in northern countries and Gemeinschaft in southern countries. Indeed, community indicators (which are assumed protective against loneliness) are more common in southern European countries, and household atomisation and solitary living (which are assumed to relate to higher loneliness) first took place in northern countries (Sundström et al., 2009). The different loneliness levels between cultural regions (such as between the Walloon and Flemish regions) shows that loneliness is not only determined by individual and relational factors but also by structural and cultural factors. Third, there is only a very small effect of age, whereby the 'older' old (eighty-five years or older) are lonelier than the 'younger' old. In this regard, research is not conclusive. On the one hand, older persons are found to be more often confronted with lacking intimate attachment figures (Vozikaki et al., 2018), more dependency and a loss of mastery and income (Van Campen et al., 2018). On the other hand, older persons appear to have a lower risk of social loneliness (Wolfers et al., 2022), which could be explained by the socio-emotional selectivity theory, which states that older persons attach more importance to the quality of contacts and are more satisfied with their social relationships (Schoenmakers et al., 2012). Fourth, although women are in general lonelier than men (model 1), our analyses show that this can be explained by their worse health situation (model 2). Fifth, the last model shows that people in the two highest income deciles are less lonely than those in the lowest income decile, which concurs with other research that states that people with a lower income or less wealth have less financial possibilities to participate (Vozikaki et al., 2018). In this respect, the higher loneliness levels of people with a low income are in part explained by their worse health situation, which again is in line with other research (Niedzwiedz et al., 2016). Next, we observe that older persons who live together with someone and who have children are considerably less lonely than those who do not. Further, a worse health situation and cognitive functioning strongly relates to higher loneliness levels, with depression having the most important effect. In this regard, research shows that this relation works in both directions: a worse health situation (e.g. mobility problems) can lead to higher loneliness levels (De Witte & Van Regenmortel, 2019a), but loneliness may also result in worse mental and physical health (e.g. depression, higher blood pressure) (Dahlberg et al., 2022). In this respect, Heinberg and Steffen (2021, p. 367) find, for example, that loneliness and social isolation, which increased during the Covid-19 crisis, affected eating behaviour: 'eating episodes and calories consumed tend to increase in times of emotional distress – particularly depression – boredom and loneliness'. Health not only has a strong effect on loneliness (and vice versa), but health also explains a significant part of the variation in loneliness according to different characteristics (e.g. the 'older' old, women and people with a migration background). This concurs with our theoretical framework, which states that certain groups have more adversities (e.g. health limitations) and less resources (e.g. lower income), negatively affecting their general resilience and loneliness. Last, we find that the prevalence of loneliness is lower for older persons who undertake more activities and who have a larger social network. This explains (in part) the detrimental effects of the imposed social restrictions to deal with the Covid-19 outbreak on loneliness among older persons.

Table 3.2: Logistic regression of European older persons (65 years and older) (2015), with not being lonely as the reference category (in adjusted log odds).

	Model 1	Model 2	Model 3
Immigrant generation (natives = ref.)			
2nd generation	0.981	0.945	0.918
1st generation	1.222 ***	1.188 ***	1.144 ***
Region (Central Europe = ref.)			
Northern Europe	0.869 ***	1.182 *	1.198 ***
Eastern and southern Europe	2.188 ***	2.169 ***	2.028 ***
Age	1.023 ***	1.006 **	1.005 **
Gender (Men = ref.)			
Women	1.402 ***	1.041	1.050

	Model 1	Model 2	Model 3
Net household income (Decile 1 = ref.)			
Decile 2	0.977	1.076	1.074
Decile 3	0.906	1.022	1.017
Decile 4	1.103	1.363	1.368
Decile 5	0.843 ***	1.005	0.987
Decile 6	0.905 ***	1.133	1.144
Decile 7	0.702 ***	0.897	0.903
Decile 8	0.776 ***	1.012	1.045
Decile 9	0.607 ***	0.772 ***	0.790 ***
Decile 10	0.616 ***	0.786 *	0.796 ***
Household size (1 = ref.)			
>1	0.448 ***	0.441 ***	0.435 ***
Having a child/children (No = ref.)			
Yes	0.785 ***	0.763 ***	0.814 *
ISCED-97 (Upper secondary = ref.)			
Pre-primary	1.326 **	0.940 ***	0.863 ***
Primary	1.138 ***	0.939	0.872
Lower secondary	1.134 ***	1.047 *	0.977
Post-secondary	0.814	0.850	0.844
First stage of tertiary	0.785	0.907	0.900
Second stage of tertiary	1.244	1.367	1.413
Self-perceived health (US-scale) (Good = ref.)			
Excellent		0.916 ***	0.971 ***
Very good		0.861 ***	0.870 **
Fair		1.188 ***	1.158 ***
Poor		1.053 **	1.030 **
Number of mobility limitations		1.037 ***	1.045 ***
Euro Depression scale		1.427 ***	1.425 ***
Memory test (good = ref.)			
Excellent		0.805 **	0.796 **
Very good		0.924 *	0.942
Fair		1.227 ***	1.235 **
Poor		1.209 ***	1.197 ***
Number of activities			0.959 ***
Social network size			0.933 ***
N	22,700	22,700	21,499
Pseudo R (Nagelkerke)	0.13	0.28	0.28

χ^2-test: *p<0.1; **p<0.05; ***p<0.01.

4.   Empowerment as a way to tackle loneliness

4.1   Developing effective loneliness interventions

Our theoretical framework shows that loneliness is a complex phenomenon that comes in multiple forms (e.g. social and emotional loneliness) and is determined by a complex interplay of individual (e.g. health), relational (e.g. network size) and contextual factors (e.g. culture). Subsequently, we have seen that the older population is a heterogeneous one and that feelings of loneliness affect some groups more than others (e.g. women, people with a migration background). From this, we conclude that one-size-fits-all interventions to tackle loneliness do not exist. Rather, we need a wide range of interventions that are tailored around the unique needs of the individual. Interventions should not only take into account the specific characteristics of the loneliness problem (e.g. type, cause, duration) but also the qualities (e.g. subjective perceptions, needs and possibilities) and context (e.g. access to health and social care, culture) of the person (De Witte & Van Regenmortel, 2019b). Moreover, for a loneliness intervention to be successful, the older person must (1) be aware of his or her loneliness, (2) be willing to deal with it and (3) be able to participate in the intervention (Fokkema & van Tilburg, 2007). In sum, loneliness interventions can focus on different types of loneliness, target groups, intervention strategies (e.g. improving social relations to the desired level, lowering standards or accepting a discrepancy), intervention types (e.g. group setting, one-on-one interventions) and in various settings (e.g. retirement homes, caring neighborhoods).

4.2   Empowerment principles as a guide for interventions

Empowerment starts from a strengths-based perspective, which is particularly useful to guide the development of interventions for vulnerable groups, such as older persons who feel lonely. Indeed, as previously described, older persons are often confronted with increasing adversities (e.g. death of a partner, health problems) and decreasing resources (e.g. a declining social network), through which their possibilities to use primary control strategies decrease and secondary control processes become more promising. Therefore, the emphasis of empowerment that all older persons can have mastery and lead an autonomous life, despite several age-related adversities and dependencies, is crucial for loneliness interventions.

> *It is important not just to consider approaches that ameliorate the losses associated with older age, but also those that may reinforce recovery, adaptation and psychosocial growth.* (WHO, 2015, p. 25)

Therefore, focusing on what people can still do and accepting certain limitations is crucial from a strengths-based perspective. Indeed, it is not only important to enhance social relations (primary control), but in some instances also to lower standards or accept a discrepancy between the actual and desired situation (secondary control). Further, since older persons are increasingly confronted with age-related adversities, the empowerment framework builds on the resilience of older persons. Such a strength-based approach avoids unnecessary dependency and positively affects resilience and connectedness (Ten Bruggencate et al., 2018), through which feelings of loneliness decrease.

Loneliness interventions that aim to enhance strength and general resilience can focus on factors on the individual, relational and structural level, since both the causes of loneliness and sources of strength can be found on these levels (De Witte & Van Regenmortel, 2019b). This is in line with the empowerment framework, which stresses the shared responsibility of individual, relational and structural factors with respect to loneliness. As a result, all stakeholders (i.e. older persons, the social network, professionals, policymakers) can help to alleviate loneliness by creating so-called enabling niches, 'safe and warm places in which people are respected and not stigmatized, and be encouraged to grow', that help to prevent and alleviate feelings of loneliness (Van Regenmortel, 2015). In this respect, they can take the empowerment principles into consideration when developing or evaluating loneliness interventions, such as strength in and through connection, a positive stance, participation, inclusiveness and an integral perspective. Further, they can also appeal to specific methods of action that stimulate empowerment such as structuration, coordination, proactive action and outreaching. These guiding principles can be used as quality criteria to evaluate interventions, as well as to develop individual empowering policy, practice and research (See Chapter 8).

4.3   Bras dessus Bras dessous: An empowering intervention to alleviate loneliness

Bras dessus Bras dessous (BdBd) is a social work organisation that applies various empowerment principles and methods of action to alleviate feelings of loneliness among older persons in Brussels, Belgium. Based on qualitative research methods, we discuss how this organisation tries to enhance the resilience and mastery of its participants and in that way alleviate feelings of loneliness (De Witte & Van Regenmortel, 2019b).

The development of Bras dessus Bras dessous

In 2015, BdBd was created in response to three observations. First, citizens of a specific neighbourhood in Brussels indicated that older persons went outside less often because of feelings of loneliness, a general emptiness surrounding them, mobility problems, fear of going out and because they felt like there was no point in going out. Second, professionals of about thirty organisations who are active in that neighbourhood (family help, social services, and medical houses, for example) stated that they did not have sufficient time to simply chat with older persons (through which they could detect needs). This negatively affected the possibilities of older persons to safeguard their quality of life and to remain in their own home and neighbourhood. Third, BdBd observed that many people were willing to engage and strengthen the social and intergenerational bond with older persons in their neighbourhood.

Based on these observations, BdBd was created. This organisation supports lonely and socially isolated older neighbours (*beneficiaries*) by realising intergenerational encounters with younger neighbours (*visitors*), through which participation and a feeling of connectedness increase. More specifically, two neighbours (a beneficiary and a visitor) regularly undertake a free activity together which gives meaning to their lives and through which their health and social network improves. The fact that there is no money involved is supposed to add to the creation of *real* connections. The beneficiaries are sixty years or older, live at home and express a feeling of loneliness or social isolation. About half of the beneficiaries have no friends or family on whom they can count. Further, most beneficiaries only have a moderate to low income, and many of them never go out alone (because they do not want to or are unable to). Visitors are younger, mostly between twenty and seventy years old.

The overall goal of BdBd is not to realise autonomy, but rather that older persons acquire a positive self-image and a feeling of control through which they can make conscious decisions about their own lives again. This is in line with our data analyses in the previous paragraphs, which show that *feeling in control* relates to lower loneliness levels. From this we conclude that BdBd was developed based on a needs assessment through which a specific target group was detected (i.e. lonely and socially isolated older persons) and an intervention strategy was chosen (i.e. improving social relations to the desired level by creating new relations). This intervention is suited for this target group because our data analyses demonstrate that both social participation and network size significantly relate to lower loneliness levels. This intervention is further also positive for the 'visitors' because our analyses show that voluntary work and doing things for other people result in more resilience and less loneliness.

Empowerment principles

BdBd adheres to the empowerment framework. Indeed, its main focus lies in stimulating *strength and connection* of the beneficiaries by focusing on the activities they want and are still able to do.

First, BdBd uses a *proactive outreaching method* to find both beneficiaries and visitors. At the outset, BdBd contacted various professional confidants of older persons in the neighbourhood where they were active (e.g. doctors, medical houses, social workers) and various small shops (e.g. pharmacies, butchers). They subsequently informed those actors about how BdBd works, and handed out flyers and posters to inform possible beneficiaries. It is important that people see those flyers and posters in various local places because often it takes some time before they dare to make contact with the organisation or even to simply realise that they feel lonely. Second, over five days, BdBd was physically present in the neighbourhood with a caravan to inform people about loneliness, social isolation and how the organisation works. They gained confidence and trust by staying several days in the same neighbourhood, which is needed to reach hard-to-reach groups (*inclusiveness*). Third, BdBd informed the public through various local information channels (local television, radio, magazines). The visitors were sought through the same channels as the beneficiaries, supplemented with word-of-mouth publicity and publicity in schools and on Facebook.

BdBd adopts an *integral and person-centred* philosophy, whereby everything starts with the wishes and needs of the participants. The participants themselves decide how and to what extent they participate in this intervention, which is an important empowerment principle. In this regard, BdBd always meets a beneficiary or visitor to understand their personal needs, wishes, desires and availability, through which the professionals obtain a holistic picture of the person. BdBd is very flexible (e.g. with respect to engagements, hours, activities) so that more individuals can participate (e.g. single-parent households with little time) (*inclusiveness*). The only engagement BdBd asks from the visitors is that they sign a volunteering contract and show proof of good conduct. Further, BdBd creates a personal file for each participant that contains information about their confidants, the activities they want to do (e.g. learn a language, go out for a walk) and their availability. Last, during this conversation, BdBd also gives information about other organisations that could help the beneficiaries if they have specific needs BdBd cannot fulfil. That way, BdBd works complementarily to other organisations.

Subsequently, BdBd matches a beneficiary with one to three visitors, based on both actors' individual preferences (e.g. availability, interests). The desire to meet each other and share an activity is essential. A good match is crucial because it increases the chance of a *positive relation* between the participants, in which trust and respect are central. Therefore, participants must be clear about their expectations and engagements. This is important because interventions are more effective when participants share values, culture and background, belong to the same generation, and have common interests, because this leads to more reciprocity and strengthens their resilience (Hagan et al., 2014). Once a match between two neighbours is made, the beneficiary and visitor meet each other, together with a professional from BdBd. A few days later, both parties indicate to BdBd if they are okay with the other person. If this is the case, they meet each other maximally once a week to do an activity together. BdBd sporadically gets in touch with both parties to verify whether the activities and encounters go well. That way, both beneficiaries and visitors can influence the intervention and participate in the decision-making process. During the activities, all involved actors who surround a beneficiary (e.g. beneficiary, visitors, doctor, children) can use a specific ICT tool which allows them to better communicate with each other. That way, they can, for example, make sure that two people do not visit the beneficiary on the same day so as to spread their social contacts.

With respect to *participation*, although beneficiaries are not structurally implicated in the evaluation of BdBd, they are sporadically formally invited to give their perspective on the intervention, and informally they are often asked about their opinions. This has already resulted in various new initiatives such as the so-called soup workshops (more on this below). Next, visitors are regularly invited to a meeting where they can share their experiences, through which they indirectly evaluate the working of BdBd. During those meetings, BdBd also informs the visitors about the working of the organisation, and external speakers are invited to talk about relevant themes. This participation is important because research demonstrates that interventions are more effective when older persons themselves are involved in the process (Cattan et al., 2005; Findlay, 2003).

As we have seen, the informal feedback from the participants led to the weekly organisation of soup workshops, where all neighbours can eat soup together and meet each other in an informal manner. This is a good example of the importance of *collaboration and coordination*. Indeed, BdBd works together with a local food store to make this happen, and various local organisations are invited to talk to the participants about their specific projects. Further, BdBd also organises other activities such as an annual meal, going to the sea and intergenerational activities. However, although these group activities have an added value, they are not the core business of BdBd because many lonely and socially isolated older persons do not want or dare to participate in group activities.

From the above, it is clear that BdBd follows a certain *structure* with both beneficiaries and visitors, and makes use of various tools such as a personal file for each participant and an ICT tool for communication. This offers transparency for all participants, which, according to the empowerment framework, enhances both involvement and participation. Indeed, structuration stresses the importance of jointly creating a methodical plan in which the possibilities of the individual and his environment are described, goals are put forward and priorities determined. Such a plan not only enhances the understanding of the loneliness problem and its solutions, but it also gives those persons a voice and offers structure and insight in what works. In sum, this intervention is a local, informal initiative that aims to stimulate encounters between neighbours and enhance the dynamic in the community.

With regard to the effects of the intervention on the beneficiaries, professionals of BdBd suggest that the beneficiaries increasingly start socialising again, which is indicated by the fact that certain pairs start calling each other on their own, some beneficiaries take contact with their children again (after a rupture), and some older persons go outside again after having been indoors for multiple years. About four out of five pairs do not stop their visits. Further, the beneficiaries are said to be happier: they take better care of themselves, they put on make-up again and their general self-image is said to improve. This is perfectly in line with the central duality of the empowerment framework, which stresses that connections result in more strength and vice versa. However, not only their mental health seems to improve, but beneficiaries also seem to use less medication and go to their general practitioner less often. According to the professionals, this intervention allows beneficiaries to stay longer in their own home. The positive effects of this intervention on the resilience and quality of life of the beneficiaries is also demonstrated by the fact that some of them become visitors after a while. Last, with respect to the effects of the intervention on the (often also lonely) visitors, the professionals suggest that their social life enhances because they go out more often, they feel better by helping others (*the power of giving*) and because this intervention gives meaning to their lives.

Nevertheless, although BdBd has some ideas about its effectiveness (mainly based on information from its professionals), it has not conducted a thorough effectiveness study. Therefore, it is crucial to study whether BdBd in fact realises a decrease in loneliness levels and which are the working mechanisms.

5. The need for tailor-made empowerment interventions

Loneliness is a complex phenomenon that comes in multiple forms and is determined by factors in the individual, relational and structural domains. Furthermore, the older population is also a heterogeneous one. As a result, one-size-fits-all interventions do not exist. Rather, we need a wide range of interventions, which should be tailored around the unique needs of the individual and based on a holistic perspective that takes individual, relational and structural factors into account. These loneliness interventions can focus on (1) network development, (2) lowering expectations with regard to the social network and (3) accepting a discrepancy between the actual and desired situation. Moreover, all involved actors that surround an older person who feels lonely can contribute to alleviating feelings of loneliness (which is in line with empowerment's idea of a shared responsibility): the older person, the social network of family and friends, professionals and policymakers.

Based on our data analyses, we detect several factors that are entwined with loneliness and on which loneliness interventions could focus. On the individual domain, loneliness relates strongly to health limitations, through which interventions could focus on enhancing the health situation of older persons (which is preventive) or on alleviating the negative impact of health limitations. In this respect, it is important to counteract depression (e.g. by providing sufficient affordable and accessible psychological support). Through psychological support, older persons can learn to lower their expectations with regard to their social network and learn to deal with grief and traumatic experiences that impede them from forming or maintaining relations. In this regard, Chapter 1 shows that vulnerable older persons are often unable to appeal to psychological support because of its financial cost. Further, mobility limitations also significantly affect loneliness among older persons because they impede older persons (e.g. with a walker or wheelchair) to use public transportation or inadequate sidewalks and because it is not always possible to use a taxi with limited financial means. Therefore, it is important to provide affordable individual transportation, and to adapt sidewalks and public transportation to the needs of older persons with mobility limitations. Moreover, taking away the negative outcomes of health limitations would not only alleviate loneliness levels: since health is distributed unequally among different groups in society (e.g. according to gender, age and migration back-ground), it would also help to counteract the inequality between those groups with respect to loneliness. On the interactional domain, loneliness appears to be strongly related to social participation and network size. Therefore, a wide range of interventions is needed that stimulate social participation, increase network size and consider the specific situation of the older person who feels lonely. Indeed, while it might be appropriate to improve the social capacities of some persons (e.g. through social skill training), for other persons it might be more beneficial to take away the contextual barriers that impede them from participating. This can be done, for example, by increasing their mobility, providing sufficient affordable (public and individual) transportation, providing access to health and social services or by providing sufficient support for family caregivers with a high burden of care, which can also increase loneliness. In this respect, interventions could also focus on people with a low income because there are still many financial barriers for participation and network creation, which result in higher loneliness levels. However, not all loneliness interventions cost money. Indeed, our analyses show that older persons who give support (to others outside the own household) are less lonely, which harmonises with the idea of *the power of giving*. Indeed, doing things for other people (e.g. volunteering, taking care of grandchildren) has beneficial effects on the quality of life of older persons and society in general. For older persons, this is an important source of strength that results in increased feelings of self-worth, self-esteem and mastery. And since the *power of giving* often includes social contact, research shows that it also stimulates network development. Last, social participation can also be enhanced by stimulating older persons to move in time to a suitable *caring neighbourhood* where there are more possibilities for social participation (see Chapter 4) or by creating empowering nursing homes that stimulate social participation of its residents by appealing more to their strengths.

   Although a variety of interventions are imaginable, we stress that empowerment is a particularly suitable framework to guide the development of loneliness interventions. Empowerment is suitable because it accentuates that older persons who are increasingly confronted with problems on various life domains can still have mastery over their own situation and environment. In this respect, empowerment's emphasis on resilience, strength and connection is crucial for interventions that aim to alleviate loneliness among older persons. Indeed, by stimulating the use of strengths, older persons who feel lonely not only have more possibilities to create a satisfying social network, but they also become psychologically more resilient through which they can more easily deal with social setbacks. And since loneliness is a shared responsibility, it is important that all involved actors support older persons to make use of their strengths and gain control, which enhances their sense of mastery and social participation. In this respect, loneliness interventions should take the empowerment principles into account to evaluate their working because these principles not only aim to enhance the general resilience of older persons but also stimulate their strength and connectedness, and in that way alleviate feelings of loneliness.

Notes

1. This paper uses data from SHARE Wave 6 (http://dx.doi.org/10.6103/SHARE. w6.800); see Börsch-Supan et al. (2013) for methodological details. The SHARE data collection has been funded by the European Commission, DG RTD through FP5 (QLK6-CT-2001-00360), FP6 (SHARE-I3: RII-CT-2006-062193, COMPARE: CIT5-CT-2005-028857, SHARELIFE: CIT4-CT-2006-028812), FP7 (SHARE-PREP: GA N°211909, SHARE-LEAP: GA N°227822, SHARE M4: GA N°261982, DASISH: GA N°283646) and Horizon 2020 (SHARE-DEV3: GA N°676536, SHARE-COHESION: GA N°870628, SERISS: GA N°654221, SSHOC: GA N°823782, SHARE-COVID19: GA N°101015924) and by DG Employment, Social Affairs & Inclusion through VS 2015/0195, VS 2016/0135, VS 2018/0285, VS 2019/0332, and VS 2020/0313. Additional funding from the German Ministry of Education and Research, the Max Planck Society for the Advancement of Science, the U.S. National Institute on Aging (U01_AG09740-13S2, P01_AG005842, P01_AG08291, P30_AG12815, R21_AG025169, Y1-AG-4553-01, IAG_BSR06-11, OGHA_04-064, HHSN271201300071C, RAG052527A) and from various national funding sources is gratefully acknowledged (see www.share-project.org).
2. For more information: http://www.share-project.org/.
3. This is based on following countries: Sweden, Denmark, Austria, Belgium, Germany, France, Switzerland, Czech Republic, Spain and Italy.
4. We distinguished between northern (Sweden, Denmark), central (Austria, Belgium, Germany, France and Switzerland) and eastern and southern Europe (Czech Republic, Spain, Italy) based on their geography.

References

Aroonsrimorakot, S., Laiphrakpam, M., Metadilogkul, O., & Konjengbam, S. (2019). Ageing, social isolation, loneliness, health, social care and longevity: insights from case studies in Thailand and India. *Ageing International, 44*(4), 371–384. https://doi.org/10.1007/s12126-019-09353-x

Bergmann, M., Kneip, T., De Luca, G., & Scherpenzeel, A. (2019). Survey participation in the survey of health, ageing and retirement in Europe (SHARE), Wave 1–7. Based on Release 7.0.0 SHARE Working Paper Series 41–2019. Max Planck Institute for Social Law and Social Policy. http://www.share-project.org/uploads/tx_sharepublications/WP_Series_41_2019_Bergmann_et_al.pdf

Börsch-Supan, A., Brandt, M., Hunkler, C., Kneip, T., Korbmacher, J., Malter, F., & Zuber, S. (2013). Data resource profile: the Survey of Health, Ageing and Retirement in Europe (SHARE). *International Journal of Epidemiology, 42*(4), 992–1001. https://doi.org/10.1093/ije/dyt088

Börsch-Supan, A. (2022). *Survey of Health, Ageing and Retirement in Europe (SHARE) Wave 6.* Release version: 8.0.0. SHARE-ERIC. Data set.

Burholt, V., Windle, G., Morgan, D. J., & CFAS Wales Team. (2017). A social model of loneliness: The roles of disability, social resources, and cognitive impairment. *The Gerontologist, 57*(6), 1020–1030. https://doi.org/10.1093/geront/gnw125

Cacioppo, S., Grippo, A. J., London, S., Goossens, L., & Cacioppo, J. T. (2015). Loneliness: Clinical import and interventions. *Perspectives on Psychological Science, 10*(2), 238–249. https://doi.org/10.1177/1745691615570616

Cattan, M., White, M., Bond, J., & Learmouth, A. (2005). Preventing social isolation and loneliness among older people: a systematic review of health promotion interventions. *Ageing & Society, 25*(1), 41–67. https://doi.org/10.1017/S0144686X04002594

Dahlberg, L., McKee, K. J., Frank, A., & Naseer, M. (2022). A systematic review of longitudinal risk factors for loneliness in older adults. *Aging & Mental Health, 26*(2), 225–249. https://doi.org/10.1080/13607863.2021.1876638

De Jong Gierveld, J., & van Tilburg, T. (2006). A 6-item scale for overall, emotional, and social loneliness: confirmatory tests on survey data. *Research on Aging, 28*(5), 582–598. https://doi.org/10.1177/0164027506289723

De Jong Gierveld, J., & van Tilburg, T. (2008). De ingekorte schaal voor algemene, emotionele en sociale eenzaamheid. [The abbreviated scale for general, emotional and social loneliness]. *Tijdschrift voor Gerontologie en Geriatrie, 39*(1), 4–15. https://doi.org/10.1007/BF03078118

De Witte, J., & Van Regenmortel, T. (2019a). *Silver Empowerment. Resilience of vulnerable elderly. A narrative research approach*. HIVA – KU Leuven. https://hiva.kuleuven.be/nl/nieuws/docs/tvr-18-tse-lssrc1-o2010-resilience-of-vulnerable.pdf

De Witte, J., & Van Regenmortel, T. (2019b). *Silver Empowerment. Loneliness and social isolation among elderly. An empowerment perspective*. HIVA – KU Leuven. https://hiva.kuleuven.be/nl/nieuws/docs/tvr-18-tse-lssrc1-o2010-loneliness-and-social.pdf

De Witte, J., & Van Regenmortel, T. (2020a). *Silver Empowerment. A quantitative picture of loneliness among elderly in Belgium and Europe*. HIVA – KU Leuven. https://hiva.kuleuven.be/nl/nieuws/docs/tvr-18-tse-lssrc1-o2010-loneliness-of-people-with.pdf

De Witte, J., & Van Regenmortel, T. (2020b). *Silver Empowerment. Family care for community-dwelling older seniors in times of corona: the power of giving and/or a burden of care?* HIVA – KU Leuven. https://hiva.kuleuven.be/nl/nieuws/docs/tvr-18-tse-lssrc1-o2010-informal-care.pdf

De Witte, J., & Van Regenmortel, T. (2021). The relationship between loneliness and migration among Belgian older adults. *Ageing International*, 1–23. https://doi.org/10.1007/s12126-021-09460-8

Dolberg, P., Shiovitz-Ezra, S., & Ayalon, L. (2016). Migration and changes in loneliness over a 4-year period: the case of older former Soviet Union immigrants in Israel. *European Journal of Ageing, 13*(4), 287–297. https://doi.org/10.1007/s10433-016-0391-2

Findlay, R. A. (2003). Interventions to reduce social isolation amongst older people: where is the evidence?. *Ageing & Society, 23*(5), 647–658. https://doi.org/10.1017/S0144686X03001296

Fokkema, T., De Jong Gierveld, J., & Dykstra, P. A. (2012). Cross-national differences in older adult loneliness. *The Journal of Psychology, 146*(1–2), 201–228. https://doi.org/10.1080/00223980.2011.631612

Fokkema, C. M., & van Tilburg, T. G. (2007). Zin en onzin van eenzaamheidsinterventies bij ouderen. [The sense and nonsense of loneliness interventions among older people] *Tijdschrift voor Gerontologie en Geriatrie, 38*(4), 161–177. https://doi.org/10.1007/bf03074846

Fuller-Iglesias, H., Sellars, B., & Antonucci, T. C. (2008). Resilience in old age: Social relations as a protective factor. *Research in Human Development, 5*(3), 181–193. https://doi.org/10.1080/15427600802274043

Gerino, E., Rollè, L., Sechi, C., & Brustia, P. (2017). Loneliness, resilience, mental health, and quality of life in old age: A structural equation model. *Frontiers in psychology, 8*, 2003. https://doi.org/10.3389/fpsyg.2017.02003

Hagan, R., Manktelow, R., Taylor, B. J., & Mallett, J. (2014). Reducing loneliness amongst older people: a systematic search and narrative review. *Aging & Mental Health, 18*(6), 683–693. https://doi.org/10.1080/13607863.2013.875122

Heinberg, L. J., & Steffen, K. (2021). Social isolation and loneliness during the COVID-19 pandemic: impact on weight. *Current Obesity Reports, 10*(3), 365–370. https://doi.org/10.1007/s13679-021-00447-9

Holt-Lunstad, J., Smith, T. B., Baker, M., Harris, T., & Stephenson., D. (2015). Loneliness and social isolation as risk factors for mortality: A meta-analytic review. *Perspectives on Psychological Science, 10*(2), 227–237. https://doi.org/10.1177/1745691614568352

Janssen, B. M., (2013). *Resilience and old age: Community care from an insider and empowerment perspective* [Doctoral dissertation, Vrije Universiteit Amsterdam].

Keung Wong, D. F., Li, C. Y., & Song, H. X. (2007). Rural migrant workers in urban China: living a marginalised life. *International Journal of Social Welfare, 16*(1), 32–40. https://doi.org/10.1111/j.1468-2397.2007.00475.x

Luthar, S.S., Cicchetti, D., & Becker, B. (2000). The construct of resilience: a critical evaluation and guidelines for future work. *Child Development, 71*(3), 543–562. https://www.jstor.org/stable/1132374

Marquez, J., Goodfellow, C., Hardoon, M. D., Inchley, J., Leyland, A., Qualter, P., Simpson, S. A., & Long, E. (2021). Loneliness in young people: A multilevel exploration of social ecological influences and geographic variation. *Journal of Public Health.* https://doi.org/10.1093/pubmed/fdab402

Meisters, R., Westra, D., Putrik, P., Bosma, H., Ruwaard, D., & Jansen, M. (2021). Does loneliness have a cost? A population-wide study of the association between loneliness and healthcare expenditure. *International Journal of Public Health, 2.* https://doi.org/10.3389/ijph.2021.581286

Niedzwiedz, C. L., Richardson, E. A., Tunstall, H., Shortt, N. K., Mitchell, R. J., & Pearce, J. R. (2016). The relationship between wealth and loneliness among older people across Europe: Is social participation protective? *Preventive Medicine, 91*, 24–31. https://doi.org/10.1016/j.ypmed.2016.07.016

O'Rourke, H. M., Collins, L., & Sidani, S. (2018). Interventions to address social connectedness and loneliness for older adults: a scoping review. *BMC geriatrics, 18*(1), 1–13. https://doi.org/10.1186/s12877-018-0897-x

Peplau, L. A., & Perlman, D. (1979). Blueprint for a social psychological theory of loneliness. In M. Cook & G. Wilson (Eds.), *Love and attraction: An interpersonal conference* (pp. 101–110). Pergamon.

Perlman, D., & Peplau, L. A. (1981). Toward a social psychology of loneliness. *Personal relationships, 3*, 31–56.

Pruchno, R., & Carr, D. (2017). Successful aging 2.0: Resilience and beyond. *The Journal of Gerontology: Series B, 72*(2), 201–203. https://doi.org/10.1093/geronb/gbw214

Schoenmakers, E. C., van Tilburg, T. G., & Fokkema, T. (2012). Coping with loneliness: what do older adults suggest?. *Aging & Mental Health, 16*(3), 353–360. https://doi.org/10.1080/13607863.2011.630373

Siriwardhana, C., Ali, S. S., Roberts, B., & Stewart, R. (2014). A systematic review of resilience and mental health outcomes of conflict-driven adult forced migrants. *Conflict and Health, 8*(1), 1–14. https://doi.org/10.1186/1752-1505-8-1

Smith, B. J., & Lim, M. H. (2020). How the COVID-19 pandemic is focusing attention on loneliness and social isolation. *Public Health Research & Practice, 30*(2), 3022008. https://doi.org/10.17061/phrp3022008

Steyaert, J., & Heylen, L. (2021). *Eenzaamheid* [Loneliness]. Bond Zonder Naam.

Sundström, G., Fransson, E., Malmberg, B., & Davey, A. (2009). Loneliness among older Europeans. *European Journal of Ageing, 6*(4), 267–275. https://doi.org/10.1007/s10433-009-0134-8

Takagi, E., & Saito, Y. (2015). Older parents' loneliness and family relationships in Japan. *Ageing International, 40*(4), 353–375. https://doi.org/10.1007/s12126-015-9219-1

Tele-Onthaal (2021). *Jaarcijfers 2020* [Annual numbers 2020]. Tele-Onthaal.

Ten Bruggencate, T., Luijkx, K. G., & Sturm, J. (2018). Social needs of older people: a systematic literature review. *Ageing & Society, 38*(9), 1745–1770. https://doi.org/10.1017/S0144686X17000150

Van Campen, C., Vonk, F., & van Tilburg, T. (2018). *Kwetsbaar en eenzaam?* [Vulnerable and lonely?] Sociaal en Cultureel Planbureau.

Van Regenmortel, T. (2015). Empowerment en (maatschappelijk) opvoeden [Empowerment and (societal) education)]. In C. Gravesteijn & M. Aartsma (Eds.), *Meer dan opvoeden. Perspectieven op het werken met ouders* [More than educating. Perspectives on working with parents] (pp. 51–64). Coutinho.

van Tilburg, T. G., & Fokkema, T. (2021). Stronger feelings of loneliness among Moroccan and Turkish older adults in the Netherlands: in search for an explanation. *European Journal of Ageing, 18*(3), 311–322. https://doi.org/10.1007/s10433-020-00562-x

Vandenbroucke, S., Lebrun, J.-M., Vermeulen, B., Declercq, A., Maggi, P., Delye, S., & Gosset, C. (2012). *Oud word je niet alleen. Een enquête over eenzaamheid en sociaal isolement bij ouderen in België.* [You don't get old alone. A survey on loneliness ansd social isolation among older persons in Belgium]. Fondation Roi Baudouin.

Victor, C., Scambler, S. J., Shah, S., Cook, D. G., Harris, T., Rink, E., & De Wilde, S. (2020). Has loneliness amongst older people increased? An investigation into variations between cohorts. *Ageing and Society, 22*(5), 585–597. https://doi.org/10.1017/S0144686X02008784

Visser, M. A., & El Fakiri, F. (2016). The prevalence and impact of risk factors for ethnic differences in loneliness. *The European Journal of Public Health, 26*(6), 977–983. https://doi.org/10.1093/eurpub/ckw115

Vozikaki, M., Papadaki, A., Linardakis, M., & Philalithis, A. (2018). Loneliness among older European adults: Results from the survey of health, aging and retirement in Europe. *Journal of Public Health, 26*(6), 613–624. https://doi.org/10.1007/s10389-018-0916-6

Ward, M., May, P., Normand, C., Kenny, R. A., & Nolan, A. (2021). Mortality risk associated with combinations of loneliness and social isolation. Findings from The Irish Longitudinal Study on Ageing. *Age and Ageing, 50*(4), 1329–1335. https://doi.org/10.1093/ageing/afab004

Weiss, R. (1973). *Loneliness: The experience of emotional and social isolation.* MIT Press.

WHO (2015). World report on ageing and health. WHO.

Wilson, D. K., Bamishigbin Jr, O. N., Guardino, C., & Schetter, C. D. (2021). Resilience resources in low-income Black, Latino, and White fathers. *Social Science & Medicine, 282*, 114139. https://doi.org/10.1016/j.socscimed.2021.114139

Wolfers, M. E., Stam, B. E., & Machielse, A. (2022). Correlates of emotional and social loneliness among community dwelling older adults in Rotterdam, the Netherlands. *Aging & Mental Health, 26*(2), 355–367. https://doi.org/10.1080/13607863.2021.1875191

Wu, Z., & Penning, M. (2015). Immigration and loneliness in later life. *Ageing & Society, 35*(1), 64–95. https://doi.org/10.1017/S0144686X13000470

CHAPTER 4

THE IMPORTANCE OF NEIGHBOURHOOD-ORIENTED CARE FOR THE QUALITY OF LIFE AND EMPOWERMENT OF OLDER PERSONS

Leen Heylen

1.   The neighbourhood: Back from the past

The neighbourhood is back from the past when it comes to facing the challenges of an ageing population (Thomése et al., 2019). This increasing focus corresponds with the rise of the policy concept of ageing in place (Bigonnesse & Chaudhury, 2021). Ageing in place is not only preferred by older persons themselves, as a symbol of autonomy and independence, but it is also preferred on a policy level as a cost-saving solution to the healthcare challenges corresponding with the ageing of the population (Bigonnesse & Chaudhury, 2021). In addition, the neighbourhood, and more specifically neighbours, have gained importance as potential informal care providers (Thomése et al., 2019; Volckaert et al., 2020).

This dual trend merged into concepts such as neighbourhood care, caring neighbourhoods and active caring communities that guide local and regional policy on ageing in Flanders, the northern region of Belgium (Volckaert et al., 2020). In other countries around the world, the community as a field of policy action has gained importance as well (Vandesande, 2020). The World Health Organization (WHO) can be considered a significant driver of this tendency (Volckaert et al., 2020) because it has introduced both the policy concept of age-friendly cities and communities (WHO, 2007) as well as the conceptual framework on integrated people-centred healthcare (Bigonnesse & Chaudhury, 2021; WHO, 2016).

However promising, as both the built environment and neighbourly support have been shown to be of significant importance for the well-being of older persons (Thomése et al., 2019), there are also some challenges and potential pitfalls on the road towards the implementation of neighbourhood-oriented care. In this chapter, we elaborate on the potential of the policy concept of 'neighbourhood-oriented care' to add to the general well-being and empowerment of vulnerable older persons, but we also explore the pitfalls, boundaries and preconditions when putting this policy concept into practice.

Hereby, our guiding question is: does it empower older persons? As stated in Chapter 1, we build on the following definition of empowerment:

> *empowerment is a strengthening process whereby individuals, organisations and communities gain mastery over their own situation and their environment through the process of gaining control, sharpening the critical awareness and stimulating participation.* (Van Regenmortel, 2011)

We first situate the policy concept and disentangle what it actually intends. Next, we focus on the empowering aspects of the policy concept with the guiding definition of empowerment (see Chapter 1) in mind: which aspects have the potential to strengthen individuals, and specifically older persons, to gain mastery over their own situation and environment? In addition, we also take a closer look at potential pitfalls and boundaries accompanied with the translation of the policy concept into practice: where does it risk undermining the empowerment of older people? Specific attention is paid to the impact of the Covid-19 crisis on neighbourhood-oriented care and the empowerment of older persons. Throughout the chapter, we start from the Flemish policy concept on neighbourhood-oriented care. We situate this policy concept within an international framework and build on both national policy-oriented and international academic publications in this chapter in order to reflect on the empowering features of neighbourhood-oriented care for older persons.

2.   The policy concept 'neighbourhood-oriented care'

2.1   The rise of the neighbourhood as a policy tool

The rise of the neighbourhood as a geographical policy scope in facing the challenges of the ageing population can first of all be connected to the overall thriving policy concept of 'ageing in place' (Bigonnesse & Chaudhury, 2021; Volckaert et al., 2020). On the one hand, older people prefer to age in place, in their familiar neighbourhood. On the other hand, economic reasons also drive this policy choice (Bigonnesse & Chaudhury, 2021). Due to the ageing of the population, the need for care will rise, and therefore the costs of care as well (Volckaert et al., 2020). As policymakers promote ageing in place, the place where people live correspondingly gained policy attention. Place is a central concept in international ageing policies nowadays (Drilling et al., 2021).

When we turn to the international policy level, two of the WHO's policy frameworks can be connected to this rising attention of (inter)national ageing policies towards the concept of neighbourhood-oriented care (Bigonnesse & Chaudhury, 2021). The first is the policy framework of age-friendly cities and communities, launched in 2006 (Rémillard-Boilard, 2019). As the WHO (2007) states: 'an age-friendly city encourages active ageing by optimizing opportunities for health, participation and security in order to enhance quality of life as people age' (p. 1). Cities and communities are encouraged to build age-friendly environments, according to eight domains which were distinguished to enhance age-friendliness. Among these are, apart from domains such as community support and health services and social partici-pation, 'place-based' domains such as as outdoor spaces and building and housing. A specific checklist was created as well as a guide to assess the level of age-friendliness of cities, a tool frequently used by cities and communities. This global policy promotes an integrated response, including the spatial context of ageing, to address the challenges accompanied with the ageing of the population (Rémillard-Boilard, 2019).

A second policy framework by the WHO which can be connected to the policy concept of neighbourhood-oriented care is the framework on integrated people-centred health services. The WHO defines integrated people-centred health services as 'putting people and communities, not diseases, at the centre of health systems, and empowering people to take charge of their own health rather than being passive recipients of services' (n.d.). In the centre of the concentric model representing this framework is the individual person. This first circle around the person refers to self-care. The family is located in the next circle: this circle refers to care provided by family, friends and acquaintances. A third circle comprises care and support by the community. Surrounding these three circles is the fourth circle of professional health services.

To implement this model, the WHO (n.d.) formulated a framework of five interwoven general strategies. Specifically the first strategy is of interest with respect to this chapter: 'engaging and empowering people'. As the WHO states:

this goal seeks to unlock community and individual resources for action at all levels. It aims at empowering individuals to make effective decisions about

their own health and at enabling communities to become actively engaged in
co-producing healthy environments, providing care services in partnership
with the health sector and other sectors, and contributing to healthy public
policy. (WHO, n.d.)

Here, the community, as the third circle of the conceptual model, comes
forward. Within this circle, we can situate the rising attention by policymakers
for the neighbourhood. Indeed, with regard to empowering and engaging communities, the strategic approach the WHO pushes aims to help to
build confidence, trust and mutual respect as well as the creation of social
networks within these communities. The aim is to strengthen the capacity
of communities to organise themselves in this manner and also to generate
changes in their own living environments (WHO, n.d.).

Where the age-friendly city programme promotes the spatial aspect of
policies for older people (Bigonnesse & Chaudhury, 2021), the model of
person-centred and integrated care broadens the target group of care to all
persons with a need for care and support within communities, regardless
of their age. Also, the community and civil society are explicitly put to the
fore as sources of care and support (Volckaert et al., 2020). For Flanders, the
WHO framework on person-centred healthcare guided the policy reform of
primary care (Agentschap Zorg & Gezondheid, 2017; Volckaert et al., 2020).
Here, the community, and more specifically the neighbourhood, comes to
the forefront. Applied to the regional context of Flanders, this resulted in the
policy concept of caring neighbourhoods and neighbourhood-oriented care
(Agentschap Zorg & Gezondheid, 2017; Vandeurzen, 2018).

2.2   The policy concept of neighbourhood care disentangled

Neighbourhood-oriented care or caring communities and neighbourhoods
are broad concepts, often interpreted as well as implemented in different ways
(Vandesande, 2020). The Flemish government defines a 'caring neighbourhood' as follows:

a caring neighbourhood is one in which people, regardless of age and major or
minor support needs in several areas of life, can (continue to) live comfortably in
their home or familiar environment. It is a neighbourhood where young and old
live together, where people feel good and secure, where quality of life is central,
where residents know and help each other, where individuals and families with
large and small support needs receive support and where services and facilities
are accessible and available. (Beke, 2021, slide 4)

Smetcoren et al. (2019, p. 104) correspondingly speak of an 'active caring community' in Brussels as 'an environment able to support frail older people to "age in place"'. This is more specifically understood as

> *a community supporting ageing in place; where residents of the community know and help each other; where meeting opportunities are developed; and where individuals and their informal caregivers receive care and support from motivated professionals.* (Smetcoren et al., 2019, p 104)

'Neighbourhood-oriented care' can be understood as a guiding organisational model to build 'caring neighbourhoods' (Heylen & Gryp, 2020). The Flemish policy level defines neighbourhood-oriented care as

> *care that is aimed at strengthening social cohesion, at meeting needs for care and support from the neighbourhood, at directing users to appropriate care and support if necessary, or at taking care of this themselves, but also at actively involving the neighbourhood in the operation of the facility through active cooperation at the local level, in line with the local social policy plan, under the direction of local government.* (Woonzorgdecreet, 2019, art. 4, § 2)

In these conceptualisations of 'caring neighbourhoods' and 'neighbourhood-oriented care', we can distinguish several common features guiding the current practice of care in general and specifically for older persons (Heylen & Gryp, 2020). These conceptualisations have in common that they focus on the geographical level, the meso level of the neighbourhood and on the immediate vicinity of people as a field of action for care and support. They also imply a holistic view: the person, with individual needs, is at the centre of this policy approach. Correspondingly, they also strive for an integrated approach across several policy areas. In addition, the conceptualisations do not focus on specific age groups, promoting an inclusive approach irrespective of age. They also acknowledge citizens, neighbours, neighbourhood networks and community organisations, for example, as key players in care (Vandensande, 2020; Volckaert et al., 2020). While this was already the case for family caregivers, these categories of informal care providers are also increasingly coming to the foreground (see also Chapter 5).

This view on care from a neighbourhood perspective offers several opportunities to address some of the needs of an ageing population. However, it also starts from some implicit assumptions about both older persons and our current society, which do not necessarily correspond with the social reality (Thomése et al., 2019; Volckaert et al., 2020).

In the following, we first elaborate on the opportunities of approaching care and support for older persons from a neighbourhood perspective. Second, we disentangle the implicit assumptions of this policy approach and question the impact on the quality of life of older persons and their empowerment. We also take a look at the impact of the Covid-19 crisis on neighbourhood-oriented care in practice. To conclude, we formulate some policy recommendations on how this policy concept can be translated into practice in a manner which actually empowers older persons in our society.

3.   The policy concept challenged: Does neighbourhood-oriented care empower older persons?

3.1   Opportunities for empowerment

Where you live matters

When we disentangle what the concept 'neighbourhood-oriented care' intends, one of its implicit assumptions is that the neighbourhood, the place where you live, exerts influence on the well-being of its residents, irrespective of their individual characteristics (Albeda & Oosterlynck, 2018). We call this 'neighbourhood effects'. Neighbourhood effects can be defined as

> *the idea that living in deprived neighbourhoods has a negative effect on residents'*
> *life chances over and above the effect of their individual characteristics.* (van
> Ham et al., 2012, p. 1)

Galster (2012) broadly distinguishes four rubrics or types of neighbourhood effects: (1) social interactive, (2) environmental, (3) geographical and (4) institutional.

The social interactive mechanisms refer to social processes endogenous to neighbourhoods (Galster, 2012), which can encompass several mechanisms. For example, personal norms or attitudes can be affected by contact with neighbours. Also, the degree of social cohesion in the neighbourhood can affect individual well-being. The environmental mechanisms refer to the effects of the surroundings, both natural and human-made attributes of the neighbourhood, on the mental or physical health of its residents. Examples are exposure to violence, the physical environment (e.g. noise, green) and toxic exposure. The geographical neighbourhood effects are about the effects of the geographical location of a neighbourhood affecting the life courses of the inhabitants. They do not arise within the neighbourhood itself, but are relative to larger-scale political and economic forces (Galster, 2012). An example is the 'spatial mismatch': a mismatch between the supply and demand of, for example, jobs but also of care, support and services. Another example is inferior public services, simply because the local community has poor tax base resources compared to other local communities in the neighbourhood. Institutional mechanisms, to conclude, involve actions by those who control important institutional resources located in the neighbourhood or points of interface between residents and vital markets. Examples are the presence and access to high-quality private, non-profit or public institutions, the presence of local market players as fresh food markets or, on the other side, fast food restaurants or general territorial stigmatisation due to, for instance, the history of the neighbourhood, in its turn potentially affecting the self-esteem of the inhabitants (Galster, 2012).

The general implicit rationale behind neighbourhood-oriented care can be related to these neighbourhood effects. The meso level, and more specifically the manifestation of neighbourhood effects, is acknowledged as one of the mechanisms or potential policy tools to add to the well-being of older people.

It is precisely this geographic proximity that is important for people who, due to health or other problems such as financial constraints, are limited in their mobility. Older persons, who are often confronted with multimorbid-ity, are an important group in this respect (Thomése et al., 2019). Simply put, where you live matters, specifically in old age (Prattley et al., 2020). The environmental gerontology literature points to several reasons why the neighbourhood contributes to the well-being of older people.

First of all, the built environment and proximity of services and amenities positively affects the quality of life of older persons (Bigonnesse & Chaudhury, 2021). As the length of time spent at home and in the immediate surround-ings is significantly higher among this age group, their dependency on their immediate built environment increases (Thomése et al., 2019). The presence or absence of certain public services or facilities can therefore have a positive or negative effect on the residents' well-being. Think, for example, of the presence of a local service centre for meeting other people. People who feel good in their neighbourhood and who are satisfied with the local amenities, for example, feel lonely less often (Kearns et al., 2015; Kemperman et al., 2019).

The overall accessibility of the neighbourhood environment – namely, the presence of pavements and the accessibility of public spaces and parks matters (Bigonnesse & Chaudhury, 2021). This can have an impact on the health and meeting opportunities of older persons. Investing in these 'neighbourhood effects' from a policy level therefore offers opportunities to contribute to the general objective of a caring neighbourhood.

The neighbourhood's profile in terms of deprivation matters. In low-risk neighbourhoods in the city of Brussels, for example, older persons' needs focused more on formal care and the quality of care, whereas in high-risk neighbourhoods, informal care and access to care mattered more (Verté et al., 2018). On the negative side, neighbourhood deprivation tends to correlate with social exclusion in later life (Prattley et al., 2020).

The attachment to place is also considered an important dimension of ageing well (Thomése et al., 2019). The length lived in a neighbourhood positively affects the emotional bond of older persons with the neighbourhood (Thomése et al., 2019). It is this sense of belonging which is associated with lower levels of social exclusion (Prattley et al., 2020). A lower level of attachment to the neighbourhood among older persons has been found to relate to higher levels of loneliness (Kemperman et al., 2019).

In addition, as people age, the neighbourhood gains importance as a source of social contact and social support (Kemperman et al., 2019; Thomése et al., 2019). Neighbours are important sources of support for older people (Volckaert et al., 2020). Not only the actual support among neighbours matters but also the latent support: knowing that there are people around in case of need or problems and that people are keeping an eye on you is associated with lower levels of loneliness as well (Kearns et al., 2015).

All these neighbourhood features are interrelated and related in multiple ways to the general well-being of older persons (Bigonnesse & Chaudhury, 2021; Drilling et al., 2021). For example, the built environment and proximity of services and amenities positively affects both older persons' sense of belonging and number of social contacts.

To summarise, by recognising not only the individual micro level but also the meso level of the neighbourhood as a means of meeting the challenges of the ageing population, the concept of neighbourhood-oriented care offers policymakers additional tools to empower older persons and strengthen their participation. Related to the increasing focus on the neighbourhood as a field of policy action, we can discern a first opportunity for the empowerment of older persons – namely, the focus on the geographical, nearby residential environment of people in need of support.

Beyond ageism

Neighbourhood-oriented care is also an inclusive approach: it focuses on everyone in the neighbourhood, each resident with unique needs and demands. This inclusive view has the potential to work across specific target groups (a categorical approach) such as the often targeted group of dependent oldest old adults living alone. This inclusive approach offers a starting point to counteract discrimination or stereotyping, as older people know it in the form of ageism. Ageism is the systematic stereotyping and discrimination of people simply because of their age (Johnson, 2005). Due to the increased life expectancy, ageism not only manifests itself in our current society as a fear of growing old but also as a fear of growing old with a physical disability. Illness and dependency are being problematised, where active ageing, autonomy and independency are being promoted, resulting in a simplistic dichotomy between the actively involved healthy older persons and dependent older persons (Boudiny & Mortelmans, 2011). Discriminating and stereotyping dependent older persons fosters the societal and social exclusion of dependent older persons in need of care. In addition, as some older persons internalise these negative age stereotypes, this ageism can have a detrimental impact on their self-esteem (Burholt et al., 2020).

In the reasoning of neighbourhood-oriented care, older persons are not only addressed as people perhaps in need of care due to their dependency but also as potential care providers or supporters. After all, one of the key elements of neighbourhood-oriented care is its focus on mutual, informal neighbourly support. This kind of support is built on a strengths perspective and the concept of reciprocity. In this respect, the empowerment paradigm emphasises that vulnerability can go hand in hand with mastery over one's life and that reciprocity enables empowerment (see also Chapter 1). If people are able to give, and not only receive, their self-esteem rises (De Witte & Van Regenmortel, 2019, 2020; Heylen & Lommelen, 2016). This relational conceptualisation of care in the neighbourhood can be considered as a way forwards in moving beyond the simplistic, artificial dichotomy between caregiver and care recipient (Smetcoren et al., 2019). Subsequently, moving beyond this simplistic dichotomy has the potential to empower older persons and, on a societal level, move beyond a stereotypical view on old age.

Acknowledgement of the importance of 'weak ties'

Not only neighbours as a source of mutual support are gaining importance as people age; the social fabric of a neighbourhood in general matters as well (Bigonnesse & Chaudhury, 2021). Regular contacts with neighbours, a hello from a neighbour, an accidental encounter with acquaintances, a chat with a shopkeeper all shape the social fabric of a neighbourhood (Bigonnesse & Chaudhury, 2021). These 'weak ties', recalling the legacy of Granovetter (1973), among neighbours can add to feelings of familiarity and safety as well as a sense of belonging and place attachment to the neighbourhood (Weijs-Perrée et al.,

2017), which all are acknowledged as key elements of ageing well (Bigonnesse & Chaudhury, 2021). In addition, they can form a bridge towards stronger relations (Heylen & Lommelen, 2016; Weijs-Perrée et al., 2017) and therefore, for some, prevent or alleviate feeling of loneliness (Kemperman et al., 2019). A British study on loneliness concluded that in deprived communities, 'neighbouring' – social interaction with others in close residential proximity – was associated with lower levels of loneliness. In addition, active acquaintance, meaning being able to stop and talk to people, was associated with lower feelings of loneliness as well (Kearns et al., 2015).

The policy concept of neighbourhood-oriented care implicitly acknowledges the importance of these ties, as it strives to strengthen the community, develop meeting opportunities and encourage residents to get to know each other. As older persons benefit from a good social fabric in their living environment, neighbourhood-oriented care has an empowering potential within this respect as well, strengthening the participation of older persons.

An holistic, transversal approach

A last opportunity that the policy concept entails is the cross-policy area view. Neighbourhood-oriented care stands for cooperation across various policy domains: not only care but also welfare and housing, mobility, urban development and so on are important policy areas that are expected to contribute to the general objective. One of the success factors identified in the development of age-friendly cities is the extent to which policies for older persons are integrated in policies of urban development and management of cities (Rémillard-Boilard, 2019). The resident of the neighbourhood, with unique care and support needs, is central; a person-centred and integrated approach is promoted, corresponding with the model of the WHO. This transversal approach, specifically introducing urban planning as a means to create healthy social communities for the older persons, can help prevent or even reduce loneliness (Kemperman et al 2019). Indeed, Chapter 3 shows that feelings of loneliness are related to various factors on the individual, relational and structural domains, such as health, income and social network characteristics as well as wealth, culture and the region where people live.

3.2 From policy to practice: A road full of pitfalls

Whereas the policy concept of 'neighbourhood-oriented care' offers several opportunities to empower older persons, there are also challenges, pitfalls, boundaries and risks on the road towards more caring neighbourhoods.

Where you live matters

A first important issue to keep in mind is that not all neighbourhoods are good environments to age in place (Thomése et al., 2019), and this for several reasons (see also the theory on 'neighbourhood effects').

As mentioned above, the level of deprivation of a neighbourhood can have an impact on the well-being of older persons. Victor and Pikhartova (2020) conclude that older persons' loneliness was higher in the most deprived areas in the UK, and this independent of individual-level factors. In addition, these deprived neighbourhoods are often characterised by a high population turnover, which in turn can have detrimental effects on the social networks and relationships of the long-term residents (Smetcoren et al., 2019).

Also, the proximity of amenities and services matter. The general tendency of the disappearance of local grocery shops, specifically in the countryside, across Europe can therefore have a negative effect on older persons well-being as well. As a result of the disappearance of the local grocery shop, older persons not only lose access to food close to their door but also a place for approachable contact in the neighbourhood. These 'food deserts' can therefore have a detrimental effect on older persons' well-being (Volckaert et al., 2019).

But also not everyone lives in a neighbourhood or has a neighbour. When we look at Flanders, it is important to note its dispersed building environment. Flanders has about 13,000 km of ribbon development, where about a quarter of the Flemish population lives. 6 per cent of the Flemish population live in scattered settlements (Pisman et al., 2018). In addition, almost 28 per cent of the Flemish population live in a place with an insufficient mix of basic facilities within walking or cycling distance, the so-called food deserts. Among them are many people over sixty-five (Volckaert et al., 2019). These type of built environments are not conducive to building strong, close-knit networks of neighbours.

To summarise, although the concept of neighbourhood-oriented care has a great deal of potential, the spatial planning can be a deal-breaker.

Nostalgia as a misleading driver

When it comes to 'neighbourly help', the bar generally tends to be set too high. Nostalgia can be a misleading driver for change in this respect (Volckaert et al., 2020). For one, having a neighbour is a first precondition for support. Next, even if you have a neighbour, this does not necessarily mean that they will actually help you when you are in need, as neighbours do not help each other spontaneously. Linders (2010) explains this by three clarifying concepts.

First of all, due to what she calls 'the hesitation to ask for help', people in need of care are often reluctant or hesitant to ask others for help. Second, she found that most people are willing to help others but hesitate to help others. We generally do not want to interfere in other peoples' lives, specifically those who we only know superficially (as is often the case with neighbours). We generally want to respect peoples' privacy. Third, even if people offer to help, people in need of care are mostly reluctant to accept the help offered. This is problematic because Chapter 1 demonstrates that 'acceptance of help and support' is an important building block of resilience among older persons. The 'hesitation to ask for help', the 'hesitation to help each other' and the 'reluctance to accept help' are barriers for informal support among neighbours (Linders, 2010). To illustrate: 14 per cent of the Flemish adult population (eighteen years or older) found it (very) difficult to get practical help from neighbours if they should need it; 42 per cent think it is possible; 44 per cent think it is (very) easy. Those who found it difficult are significantly more lonely (Steyaert & Heylen, 2021).

Only when efforts are made to facilitate social contacts and neighbours learn to get to know each other can neighbourly help follow (Heylen & Lommelen, 2016). And even in that case, when neighbours do help each other, this help is usually limited to 'minor help'. This concerns more sporadic help such as helping out in the garden, doing the shopping, having a chat and keeping an eye on each other. Help on a regular basis or more intensive help, such as help with personal care, for example, is usually not included (Heylen & Lommelen, 2016; Volckaert et al., 2020). Keeping a certain psychological distance is preferred among neighbours (Volckaert et al., 2020). This type of support can therefore take shape in many ways and is valuable, but it also has its limits.

Nevertheless, the bar generally tends to be set too high for this kind of neighbourly support. In this respect, Thomése et al. (2019) point to a discrepancy between what a 'community' actually is and what people (including policymakers but also some researchers) feel it should be. There thus tends to be a discrepancy between the empirical observation of research on communities (e.g. in terms of contact among neighbours, actual support), on the one hand, and normative description, what people feel it should be, on the other hand (Heylen & Lommelen, 2016; Thomése et al., 2019). Volckaert et al. (2020) suggest this could be specifically the case in more rural areas, where people tend to believe in a Gemeinschaft idea of their community, a community with strong affectionate ties, ignoring the fact that rural areas have changed over the past decade. This is in line with the observation in Chapter 3 that people in southern European countries, where indicators of community and Gemeinschaft are more common, are nevertheless lonelier than those in northern and central European countries, where household atomisation and solitary living took place earlier.

To summarise, nostalgia can therefore be a misleading driver when putting policy into practice. Setting the bar of neighbourly support and networks within communities too high can lead to an overestimation of both the willingness to as well as the extent to which neighbours help and support each other.

The danger of reinforcing inequalities

A next pitfall we can distinguish is the danger of reinforcing inequalities among neighbours or even fostering new inequalities.

On the one hand, neighbourhood-oriented care acknowledges neighbours as actors in mutual support and care, which can have positive effects on the well-being of older persons. On the other hand, by appealing to the caring attitude of citizens such as neighbours, local residents and informal carers, the responsibility of the professional is in danger of being pushed into the background. More emphasis is implicitly placed on the citizen as care provider: for him- or herself, as a neighbourhood resident, as an informal caregiver. This view stems from the WHO's concentric model, which also lies behind the Flemish policy (Volckaert et al., 2020). Within this model, the individual is central, then the informal care and support by family, friends, acquaintances and the community, followed by the circle of professional care.

However, not everyone has a social network on which they can rely in case of need. And the most vulnerable older persons are the least likely to have such a network of family, friends and neighbours to rely on (Heylen, 2011). A recent survey of 1,004 Flemish adults eighteen years and older confirmed this. Those who experience (severe) difficulties in making ends meet experience significantly less social support compared to those who found it (very) easy (Steyaert & Heylen, 2021). The concentric WHO model, which is the guiding framework of the Flemish policy on care, tends to facilitate a 'deficit thinking' in this respect (Thys, 2018): this view feeds the perception that individuals who lack an informal support network from neighbours have a 'deficit'. Those who are vulnerable and lack a social network risk being marginalised (Rémillard-Boilard, 2019).

In addition, as mutual support is strongly emphasised in the conceptualisation of neighbourhood-oriented care, we have to be aware that not all older persons have the capacity to take overt, active roles within the community (Bigonnesse & Chaudhury, 2021). Perhaps they lack the social skills or simply do not attach much importance to social contacts in the neighbourhood (Machielse, 2015).

On a neighbourhood level, the question is raised whether people in deprived neighbourhoods are able to support one another. Here again, a risk of social exclusion arises. Also, those who lack a neighbour, simply because they don't live in what policymakers perceive as a neighbourhood, risk being overlooked (Heylen & Gryp, 2020).

The question can be therefore be raised how inclusive this policy actually is in practice (Rémillard-Boilard, 2019) and whether a negative side effect of this policy is the reinforcement of existing or the creation of new forms of social exclusion at old age, dividing the included and the excluded (Thomése et al., 2019).

4.   The Covid-19 crisis and neighbourly support

The Covid-19 crisis in 2020–2021 had a major impact on the social life of the older persons and the population in general. Feelings of loneliness increased across all ages (Steyaert & Heylen, 2021). An online survey on social relations and support among the Flemish adult (eighteen and over) population during the Covid-19 crisis confirmed that many people lacked social support (Steyaert & Heylen, 2021). A three-item scale measuring social support (OSLO Social Support Scale) (Kocalevent et al., 2018) was included in the survey (Bond Zonder Naam, 2021). Based on this scale, 1,044 respondents were classified in three categories: limited social support (26 per cent), average social support (53 per cent) and strong social support (21 per cent). Limited social support means that respondents have no one or almost no one they can turn to when they are in trouble, it is difficult for them to ask neighbours for practical help when this is needed, and there are no or few people around them who pay attention to what they are doing.

Vulnerable respondents experienced limited social support significantly more often. Poor health, a difficult financial situation, a lower level of education and living alone go hand in hand with limited social support. When we look at neighbourly contact and support, as many as 32 per cent of respondents with limited social support never have contact with their neighbours. For respondents with strong social support networks, this is only 5 per cent. In addition, among the latter, the contact frequency with neighbours increased significantly during the second lockdown compared to those with limited social support.

Various local authorities in Flanders and in other countries, but also citizens, started initiatives in their neighbourhoods to support and help others in their neighbourhood and communities during the Covid-19 crisis, including older persons: from phone calls to people over eighty to help with groceries and to donating laptops for families in poverty, among other actions

(Plovie & Heylen, 2020) (see also Chapter 5). An online survey among citizens during the first lockdown in Belgium (April–May 2020) on these initiatives discovered that people generally tend to support neighbours they already know (Plovie & Heylen, 2020). Keeping in mind that precisely the most resourceful people have the largest support networks, this implied that the more vulnerable inhabitants also fell between the cracks of the informal neighbourhood networks during the Covid-19 crisis.

Some people, and specifically the most vulnerable, did not benefit from the wave of informal initiatives in their neighbourhood during the Covid-19 crisis. People's commitment is generally great, but it is mainly focused on those they already know. This type of 'direct' or 'warm' solidarity, situated in the informal, private sphere of the community, clearly has its limits. It is based on moral values and norms and appeals to citizens' moral duty to care for each other (Plovie & Heylen, 2020). In this view on solidarity, citizens themselves choose who they support or not (Oosterlynck, 2018).

When it comes to putting neighbourhood-oriented care into practice during the Covid-19 crisis, the lesson learned is that, in order to empower vulnerable older persons, governments and professionals (as a form of 'indirect' or 'cold' solidarity) play a key role in mitigating the inequalities inherent in the social networks of older persons by reaching out to vulnerable older persons (Plovie & Heylen, 2020).

5. Conclusion: Towards an empowering neighbourhood-oriented care concept

The recognition of the neighbourhood as a field of action for ageing policies to address the challenges of the ageing population is booming. In this chapter, we have mapped out both the opportunities that come with neighbourhood-oriented care and its challenges, limitations and pitfalls. Empowerment of older persons was our guiding principle.

We distinguished several general opportunities for empowerment. First of all, the neighbourhood, the place where you live, does matter in old age, as environmental gerontology argues. The living environment has the power to empower people. Place-based policies on care therefore inherently have an empowering potential for older persons.

In addition, the inclusive view behind neighbourhood-oriented care can address ageism in our societies. By moving beyond a categorical approach to care and support and explicitly focusing on mutual support in the neighbour-hood, we can consider older persons as both residents perhaps in need of care and support as well as residents who can support others. Focusing on the power of giving is a key strategy to empower older persons in this respect (De Witte & Van Regenmortel, 2019, 2020).

In neighbourhood-oriented care, the focus not only lies on mutual support but also on strengthening the social cohesion in the nearby environment of older persons. These weak ties are known to be of importance as one ages. From a small encounter at the local grocery shop to wishing each other a good day on the street, these interactions all matter in enhancing older persons' sense of belonging.

At a policy level, neighbourhood-oriented care strives for a holistic, transversal approach. This transversal approach can have an empowering effect on older persons because bridging several policy domains, and specifically urban planning with care, has the potential to contribute to their well-being, specifically in the prevention and reduction of loneliness among older persons.

On the other hand, we also distinguished some challenges and pitfalls corresponding to this booming attention on the neighbourhood. First of all, not all neighbourhoods are good places to age well, and this for several often intertwined reasons like deprivation, food deserts, the built environment and the absence of green areas in the neighbourhood. In addition, nostalgia can be a misleading driver in putting policy into practice. There tends to be a discrepancy between what policymakers, and also researchers, believe a community should be and the empirical social reality. Specifically, the bar for mutual support among neighbours generally tends to be set too high. Both policymakers and professionals have to be aware of the limits of this type of support in both prevalence and intensity. Putting the policy of neighbourhood-oriented care into practice also risks reinforcing or establishing inequalities among older persons.

These challenges and potential pitfalls do not mean, however, that we should abort the concept of 'neighbourhood-oriented care'. It can offer a stepping stone for tackling many of the challenges associated with an ageing population and has the potential to contribute to the empowerment of older persons.

The fact that many local authorities and healthcare organisations see these opportunities is demonstrated by the growing number of practices that have emerged under this broad heading in recent years (De Donder et al., 2021). However, further implementation in practice requires a number of preconditions to truly meet the needs of the older persons and to empower them.

An important precondition is that the spatial dimension of ageing explicitly has to be taken into account for persons to age well in place (Thomése et al., 2019). Therefore, it is important to recognise that not every neighbourhood is a good place to grow old. In practice, this also means having an eye for the inequalities between neighbourhoods (Prattley et al., 2020). Some deprived neighbourhoods will require efforts to compensate for these inequalities as far as possible. This implies that actions and interventions under the heading of neighbourhood-oriented care explicitly have to pay attention to this spatial dimension: how does the level of deprivation affect ageing well; are there enough basic amenities in the neighbourhood; what is the age-friendliness of the neighbourhood? Actions and interventions on urban planning should therefore also be acknowledged by policymakers as interventions on neighbourhood-oriented care. Those older persons who do not live in what we, sometimes implicitly, consider a neighbourhood should not be forgotten either. In the short term, this requires a focus on outreaching social work. In the long term, the concept of moving in time can be of guidance: this means making an effort to move in time to an adapted home and living environment that allows for ageing in place (De Decker et al., 2018) (and therefore not in a ribbon development or in isolation). Or, as the former Flemish master builder stated at a conference on neighbourhood-oriented care organised by the Flemish government in 2019, 'Moving in time, to age well in place' (Van Broeck, 2019). Policymakers and policy domains as urban and spatial planning have a key awareness-raising role as well as a facilitating role in this respect.

Also, the role of the professional in this story of neighbourhood-oriented care should not be underestimated, nor should the role of neighbours be overestimated. The professional – whether it be the social worker of a local service centre, the home-care worker or the home-care nurse – should have professional experience and expertise in connecting and facilitating people and organisations. Working on neighbourhood-oriented care often requires a different method of working, a professional shift, but this does not make the professional redundant – on the contrary (Heylen & Lommelen, 2016). Precisely these professionals are needed to form support networks of other professionals, neighbours and informal carers around the older persons in need of care. In this respect, Thys (2018) argues for a complementary way of working that does not start from a deficit view on, for example, those who lack social networks, but to approach both informal and professional care with a positive, strengths-oriented empowering view. Self-care, informal and professional care can complement each other simultaneously, instead of professional care only intervening when self-care and informal care prove insufficient, as the concentric model of the WHO implicitly implies. This way of thinking allows us not to lose sight of the more vulnerable older people without a social network, not to approach them purely from the perspective of a deficit and to offer professional support as a matter of course (Thys, 2018).

De Donder et al. (2021) promote more cooperation and more partnerships between all relevant stakeholders of neighbourhood-oriented care within this respect. Where initiatives on neighbourhood-oriented care in Flanders currently often focus on the strengthening of social networks and social cohesion or the detection of care needs and the referral to professional care, little has yet been done to bridge the gap between these two kinds of initiatives on neighbourhood-oriented care. According to the study by De Donder et al. (2021) of thirty-five practices of caring neighbourhoods, the politicising factor is still missing. There is little or no feedback on policy. And this is precisely where there are empowering opportunities in working on neighbourhood-oriented care: working together across policy domains, from an integral, holistic approach, in accordance with the framework of the WHO on integrated and person-centred care.

Recently, the WHO launched the UN Decade of Healthy Ageing (2021–2030) (WHO, n.d.). Four action areas were defined: (1) age-friendly environments, (2) combatting ageism, (3) integrated care and (4) long-term care. When we turn to the policy concept of neighbourhood-oriented care, this approach touches on these four areas. If applied in an empowering manner, with the pitfalls and limitations in mind, neighbourhood-oriented care can offer local communities and healthcare organisations an additional tool in addressing the needs of the ageing population – in the next decade of healthy ageing and beyond.

References

Agentschap Zorg & Gezondheid. (2017). *Een geïntegreerde zorgverlening in de eerste lijn* [Integrated care in the first line]. https://www.zorg-en-gezondheid.be/sites/default/files/atoms/files/CELZ%20beleidstekst%20hervorming%20eerstelijnszorg.pdf

Albeda, Y., & Oosterlynck, S. (2018). *Over het belang van de buurt* [About the importance of the neighbourhood]. Vicinia. https://www.kenniscentrumvlaamsesteden.be/Gedeelde%20%20documenten/2018/Over%20het%20belang%20van%20de%20buurt%20-%20Ympkie%20Albeda%20en%20Stijn%20Oosterlynck.pdf

Beke, W. (2021). *Zorgzame buurten* [Caring Neighbourhoods]. https://medialibrary.uantwerpen.be/files/55242/969c96c3-b73c-483e-a94e-15077c4ca5f5.pdf?_ga=2.193769325.1788252849.1622024189-1941941047.1600685829

Bigonnesse, C., & Chaudhury, H. (2021). Ageing in place processes in the neighbourhood environment: a proposed conceptual framework from a capability approach. *European Journal of Ageing*. https://doi.org/10.1007/s10433-020-00599-y

Bond Zonder Naam (2021). *Dataset eenzaamheid in tijden van corona* [Data set loneliness in times of corona].

Boudiny, K., & Mortelmans, D. (2011, 7 1). A critical perspective: Towards a broader understanding of 'active ageing'. *Electronic Journal of Applied Psychology, 7*(1), 8–14.

Burholt, V., Winter, B., Aartsen, M., Constantinou, C., Dahlberg, L., Feliciano, V., De Jong Gierveld, J., Van Regenmortel, S., & Waldegrave, C. (2020). A critical review and development of a conceptual model of exclusion from social relations for older people. *European journal of ageing, 17*(1), 3–19. https://doi.org/10.1007/s10433-019-00506-0

De Decker, P., Vandekerckhove, B., Volckaert, E., Wellens, C., Schillebeeckx, E., & De Luyck, N. (2018). *Ouder worden op het Vlaamse platteland. Over wonen, zorg en ruimtelijk ordenen in dun bevolkte gebieden* [Growing older in the Flemish rural areas. About living, care and spatial planning in scarsely populated areas]. Garant.

De Donder, L., Hoens, S., Stegen, H., Kint, O., & Smetcoren, A.-S. (2021). *Lokaal samenwerken in zorgzame buurten* [Local collaboration in caring neighbourhoods]. Koning Boudewijnstichting.

De Witte, J., & Van Regenmortel, T. (2019). *Silver Empowerment. Resilience of vulnerable elderly. A narrative research approach.* HIVA – KU Leuven. https://hiva.kuleuven.be/nl/nieuws/docs/tvr-18-tse-lssrc1-o2010-resilience-of-vulnerable.pdf

De Witte, J., & Van Regenmortel, T. (2020). *Silver Empowerment. Family care for community-dwelling older seniors in times of corona: the power of giving and/or a burden of care?* HIVA – KU Leuven. https://hiva.kuleuven.be/nl/nieuws/docs/tvr-18-tse-lssrc1-o2010-informal-care.pdf

Drilling, M., Grove, H., Ioannou, B., & Moulaert, T. (2021). Towards a Structural Embeddedness of Space in the Framework of Social Exclusion of Older People. In K. Walsh, T. Scharf, S. Van Regenmortel, & A. Wanka (Eds.), *Social Exclusion in Later Life* (pp. 193–207). Springer.

Galster, G. C. (2012). The Mechanism(s) of Neighbourhood Effects: Theory, Evidence, and Policy Implications. In M. van Ham, D. Manley, N. Bailey, L. Simpson & D. MacLennan (Eds.), *Neighbourhood Effects Research: New Perspectives* (pp. 23–56). Springer.

Granovetter, M. S. (1973). The strength of weak ties. *American Journal of Sociology, 78*(6), 1360–1380. https://doi.org/10.1086/225469

Heylen, L. (2011). *Oud en eenzaam? Een studie naar de risicofactoren voor eenzaamheid op latere leeftijd.* University of Antwerp.

Heylen, L., & Gryp, D. (2020). Zorgzame buurten. Het antwoorden op de uitdagingen van een ouder wordende bevolking? [Caring neighbourhoods. Responding to the challenges of a population that is growing older]. *Geron, 22*(4).

Heylen, L., & Lommelen, L. (2016). *Het kleine helpen. Bouwen aan buurtnetwerken rond ouderen* [The little helping. Building on neighbourhood networks around older persons]. Politeia.

Johnson, M. L. (2005). The social construction of old age as a problem. In M. L. Johnson, *The Cambridge Handbook of Age and Ageing.* (pp. 563–574). Cambridge University Press.

Kearns, A., Whitley, E., Tannahil, C., & Ellaway, A. (2015). Lonesome towns? Is loneliness associated with the residential environment including housing and neighbourhood factors? *Journal of Community Psychology, 43*(7), 849–867. https://doi.org/10.1002/jcop.21711

Kemperman, A., van den Berg, P., Weijs-Perrée, M., & Uijtdewillegen, K. (2019). Loneliness of older adults: social network and the living arrangement. *International Journal of Environmental Research and Publich Health, 16*(3), 406. https://doi.org/10.3390/ijerph16030406

Kocalevent, R., Berg, L., Beutel, M., Hinz, A., Zenger, M., Härter, M.,&. Brähler, E. (2018). Social Support in the General Population: standardization of the Oslo social support scale (OSSS-3). *BMC Psychology, 6*(1), p. 31. https://doi.org/10.1186/s40359-018-0249-9

Linders, M. (2010). *De betekenis van nabijheid. Een onderzoek naar informele zorg in een volksbuurt* [The meaning of proximity. A study about informal care in a working class neighbourhood].

Machielse, A. (2015). The Heterogeneity of Socially Isolated Older Adults: A Social Isolation Typology. *Journal of Gerontological Social Work, 58*(4), 338–356. https://doi.org/10.1080/01634372.2015.1007258

Oosterlynck, S. (2018). Solidariteit. In F. Dhont, *Gemeend* (pp. 51–58). Socius.

Pisman, A., Vanacker, S., Willems, P., Engelen, G., & Poelmans, L. (2018). *Ruimterapport Vlaanderen.* Departement Omgeving.

Plovie, E., & Heylen, L. (2020). *Buurtzorg in crisistijd: wie al heeft, zal nog meer krijgen* [Neighbour-hood care in times of crisis: who already has, will receive even more]. Sociaal.net. https://sociaal.net/achtergrond/buurtzorg-in-crisistijd-wie-al-heeft-zal-nog-meer-krijgen/

Prattley, J., Buffel, T., Marshall, A., & Nazroo, J. (2020). Area effects on the level and development of social exclusion in later life. *Social Science & Medicine, 246*, article 112722. https://doi.org/10.1016/j.socscimed.2019.112722

Rémillard-Boilard, S. (2019). The development of age-friendly cities and communities. In T. Buffel, S. Handler, & C. Phillipson, *Age-friendly Cities and Communities. A Global Perspective* (pp. 13–29). Policy Press.

Smetcoren, A.-S., De Donder, L., Duppen, D., De Witte, N., Vanmechelen, O., & Verté, D. (2019). Towards an 'active caring community' in Brussels. In T. Buffel, S. Handler, & C. Phillipson, *Age-friendly cities and communities. A global perspective* (pp. 97–118). Policy Press.

Steyaert, J., & Heylen, L. (2021). *Eenzaamheid*. Bond Zonder Naam.

Thomése, F., Buffel, T., & Phillipson, C. (2019). Neighbourhood change, social inequalities and age-friendly communities. In T. Buffel, S. Handler, & C. Phillipson (Eds.), *Age-friendly cities and communities* (pp. 33–49). Policy Press.

Thys, R. (2018). *De zorgkracht van persoonlijke netwerken. Een onderzoek naar de aanwezigheid van ondersteuning en zorg in het sociaal netwerk van vijf groepen Brusselaars* [The power of care of personal networks. A research about the presence of support and care in the social network of five groups of persons from Brussels]. Kenniscentrum Welzijn Wonen Zorg.

Van Broeck, L. (2019). Inspiratiedag Zorgzame buurten [Inspiration day caring neighbourhoods]. Agentschap Zorg & Gezondheid.

van Ham, M., Manley, D., Bailey, N., Simpson, L., & Maclennan, D. (2012). Neighbourhood Effects Research: New Perspectives. In M. van Ham, D. Manley, N. Bailey, L. Simpson, & D. Maclennan (Eds.), *Neighbourhood Effects Research: New Perspectives* (pp. 1–21). Springer.

Van Regenmortel, T. (2011). Lexicon van empowerment. Marie Kamphuis-lezing [Lexicon of empowerment. Marie Kamphuis Lecture], Marie Kamphuis Stichting.

Vandesande, T. (2020). Starting the Transition Towards Integrated Community Care 4all. *International Journal of Integrated Care, 20*(2), 18, 1–3. https://doi.org/10.5334%2Fijic.5553

Vandeurzen, J. (2018). *Inspiratienota zorgzame buurten.* [Inspiration Note Caring Neighbourhoods] Vlaamse Overheid.

Verté, E., De Witte, N., Verté, D., Kardol, T., & Schol, J. (2018). An environmental approach to frailty management: needs of older people to age in place. *International Journal of Integrated Care, 18*(S2), A287, 1–8. http://dx.doi.org/10.5334/ijic.s2287

Victor, C., & Pikhartova, J. (2020). Lonely places or lonely people? Investigating the relationship between loneliness and place of residence. *BMC Public Health, 20*, 778. https://doi.org/10.1186/s12889-020-08703-8

Volckaert, E., De Decker, P., & Leinfelder, H. (2019). Met de rollator om brood? Het vergrijzingsvraagstuk en voedingswoestijnen in Vlaanderen. [With the walker for bread? The issue of demographic ageing and food deserts in Flanders] *Ruimte, 43*, 24–29. http://hdl.handle.net/1854/LU-8640975

Volckaert, E., Schillebeeckx, E., & De Decker, P. (2020). Beyond nostalgia: Older people's perspectives on informal care in rural Flanders. *Journal of Rural Studies*. https://doi.org/10.1016/j.jrurstud.2020.07.006

Weijs-Perrée, M., Van den Berg, P., Arentze, T., & Kemperman, A. (2017). Social networks, social satisfaction, and place attachment in the neighbourhood. *4*(3), 133–151. https://doi.org/10.18335/region.v4i3.194

Woonzorgdecreet (2019). https://codex.vlaanderen.be/Zoeken/Document.aspx?DID=103163
    9&param=inhoud&ref=search&AVIDS=1372786,1372787,1372788,1372843,1372836,13
    72822,1372824,1372831,1372835,1372844,1372845,1372864

WHO (2007). *Global Age-friendly Cities: a guide.* WHO.

WHO (2016). *Framework on integrated, people centred health services. Report by the Secretariat.* WHO.

WHO (n.d.). *About the five strategies.* https://www.who.int/servicedeliverysafety/areas/people-
    centred-care/five-strategies/en/

WHO (n.d.). *What are integrated people-centred health services?*

WHO (n.d.) *What is the UN Decade of Healthy Ageing? https://www.who.int/initiatives/decade-
    of-healthy-ageing*

CHAPTER 5
AN INTERPLAY OF FORMAL AND INFORMAL CARE: STRENGTHS AND CHALLENGES FROM AN EMPOWERMENT PERSPECTIVE

Benedicte De Koker, Leen Heylen, Dimitri Mortelmans &
Anja Declercq

1. Introduction

Most care for older persons who are ill or disabled is provided by informal caregivers (Suanet et al., 2012).[1] Many of these informal caregivers provide care in 'mixed care arrangements', together with formal care services. As in many other European countries, there is a growing awareness of the importance of the role of informal caregivers and the necessity of ensuring adequate support in Flanders (Belgium). A strengthening environment and sufficient resources are vital for the process of empowerment and the resilience of informal caregivers and older persons (Janssen et al., 2011; Sakanashi & Fujita, 2017). As Chapter 1 pointed out, resilience can be defined as 'patterns and processes of positive adaptation and development in the context of significant threats to an individual's life or function' (Janssen, 2013, p. 21). Empowering informal caregivers, for instance by acknowledging them as an equal partner in the care team, strengthens their resilience. Formal care can provide respite for the informal caregiver and specialised care an informal caregiver does not have the formation for. Working together in a partnership can be a 'win' for all those involved, including formal caregivers.

However, there are several barriers for persons with care and support needs and their informal caregivers to make use of formal support. Some studies (e.g. De Koker, 2018) even associate the presence of formal support with greater burdens on informal caregivers. In this chapter, we explore this 'support paradox' and its caveats to overcome this. Informal care is not only provided by family caregivers. Neighbours and, more broadly, citizen initiatives for care are gaining importance as well (de Jong et al., 2014). We also explore how formal care can collaborate with these 'new forms' of informal care, taking into account their specific nature. In this case as well as with family caregiving, the well-intended logic of the health and welfare sector taking over and fitting the initiatives into the traditional structure of formal care (with planning, steering, regulations, etc.) should be avoided.

The Covid-19 pandemic posed several challenges for informal caregivers and the interplay between formal and informal care. We discuss some recent studies in Flanders on this topic and the implications for policy and practice.

2. Informal caregiving in Flanders, Belgium from an international perspective

In Belgium, there is a growing awareness of the importance of informal care for the long-term care system. Informal care is considered an intrinsically valuable social phenomenon and a prerequisite for ageing in place. Public authorities in Belgium have been advocating an active policy of support for informal caregivers (Criel et al., 2014). As a consequence, in 2016 the first policy plan for informal care (2016–2020) was launched.

According to data from the European Quality of Life Survey, 30 per cent of adults in Belgium self-report as informal caregivers. This is the highest prevalence in the EU, after Greece. Also, the biggest difference between men and women is found in Belgium, where 13 per cent more women than men provide care (Zigante, 2018). Figure 5.1 demonstrates that when it comes to the intensity of caregiving, Belgian caregivers spend on average eleven hours a week on their caregiving tasks. In all countries, the intensity of caregiving has increased over the years.

From an international perspective, the use of formal home-care services among older people in Flanders is also high. In a comparison of eleven European countries, Suanet et al. (2012) report that Belgium has the highest percentage of older people combining formal and informal care – around 13 per cent. Stated reasons include the high availability of home-based services as well as a relatively strong familial culture (Suanet et al., 2012). In general, the Belgian long-term care system is a mixed system with extensive and diverse publicly financed formal care services. The system is also characterised by freedom of choice. Many organisations of diverse political or religious backgrounds are involved in home care within the same geographic area, and users are free to select the organisation they want to receive care from (De Almeida Mello, 2018; De Koker, 2018). This has advantages, but it also renders

Figure 5.1: Intensity of care (average hours/week) among informal caregivers in Europe

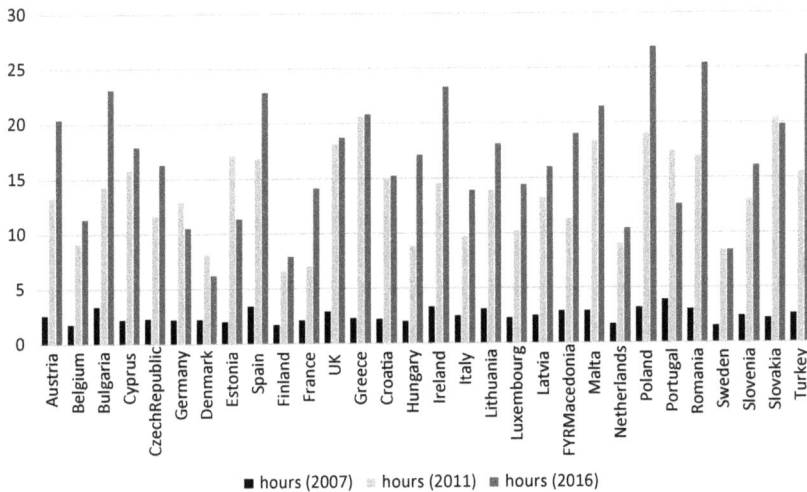

Source: European Quality of Life Survey

communication and coordination of care more difficult and complicated. Integrated care and continuity of care therefore become important elements of quality. A coordinated follow-up is essential for creating, updating and evaluating the care plans at different times and by different care professionals (De Almeida Mello, 2018). Collaboration between formal and informal actors in a broad sense is also important to provide proactive integrated care and to make sure that care is tailored to the individual needs of care recipients (Gobbens, 2017; De Witte & Van Regenmortel, 2019).

3.   Conceptual framework

The interplay between formal and informal care is a topic of increasing research attention. Many studies have focused on patterns of service usage among older persons and the question whether the two types of care function as complements or rather as substitutes (e.g. Geerts & Van den Bosch, 2012; Litwin & Attias-Donfut, 2009). Less attention has been paid to the perceptions of informal caregivers with regard to the use of formal services and how this relates to their empowerment. Insight into these experiences is, however, essential for being able to offer services that are suited to the needs of both clients and their caregivers as well as to create a supportive environment.

In their literature review, Sakanashi and Fujita (2017, p. 2) mention the support of professionals as a major factor for promoting empowerment in family caregivers. Empowerment for family caregivers is defined by these authors as

> *positive control of one's mind and body, cultivating a positive attitude, proactively attempting to understand one's role as a caregiver to improve caregiving capabilities, focusing on others as well as oneself, supporting the independence of the care-receiver, and creating constructive relationships with other people surrounding them.* (Sakanashi & Fujita, 2017, p. 2)

While Skanashi and Fujita focus on the micro level and on empowering relationships, it is just as important to take into account the contextual domain. On a broader political-societal level, the accessibility of care, the availability of material resources and social policy are crucial to promote empowerment (Janssen et al., 2011).

Caregiving is a dynamic process that is based in relationships (Büscher et al., 2011; Lindahl et al., 2010). The interplay between formal and informal care has been described as a process of 'negotiating helpful action' (Büscher et al., 2011). Sims-Gould and Martin-Matthews (2010) developed a conceptual 'triadic' model to include the interactive nature of care provision. The relationship between the caregiver and professional is defined as 'assistive care', while care provided by formal home-care workers to the person in need of care is defined as 'direct care'. With regard to direct care, it is clear that care recipients are not passive receivers of formal support. Assistive care also is a bidirectional relationship that can benefit both informal caregivers and formal caregivers. In a triadic approach, all three roles are acknowledged and valued in terms of associated responsibilities and needs. Each party 'brings to the equation a dedication to participate as a respectful and valuable care team member' (Talley & Crews, 2007, p. 227).

Informal caregiving is also often studied from a stress-theoretical perspective. This implies that formal services are also assumed to be a source of support for informal caregivers (De Koker, 2018). It is often hypothesised that an increased use of formal services will reduce caregiver burden and alleviate the negative effects of caregiving (Yates et al., 1999). The relationship between the presence of formal home-care services and caregiver outcomes, however, is not straightforward. Formal home care apparently does not automatically result in 'relief' or a lower burden for informal caregivers (De Koker, 2018; Roelands et al., 2008; Wiles, 2003). Quantitative studies (including in Flanders) have reported that the perceived burden of informal caregivers can even be higher when formal services are in place than when they are not (De Koker, 2018; Sussman & Regehr, 2009). There are several reasons for why this might be the case. First, it could be that caregiver burden prompts (rather than results from) the use of formal help. Previous studies that considered the impact of caregiver burden as a risk factor for the use of formal community services have found that caregivers sometimes exhaust their resources before turning to formal help. Second, the methodological quality of existing research has been criticised, with major issues including the failure to examine multiple outcome variables, the lack of differentiation between types of services and the need to identify moderators of intervention effectiveness (Sörensen et al., 2002). Third, Nolan et al. (2003) argue that a predominant focus on stress and burden is too narrow, overlooking aspects of caregiving dynamics and the interplay between formal and informal care. In the next section, we will turn to this 'support paradox' in more detail.

4. Support paradox

A central theme in the study by De Koker (2018) is the 'ambivalence' of informal caregivers regarding the use of formal home care. In this study, focus groups with spouses and adult children providing care for an older person, while also using formal support, showed that formal support can be helpful for informal caregivers by providing task relief, temporary respite and assurance. At the same time, such services confront informal caregivers with negative consequences, especially a loss of privacy and autonomy as well as the need to monitor the quality of care. This can be perceived as stressful, especially for co-residing caregivers. Home is a private space in which people can live according to their own habits and wishes (Lindahl et al., 2010). Given that home care involves having 'strangers' come into the home and provide services (often of an intimate nature), it presents a challenge to all those involved. Starting to use formal support represents a significant and often difficult transition for both clients and informal caregivers. Many caregivers in the De Koker's study (2018) reported having felt resistance on the part of the care recipient to bringing in 'help from outside'. The caregivers found it difficult to cope with this resistance, as they wished to respect the preferences of their parents or spouses. Several caregivers mentioned they had experienced the introduction of formal support as a failure. They felt as if they were abandoning the older person and they had failed to live up to the expectations of being a 'good' spouse or child. Third parties (e.g. other family members, healthcare practitioners and social workers) played an important role in overcoming this resistance. People who insisted on the use of outside assistance were helpful in the process of acknowledging the need for formal support for both caregivers and older people. Sharing the responsibility for this decision seemed to 'legitimise' the use of support. It is clear that the care recipients played an active role in the process of introducing formal support, either by holding back or by promoting the use of such services. Several husbands mentioned that their wives had not wanted them to do the ironing or cleaning, preferring to leave these tasks to the formal home-care worker. Several daughters also reported that their parents preferred to be assisted by formal workers for personal care tasks, as a way of preserving their dignity. The process of becoming accustomed to formal support was easier when the care recipients had a positive attitude towards help. Once formal support was in place, informal caregivers described how it had been necessary to learn how to 'let go' and become accustomed to the idea of not doing everything themselves.

Informal caregivers struggle to find a balance between the 'benefits' and 'damages' of using formal support. From the perspective of older clients, there appears to be a 'trade-off' (Martin-Matthews, 2007). By accepting formal support, they are enabled to continue living at home for longer than would have been possible otherwise. Given that many caregivers are motivated to provide care in the home for as long as possible, they are likely to feel as if they have no 'real choice'. Because of this dependency, they may try not to be overly critical of the assistance that they receive. The ambivalence towards using formal support has also been reported in a quantitative study of Belgian caregivers for individuals with dementia (Roelands et al., 2007). While almost all the informal caregivers perceived positive effects from the assistance provided by formal home-care workers, about one in three also perceived negative consequences, including lack of control in daily scheduling and decreased privacy (Roelands et al., 2007). Concerns of informal caregivers include the limited number of hours of assistance, rotating schedules and the lack of continuity, as these caregivers are the ones who must absorb structural deficits and fill the gaps. Overall, even when support is in place, informal caregivers feel a 'never-ending' responsibility for the well-being of the older person and the organisation of care. Informal caregivers are not merely 'users' of formal support. They are also often in charge of coordinating it, which involves hiring services and monitoring the quality of direct care.

From the perspective of the informal caregivers and older persons, continuity of staff is very important. Having one or two formal home-care workers allows care recipients to feel more comfortable about support and to develop a relationship of trust. Once formal home-care workers and care recipients had enough time to become acquainted with each other, the initial resistance often transformed into an appreciation of the presence of support. In this respect, it was remarkable to note that several spouses described how home-care workers had become like friends or family over time, for themselves as well as for the care recipients. Although adult children did not use words like 'friends' or 'family', they did provide accounts of close, supportive relationships with formal home-care workers (De Koker, 2018).

A sense of being acknowledged as a co-client is an important element for the 'assistive care' relationship, meaning that professionals are willing and able to look beyond the perspective of the older person and attend to the needs of caregivers. Working together implies that both parties can count on each other. Informal caregivers who were very satisfied with the support services described this as a relationship of 'trust'. In addition to providing a good level of quality in 'direct care', such a relationship requires that formal home-care workers honour what has been agreed with the informal caregiver, as well as being easily accessible. The theme of working together refers to a reciprocal, give-and-take relationship. Some informal caregivers mentioned that they tried to make it easier for the home-care workers to do their jobs and that they expected the same on their behalf. The most commonly mentioned types of interactions involved sharing information and helping each other with practical support. Informal caregivers and formal home-care workers helped each other with tasks such as lifting the older person and devising practical solutions. Both spouses and adult children considered it important to be involved as valuable partners in care and to have their skills and knowledge recognised. This was not always the case. Several of the participants mentioned that they had been criticised or had not been taken seriously (De Koker, 2018). As mentioned by, for example, Nolan et al. (2003), it is important that informal caregivers are viewed as 'co-experts', and they should be involved in negotiations concerning the allocation and implementation of assistance, both on the organisational level and in individual situations.

Good practice: Triadic approach in general hospital Maria Middelares
There is still much to be gained in the field of preventive work with informal caregivers and preparing them for the challenges they face (De Almeida Mello, 2018). Research shows that 'key events' such as a hospitalisation cause important changes in the care triad (Lambotte et al., 2020a) and can also be opportunities to provide support. The general hospital Maria Middelares, situated in Ghent, initiated a triadic approach a couple years ago to better support persons with dementia and their caregivers during and after a hospital stay. At the intake, informal caregivers are asked whether they wish to continue to carry out several

tasks while in hospital (e.g. helping with meals, being present in case of anxiety and risk of falling, helping with dressing, sleeping over), without any obligation. Information on the preferences and the specific needs of the person with dementia is gathered in a 'my habits' document that provides staff members with valuable information on the person with dementia during their stay. Informal caregivers receive psycho-education, psychosocial support and information during the hospital stay and after discharge. A nursing team and occupational therapists, among others, provide support and education for family caregivers. Three times a year, family caregivers can participate in a psycho-education programme. This triadic approach focuses on working in local networks with other care providers (e.g. home-care organisations and social work departments of health insurance associations).

Good practice: Informal care coordinators

Several organisations and local networks are investing in the function of an informal care/family care coordinator. An informal care coordinator is a professional who individually monitors and guides informal caregivers. In addition to providing individual guidance, such a coordinator is also responsible for awareness raising, training and activities for informal caregivers (De Witte & Van Regenmortel, 2020). The research report by De Witte & Regenmortel (2020, p. 76) shows the benefits are numerous:

> indeed, those family caregivers can appeal to those coordinators to ask practical information about which services exist, but also to talk about social and ethical considerations. Indeed, the family caregivers find this role extremely valuable because those coordinators can offer a more neutral perspective on their situation which could help them make decisions (about which care to use), get all siblings in line [...]
> A family care coordinator can contact the family caregivers (and seniors) to talk about their needs and try to formulate a response. In this respect, it could be useful that all those actors belong to the same covering organisation which seems to enhance their communication.

5. About neighbours and citizen initiatives

Apart from family caregivers, neighbours and, more broadly, citizen initiatives for care are (re)gaining importance as a source of informal care as well (Soares da Silva et al., 2018; van der Knaap et al., 2019). This corresponds with the general policy goal of 'care in the community' (Plovie, 2019). Regarding the first, neighbours as informal care providers, the rise of the policy concepts of neighbourhood-oriented care and caring neighbourhoods can be considered important drivers for this increasing attention (see Chapter 4). Besides the increasing focus on neighbours as a source of informal support, citizen initiatives have boosted as well over the past several years (Soares da Silva et al., 2018). This can also be related to the increasing policy focus on informal care and the appeal from governments for citizens to engage in the community. This is not only the case in Flanders (Belgium). Other examples are the Big Society in the UK and the Dutch Social Support Act in the Netherlands (Soares da Silva et al., 2018; Plovie, 2019). The empowerment of citizens can be considered one of the underlying goals (Soares da Silva et al., 2018).

Informal care by neighbours or citizen initiatives significantly differ in nature from care by family caregivers. Neighbourly support tends to be more non-binding compared with informal care by family caregivers and less intense and frequent. Neighbourly support usually encompasses more small and spontaneous help like helping with groceries, keeping an eye on each other, emotional support and creating a sense of security (Heylen & Lommelen, 2016; Smetcoren et al., 2019). Informal care by neighbours is often characterised by a type of reciprocity (Heylen & Lommelen, 2016). This reciprocal nature has a positive, beneficial effect on both older persons and society in general: being able to give (and not only receive) positively affects the quality of life of older persons, among others, by reinforcing their connectedness with others and that way enhancing empowerment. It also increases feelings of self-worth and self-esteem and a general sense of belonging and of feeling needed by society (De Witte & Van Regenmortel, 2019; Heylen & Lommelen, 2016).

Citizen initiatives also significantly differ in nature from family caregiving. A citizen initiative is set up by the citizen, and citizens come together as a collective, a group. De Jong et al. (2014) noted a number of characteristics of citizen initiatives in the care and welfare sector in order to define them as such. For one, these types of initiatives must always be organised for and by citizens. Second, they must concern the care and welfare of citizens. Third, they have a local character and, fourth, involvement of citizens and reciprocity are key values which are also found to enhance resilience (see Chapter 1). Like other type of citizen initiatives, they start from citizens, who voluntarily want to tackle a problem (De Jong et al., 2014), in this case regarding the care and well-being of citizens. Generally, citizen initiatives arise in case of unmet needs within the society where neither the government nor the market have an adequate supply of care and support. They thereby aim to fill a care vacuum (van der Knaap et al., 2019) and take responsibility to provide public goods (Soares da Silva et al., 2018).

To summarise, both neighbourly support and citizen initiatives, as types of informal care, are characterised by their voluntary and reciprocal nature. While support by family caregivers can be burdensome (De Witte & Van Regenmortel, 2020), these types of informal care generally have predominantly positive outcomes, such as feeling connected with others and a positive self-image (De Witte & Van Regenmortel, 2019) (see also Chapter 3).

5.1 The haves and the have-nots

Although these types of informal care generally have positive effects on the well-being of the informal care providers (the neighbours and citizens involved), there are some risks involved in relying too much on them.

For neighbourly support, it is important to keep in mind that people generally tend to help others they know and with whom they feel connected. Social networks, however, are unequally distributed, and a higher socio-economic status is often correlated with stronger and larger social networks. Vulnerability, on the other hand, goes hand in hand with a higher risk for social isolation (De Witte & Van Regenmortel, 2019). Therefore, the most vulnerable are generally the least likely to receive or be involved in neighbourly support (see also Chapter 4).

A similar risk exists for citizen initiatives. Plovie (2019) interviewed 364 leading figures of Flemish citizen initiatives and compared the profile of these leading figures with the average profile of the Flemish population. The results show that more highly educated people were over-represented, and citizens with a migration background were under-represented. In addition, these groups tend to be homogeneously composed as to level of education, employment and migration background (Plovie, 2019). In this respect, van der Knaap et al. (2018) concluded in a study on citizen initiatives on care in the Netherlands that capacity for concerted action is the most important mechanism in explaining differences in the presence of citizen initiatives. This capacity refers to the social capital of the community, measured by, among others, the educational level of the inhabitants (van der Knaap et al., 2018). Citizens have to possess certain social skills and capacities to be involved in these initiatives. Not all citizens, specifically the more vulnerable among them, have developed these skills. Counting too heavily on citizens' initiatives therefore risks widening the gap between resourceful citizens and more vulnerable ones (Soares da Silva et al., 2018). Citizen initiatives themselves, however, are often not aware of these inequalities. Where they often preach to be open to everyone, this does not necessarily correspond with reality (Plovie, 2019).

5.2 The ambiguous interplay between 'new forms' of informal care and formal care

As both neighbours and citizen initiatives on care have gained importance over the past several years, their interplay with professionals has gained attention as well (Soares da Silva et al., 2018). There tends to be some friction in the cooperation and there are risks involved. First, the bottom-up nature of these types of informal care is a mismatch with the top-down logic of formal care. Specifically, citizen initiatives risk being taken over and professionalised, for example, by being integrated within an existing care structure (Braes, 2018). For neighbourly support, the risk is that expectations of this type of support become too high, for example, when support is expected on a structural, frequent basis, and neighbours tend to disengage (Heylen & Lommelen, 2016). Professionals risk placing an excessive workload on citizens, specifically in the care sector (Soares da Silva et al., 2018). Building a good interplay between these rising types of informal care and formal care therefore needs specific attention.

6. Informal care in times of Covid-19

In an article in *The Lancet* (Chan et al., 2020), informal caregivers are called the 'forgotten healthcare workers' during the Covid-19 pandemic. Indeed, there is limited knowledge about the impact of the Covid-19 pandemic on family and other informal caregivers and their support needs. Lorenz-Dant and Comas-Herrera (2022) identified five key themes in literature that highlight the impact of Covid-19 on informal caregivers of people living in the community: changes in care responsibilities, concerns about Covid-19 infections, changes in the availability of formal and informal support, and financial as well as physical and mental health implications. The authors conclude that the Covid-19 pandemic is likely to have exacerbated all the risks that are generally associated with intensive informal care, such as diminished mental and physical health, decreased ability to engage in paid employment, and lower incomes.

Lambotte et al. (2020b) present results of an online survey on experiences of informal caregivers during the first wave of the Covid-19 pandemic in Flanders. Data from 651 informal caregivers were gathered in the second half of May 2020. Results indicate that two thirds of the informal caregivers in Flanders experienced their caregiving role as more difficult than before the pandemic and that more than half spent more time on informal care. This is partly due to a reduction in professional help and support from 'secondary' informal caregivers or the social network. Informal caregivers more often than usual had the feeling of being under constant stress (56 per cent) and had trouble sleeping or were lying awake more often (45 per cent). Informal caregivers noticed that the person they cared for was more depressed, that they had more memory problems and that they took up more of their time with requests for help. Groups that reported a higher burden and required specific attention were co-resident caregivers as well as persons caring for someone with psychological problems or a handicap.

During the first lockdown, the interplay with formal services was under pressure. Lambotte et al. (2020b) found that, before the pandemic, 71 per cent of informal caregivers were (rather to very) satisfied with the level of professional help, and 12.8 per cent of the caregivers were dissatisfied. During the pandemic, the percentage of dissatisfied caregivers increased from 12.8 per cent to 22.9 per cent. When it comes to cooperation between formal and informal care, 53.5 per cent of informal caregivers were satisfied, and 20 per cent of the informal caregivers were rather or very dissatisfied.

De Witte & Van Regenmortel (2020) did a qualitative study, based on in-depth interviews of community-dwelling older persons (eighty years and older) and their family caregivers. For family caregivers of older persons with high care needs, the burden of care increased significantly because they took over various tasks that had been carried out by professionals and other family caregivers before the pandemic, and because many forms of respite care were no longer available. Family caregivers of older persons with high care needs are confronted with a burden of care, which results from the pressure of constantly having to be available, seeing close ones deteriorate, feelings of guilt, a lack of flexibility and demonstrated appreciation from the older persons, and, for partners, also social isolation and feelings of loneliness. Older persons themselves indicate that, although they are in general very satisfied with informal care, some of them do have trouble asking their close ones for support.

Regarding new forms of informal care, the Covid-19 crisis boosted new initiatives among neighbours and citizens across the country as well, specifically during the first lockdown in the spring of 2020. Schools, care organisations and citizens did groceries for their neighbours, helped in the garden and made face masks for professional care providers, for example. Several cities and municipalities launched several online and offline initiatives to connect citizens who were willing to help with citizens in need of help (Plovie & Heylen, 2020).

During this first lockdown, an online survey was conducted on solidarity and support among citizens at the time (Plovie & Heylen, 2020). Across

Flanders (Belgium), 2,057 adults (eighteen years or older) participated. When we look at those who received help from their neighbours, there are interesting differences. Women received neighbourly help more often than men, and university graduates received help more often than those with a secondary education degree. There were no differences according to age, health, financial difficulties and work situation. This means that those who were expected to be in need of care (due to, for example, their health situation or financial difficulties) did not necessarily receive more support from neighbours. Contrarily, the higher educated were more likely to receive help from their neighbours. Building too strongly on this type of informal care risks reinforcing or creating new inequalities in social support: those who already have will receive even more; those who don't will receive even less (see also Chapter 4). This was also the case during the Covid-19 crisis. When we turn to the results for initiatives on care and support citizens took on themselves or were involved in, the hypothesis again was confirmed that people generally tend to support people they know. Family and neighbours with whom they have a good relationship were the main target groups. Next were friends and acquaintances. Everyone in the street or neighbourhood or specifically neighbours with a vulnerable profile had the lowest score and were thus the least likely to be supported. Interestingly, those who were engaged in more informal initiatives, not initiated by a local authority or organisation, were less likely to support vulnerable people (Plovie & Heylen, 2020). On the other hand, this implies that formal organisations, like a local authority, do have an important role in the democratisation of these citizen initiatives (Plovie, 2019).

7. Discussion and conclusion

Informal caregiving is a matter of growing interest. The interplay of formal and informal care and questions concerning how best to support informal caregivers are an important part of current discussions on the sustainability of the long-term care system (Anthierens et al., 2014). Over the past decade, informal caregivers have increasingly been recognised as 'partners' and persons with their own needs, but there still is some work to do. The paradox of support that does not always help, despite all the efforts of care providers is a reality and requires new ways of working (Driessens et al., 2016). As research and several good practices demonstrate, professionals can support and facilitate the empowerment process of older people and their family by creating enabling conditions (Sakanashi & Fujita, 2017).

Several of the themes mentioned in this chapter can be related to the framework of Van Regenmortel (2020). Strengthen, connection, trust and resistance to disempowering practices are four pillars of empowerment. Connection and trust are prerequisites for positive outcomes of the 'interplay'. Stable and trusting relationships between the client, professionals and informal caregivers, and the recognition of everyone's role in the 'care triad', is essential. Approaching informal caregivers as co-experts and 'people with their own needs' is relatively new, and the systematic assessment of caregivers' needs remains far from routine (Lamura et al., 2008). Guberman et al. (2012, p. 212) state that baby boomer caregivers 'have a better understanding of their rights, seek precise and complete information, and question norms'. This generation clearly states their needs, compared to older spouse caregivers 'who expect and ask little'. At the meso and macro level, it is important that home-care policies include policies designed to support and empower informal caregivers. As argued by Sims-Gould and Martin-Matthews (2010), a comprehensive caregiver support policy should be inclusive of home-care policy and vice versa. Triadic care asks for time and specific strategies, for example, to share information and provide specific support. The Covid-19 pandemic shows that much more is necessary to make informal care more visible and to mitigate the risks of overload, diminished well-being and psychosocial as well as financial hardship (De Witte & Van Regenmortel, 2020).

Specific attention is needed for new forms of informal care, such as neighbourly support and citizen initiatives on care. For one, the expectations of this type of informal care have to be realistic. The bar, often set by policymakers and professionals, should not be too high. This kind of support is often less frequent and of a more voluntary, ad hoc nature. Nevertheless, this kind of care and support can be very empowering for older persons. It can enhance their self-esteem and sense of belonging. Being able to give and to contribute to society has positive effects on people's general well-being and their empowerment (De Witte & Van Regenmortel, 2020).

Second, for these types of informal care, we have to be aware of the risks of social exclusion. Both neighbourly support (see also Chapter 4) and citizen initiatives are generally more reserved for citizens who are better off. The most vulnerable citizens are less often involved in these informal care networks. Professionals have a key role in counteracting these inequalities. Initiatives organised or facilitated by local authorities or professional organisations have the potential to broaden the coverage of informal support networks and to include more vulnerable citizens or those who lack the social skills (Heylen & Lommelen, 2016). In addition, professionals can play an important role in strengthening citizen initiatives on several aspects such as partnerships with other stakeholders, addressing the homogeneity of these groups and making room for a diversity of opinions in order to increase the democratic nature of citizen initiatives in this manner (Plovie, 2019).

Third, strengthening the cooperation and partnership between this kind of informal care and formal care can be a valuable way to address the increasing needs of the ageing population. As informal care providers such as neighbours or citizens involved in initiatives often are well informed of the care needs in their neighbourhood, they can be of great importance in guiding people towards professional care and support (Braes, 2018). However, in building these partnerships, both policymakers and professionals should take care not to take over these bottom-up, informal initiatives, but respect their informal, often organic nature, which is often their actual power. Acting on the basis of equity is a guiding, empowering principle in this respect. Specific attention is needed for the relationship between citizen initiatives in care and professional actors, as citizen initiatives are relatively new. How can the partnership between citizen initiatives and the professional care and welfare sector be shaped in practice with respect for one another's individuality? And how can this be done without the, admittedly well-intentioned, logic of the health and welfare sector taking over and citizen initiatives being fitted into the traditional structure of care (with planning, management, regulations, etc.) (Braes, 2018)? In this respect, Braes (2018) argues for complementarity and partnerships in which professional actors and the government can play a supporting and facilitating role.

The Covid-19 pandemic has boosted new initiatives among neighbours and citizens across the country. At the same time, it became clear that the interplay with formal care needs further attention. Given the high pressure on informal caregivers, it is essential to make them more visible, to create a strengthening environment and to mitigate the risks of overload, diminished well-being and psychosocial as well financial hardship.

Notes

1.   We use the term 'informal caregiver' to refer to persons providing care to their relatives, friends and neighbours, and the terms 'formal care/caregiver' and 'professional caregiver' to refer to professionals providing care that is paid and which they provide in the context of a professional organisation.

References

Anthierens, S., Willemse, E., Remmen, R., Schmitz, O., Macq, J., Declercq, A., Arnaut, C., Forest, M., Denis, A., Vinck, I., Defourny, N., & Farfan-Portet, M. (2014). *Support for informal caregivers – an exploratory analysis. KCE Report 223.* Belgian Healthcare Knowledge Centre (KCE).

Braes, T. (2018). Burgerinitiatieven in zorg: volwaardig en evenwaardig onderdeel van een zorg- en welzijnsecosysteem? [Neighbourhood initiatives in care: full and equal part of an ecosystem of care and well-being]. *Tijdschrift voor Sociologie, 39*(1), 60–64.

Büscher, A., Astedt-Kurki, P., Paavilainen, E., & Schnepp, W. (2011). Negotiations about helpfulness – the relationship between formal and informal care in home care arrangements. *Scandinavian Journal of Caring Sciences, 25*(4), 706–715. https://doi.org/10.1111/j.1471-6712.2011.00881.x

Chan, E. Y. Y., Gobat, N., Kim, J. H., Newnham, E. A., Huang, Z., Hung, H., Dubois, C., Hung, K., Wong, E., & Wong, S. Y. S. (2020). Informal home care providers: the forgotten health-care workers during the COVID-19 pandemic. *The Lancet, 395*(10242), 1957–1959. https://doi.org/10.1016%2FS0140-6736(20)31254-X

Criel B., Vanlerberghe V., De Koker B., Decraene B., Engels E., Waltens R. (2014). Informal Home Care for Elderly in Belgium: A Study on the Features and Challenges of Informal Care at Local Level. *Community Mental Health Journal.* https://doi.org/10.1007/s10597-014-9696-9.

De Almeida Mello, J. (2018). *The use of the interRAI Home Care instrument in the evaluation of care for frail older people: a follow-up study* [Doctoral dissertation, KU Leuven].

De Jong, F., Feliksdal, D., Turnhout, S., & Molenaar, A. (2014). *Burgerinitiatieven in zorg en welzijn* [Neighbourhood initiatives in care and well-being]. Vilans.

De Koker, B. (2018). *Variaties op mantelzorg. De inzet en beleving van mantelzorgers in de context van de vermaatschappelijking van de zorg.* [Variations on informal care. The commitment and experience of informal caregivers in the context of the socialization of care] [Doctoral dissertation, University of Antwerp].

De Witte, J., & Van Regenmortel, T. (2019). *Silver Empowerment. Resilience of vulnerable elderly. A narrative research approach.* HIVA – KU Leuven. https://hiva.kuleuven.be/nl/nieuws/docs/tvr-18-tse-lssrc1-o2010-resilience-of-vulnerable.pdf

De Witte, J., & Van Regenmortel, T. (2020). *Silver Empowerment. Family care for community-dwelling older seniors in times of corona: the power of giving and/or a burden of care?* HIVA – KU Leuven. https://hiva.kuleuven.be/nl/nieuws/docs/tvr-18-tse-lssrc1-o2010-informal-care.pdf

Driessens, K., Vansevenant, K., & Van Regenmortel, T. (2016). 10 jaar Bind-Kracht. Verbindende hulpverlening in verdelende tijden. [10 years of Bind-Kracht. Connecting aid in divisive times] *Sociaal.net.* https://sociaal.net/analyse-xl/10-jaar-bind-kracht/

Geerts, J., & Van den Bosch, K. (2012). Transitions in formal and informal care utilisation amongst older Europeans: the impact of national contexts. *European Journal of Ageing, 9*(1), 27–37. https://doi.org/10.1007/s10433-011-0199-z

Gobbens, R. (2017). *Health and well-being of frail elderly. Towards interventions that really count!* Inholland University of Applied Sciences.

Guberman, N., Lavoie, J., Blein, L., & Olazabal, I. (2012). Baby boom caregivers: Care in the age of individualization. *The Gerontologist, 52*(2), 210–218. https://doi.org/10.1093/geront/gnr140

Heylen, L., & Lommelen, L. (2016). *Het kleine helpen. Bouwen aan buurtnetwerken rond ouderen* [The little helping. Building on neighbourhood networks around older persons]. Politeia.

Janssen, B. M., Van Regenmortel, T., & Abma, T. A. (2011). Identifying sources of strength: resilience from the perspective of older people receiving long-term community care. *European journal of ageing, 8*(3), 145–156. https://doi.org/10.1007/s10433-011-0190-8

Janssen, B. M. (2013). *Resilience and old age: Community care from an insider and empowerment perspective* [Doctoral dissertation, Vrije Universiteit Amsterdam].

Lambotte, D., Smetcoren, A. S., Zijlstra, G. R., De Lepeleire, J., De Donder, L., & Kardol, M. J. (2020a). Meanings of care convoys: The structure, function and adequacy of care networks among frail, community-dwelling older adults. *Qualitative Health Research, 30*(4), 583–597. https://doi.org/10.1177/1049732319861934

Lambotte, D., De Koker, B., De Bruyne, N., & De Witte, N. (2020b). *De beleving van mantelzorgers in tijden van COVID-19* [The experience of caregivers in times of COVID-19]. HOGENT. https://hogent.be/sites/hogent/assets/File/Onderzoeksrapport%20Mantelzorg%20in%20 tijden%20van%20COVID-19.pdf

Lamura, G., Mnich, E., Nolan, M., Wojszel, B., Krevers, B., Mestheneos, L., & Döhner, H. (2008). Family carers' experiences using support services in Europe: empirical evidence from the EUROFAMCARE study. *The Gerontologist, 48*(6), 752–771. https://doi.org/10.1093/geront/48.6.752

Lindahl, B., Lidén, E., & Lindblad, B. (2010). A meta-synthesis describing the relationships between patients, informal caregivers and health professionals in home-care settings. *Journal of Clinical Nursing, 20*(3–4), 454–463. https://doi.org/10.1111/j.1365-2702.2009.03008.x

Litwin, H., & Attias-Donfut, C. (2009). The inter-relationship between formal and informal care: a study in France and Israel. *Ageing & Society, 29*(1), 71–91. https://doi.org/10.1017/S0144686X08007666

Lorenz-Dant, K., & Comas-Herrera, A. (2022). The impacts of COVID-19 on unpaid carers of adults with long-term care needs and measures to address these impacts: A rapid review of evidence up to November 2020. *Journal of Long-Term Care, 2021,* 124–153. http://doi.org/10.31389/jltc.76

Martin-Matthews, A. (2007). Situating 'home' at the nexus of the public and private spheres: Ageing, gender and home support work in Canada. *Current Sociology, 55*(2), 229–249. https://doi.org/10.1177/0011392107073305

Nolan, M., Lundh, U., Grant, G., & Keady, J. (2003). *Partnerships in family care: understanding the caregiving career.* Open University Press.

Plovie, E. (2019). Burgers in beweging [Citizens in movement]. In M. Schrooten, R. Thys, & P. Debruyne (Eds.), *Sociaal schaduwwerk, over informele spelers in het welzijnslandschap* [Social shadow work, about informal actors in the well-being sector] (pp. 31–44). Politeia.

Plovie, E., & Heylen, L. (2020). *Buurtzorg in crisistijd: wie al heeft, zal nog meer krijgen* [Neighbourhood care in times of crisis: who already has, will receive even more]. Sociaal.net. https://sociaal.net/achtergrond/buurtzorg-in-crisistijd-wie-al-heeft-zal-nog-meer-krijgen/

Roelands, M., Van Oost, P., & Depoorter, A. (2008). Service use in family caregivers of persons with dementia in Belgium: psychological and social factors. *Health and Social Care in the Community, 16*(1), 42–53. https://doi.org/10.1111/j.1365-2524.2007.00730.x

Sakanashi, S., & Fujita, K. (2017). Empowerment of family caregivers of adults and elderly persons: A concept analysis. *International journal of nursing practice, 23*(5), e12573. https://doi.org/10.1111/ijn.12573

Sörensen, S., Pinquart, M., & Duberstein, P. (2002). How effective are interventions with caregivers? An updated meta-analysis. *The Gerontologist, 42*(3), 356–372. https://doi.org/10.1093/geront/42.3.356

Sims-Gould, J., & Martin-Matthews, A. (2010). We share the care: family caregivers' experiences of their older relative receiving home support services. *Health and Social Care in the Community, 18*(4), 415–23. https://doi.org/10.1111/j.1365-2524.2010.00913.x

Smetcoren, A.-S., De Donder, L., Duppen, D., De Witte, N., Vanmechelen, O., & Verté, D. (2019). Towards an 'active caring community' in Brussels. In T. Buffel, S. Handler, & C. Phillipson (Eds.), *Age-friendly cities and communities. A global perspective* (pp. 97–118). Policy Press.

Soares da Silva, D., Horlings, L., & Figueiredo, E. (2018). Citizen Initiatives in the Post-Welfare State. *Social Sciences*, 7(12), 252. https://doi.org/10.3390/socsci7120252.

Suanet, B., Broese van Groenou, M., & van Tilburg, T. (2012). Informal and formal home-care useamong older adults in Europe: can cross-national differences be explained by societal context and composition? *Ageing and Society, 32*(3), 491–515. https://doi.org/10.1017/S0144686X11000390

Sussman, T., & Regehr, C. (2009). The influence of community-based services on the burden of spouses caring for their partners with dementia. *Health & Social Work, 34*(1), 29–39. https://doi.org/10.1093/hsw/34.1.29

Talley, R. C., & Crews, J. E. (2007). Framing the public health of caregiving. *American Journal of Public Health*, 97(2), 224–228. https://doi.org/10.2105%2FAJPH.2004.059337

van der Knaap, T., Smelik, J., de Jong, F., Spreeuwenberg, P., & Groenewegen, P. P. (2019). Citizens' initiatives for care and welfare in the Netherlands: an ecological analysis. *BMC Public Health, 19*(1334). https://doi.org/10.1186/s12889-019-7599-y.

Van Regenmortel, T. (2020). Bouwen aan een wetenschappelijke basis voor sterk sociaal werk. Onderzoek dat er toe doet! [Building a scientific foundation for a strong social work. Research that matters!]. Tilburg University. https://www.tilburguniversity.edu/sites/default/files/download/TiU_200173_Oratie%20Tine%20Van%20Regenmortel-digitaal.pdf

Wiles, J. (2003). Informal caregivers' experiences of formal support in a changing context. *Health & Social care in the Community, 11*(3), 189–207. https://doi.org/10.1046/j.1365-2524.2003.00419.x

Yates, M., Tennstedt, S., & Chang, B. (1999). Contributors to and mediators of psychological wellbeing for informal carers. *Journal of Gerontology: Psychological Sciences, 54*(1), 12–24. https://doi.org/10.1093/geronb/54B.1.P12

Zigante, V. (2018). Informal care in Europe. Exploring formalisation, availability and quality. European Commission, London School of Economics and Political Science.

CHAPTER 6
MERITS OF CRITICAL MOMENTS OF DISEMPOWERMENT: ITERATIVE PRACTICES OF EMPOWERMENT AND DISEMPOWERMENT DURING PARTICIPATORY ACTION RESEARCH WITH OLDER PERSONS AS CO-RESEARCHERS

Elena Bendien, Susan Woelders, Tineke Abma

1.   PAR as a vehicle towards empowerment

Participatory action research (PAR) is often presented as a progressive way of doing research, because it is based on horizontal democracy – in other words, equal partnership between experts, researchers and end users in the process of creating new knowledge (Abma et al., 2019; Reason & Bradbury-Huang, 2007). This entails involvement of all those whose life and work are at stake during the research process. This involvement is grounded in the respect for and the need to include the voices of all people in the research in order to come to a proper understanding of our complex world. PAR and related research approaches acknowledge the capacities and strengths of people as credible knowers, even those who have not received formal training as researchers. Building on and mobilising the knowledge of people, including experiential and indigenous forms of knowledge, helps to better understand their life-world and makes research more relevant and impactful (Van Regenmortel, 2020). The egalitarian principals of PAR can empower people and entire local communities that are involved in research. But what empowerment actually means – whether the process of PAR can bring about a feeling of disempowerment as well and how empowerment and disempowerment can become entangled within research – has not been sufficiently addressed in the academic literature so far.

One of the goals of PAR is to strengthen the empowerment of people involved in research. Empowerment is a complex, relational and multilayered concept. We define it here as

> *people assuming control and mastery over their lives in the context of their social and political environment; they gain a sense of control and purposefulness to exert power as they participate in the democratic life of their community for social change.* (Wallerstein, 1992, p. 198; Van Regenmortel, 2008, 2009)

Empowerment is relational and situational; it needs to be developed and maintained on a daily basis vis-à-vis other people in particular situations and contexts (VanderPlaat, 1999; Sprague & Hayes, 2000). Empowerment also has a political dimension: societal structures may foster or hinder one's mastery over situations. Our focus in this chapter lies on the empowerment that PAR can provide to older people who are directly (as co-researchers) or indirectly involved in research. The literature on participatory research with older people is expanding, but the results that are communicated often represent the end state of the project and recommendations for further implementation elsewhere (Backhouse et al., 2016; Dewar, 2005; Gilroy, 2003). The process of PAR itself, which we see as a relational process of co-learning and co-creation, falls beyond most of the available reports.

To demonstrate the (dis-)empowerment capabilities of PAR, we need to look at it through a care-ethical or moral-relational lens (Abma & Baur, 2014; Abma et al., 2020; Jacobs, 2006). For empowerment to take place, the researchers need to establish a relationship of trust, so the co-researchers can safely learn and explore their lives. The aim of this relational approach is to strengthen the voices of the co-researchers and to include as many perspectives as possible in the ongoing discussion during the research. PAR has an underlying normative and moral horizon, and it requires more than the proper use of methods. It aims first and foremost to create an open and safe space, or enabling niche (see Chapter 1), which enables the people involved to tell and share their stories in a setting they can trust and helps handle complicated group dynamics and unplanned shifts and needs. The prime focus is therefore to create a 'communicative space' in which everybody who is involved, including the researchers, feels mutually encouraged, respected and supported to join the process of generating knowledge. Given the complexity of this task, the facilitator needs to pay a lot of attention in order to create such a communicative space, where all voices can be expressed and all perspectives are taken seriously and explored (Abma et al., 2019).

Although empowerment is central to PAR, the pathways that set empowerment in motion through PAR have not been studied sufficiently (ICPHR position paper 3, 2020). There are some indications that PAR studies might unintentionally even have disempowering effects on co-researchers, due to internal group dynamics among the co-researchers (Groot & Abma, 2020) or politically disempowering situations (Duijs et al., 2019). In the context of PAR with older people, little is known about the empowerment potential, although there are some exceptions (Baur & Abma, 2012). In a number of PAR research projects with older persons, we encountered both processes of empowerment and disempowerment. In this chapter, we focus on how older people and other stakeholders involved in PAR shape processes of empowerment and disempowerment and what the role and responsibility of the PAR facilitator is to counter disempowerment. Our insights will add to the emerging knowledge base of PAR with older people.

2. Participatory research project 'To participate is to count'

Our data comes from a PAR project with older persons, conducted in the Dutch province Zeeland in 2017–2018. A detailed report of the impact of participatory research in this project has been published elsewhere (Bendien et al., 2020). In 2016, we as researchers were approached by a voluntary organisation called Festival of Recognition (further FoR), which was organising reminiscence sessions for people with dementia in Zeeland. Their goal was altruistic – to offer a meaningful activity to the growing number of people with dementia in their region. In cooperation with local museums, the FoR volunteers put together about seventy so-called travel bags, sets of old-fashioned objects, organised thematically, aiming to facilitate the remembering process and unlock lively conversations with older people. At the moment of the first contact, the organisation counted fifty older volunteers. It was run by older persons and had already succeeded in securing funds for their activities for five consecutive years.

2.1 A new challenge

FoR had two goals: to extend the reach of the reminiscence sessions by involving community-dwelling older persons and to ensure the continuity of the work by means of tailor-made PR activities. Beside these practical goals, the volunteers and the researchers together formulated the research question: whether and how participatory research can facilitate the participation of volunteers in the decision-making process about the activities and the future of FoR. This question reflected a shortcoming within the FoR organisation, which at that moment was almost entirely run by just two volunteers. To ensure the growth and continuity of the voluntary work, the organisation needed a more democratic structure that included closer involvement of all the FoR members. Based on these goals, the researchers and the FoR representatives prepared a research proposal, which was subsequently approved and funded by the Dutch charity fund FNO. The study lasted sixteen months (2017–2018).

2.2 Our choice for PAR

It was the researchers' idea to use PAR as a methodological design for the project. The egalitarian principles of this methodological approach appeared to match the FoR aim to redistribute the responsibilities within the organisation and to stimulate a closer involvement of the volunteers in all FoR activities. The participatory approach was presented to and discussed with the FoR board. The potential advantages of PAR that the FoR board found particularly attractive concerned the organisational structure of FoR. In the case FoR would grow, which was one of the project targets, the organisation would need more older volunteers to address the logistical issues of organising a growing number of reminiscence sessions throughout the province. So PAR was accepted by the FoR board as a methodological design of the project.

2.3 Our co-researchers

One of the FoR board members, who was also the local leader of the project, took the initiative to recruit co-researchers for the project team among the volunteers. All the volunteers were invited. No mention about the PAR methodology was made in advance, since the volunteers were not familiar with the concept. Also no inclusion or exclusion criteria were mentioned in the invitation. The invitation was repeated during the kick-off meeting, with room for questions regarding the project. Initially, ten volunteers expressed interest; they were invited to participate in the project team meetings. They were told they were free to take some time before committing themselves to the project on a permanent basis. This approach to the recruitment remained unchanged over the duration of the project. More volunteers joined the team at later stages of the project. They all had the opportunity to attend the meetings and to make up their minds about participating. The researcher's initial estimation was that the team-building process would take two or three months, given that some of the volunteers were already working together. In fact, it took about six months before the core project team emerged. Several critical moments, which we shall describe in detail later on, were responsible for that adjusted timeline. In the end, the project team consisted of seven women volunteers (aged between fifty-four and eighty-seven) and one researcher (fifty-four, first author). One of the researcher's first tasks was to explain the basic principles of PAR and to make sure they were retained. The participatory design of the project was based on the premise that the team would discuss and, if necessary, sharpen the goals of the project and decide on the course of action in close collaboration with the other FoR volunteers. The participatory design included various methods of data collection, such as participant observation, notes of team meetings, reports of brainstorming sessions with FoR volunteers, interviews and questionnaires. The data analysis, which included team members' reflections on the PAR process, was conducted during the team meetings and in the course of individual conversations between the co-researchers and the researcher.

3. Critical moments of disempowerment

Using our empirical data, we shall present four critical moments that we associate with practices of disempowerment during participatory research with older persons. We shall elaborate on their learning potential, the responsibilities of the researchers, which we call 'ethics work' (Abma, 2020; Banks & Brydon-Miller, 2018) when such moments occur, and the conditions under which they may be 'turned around' to create a positive impact on all parties involved.

We call these *critical and ethically salient moments* because certain perspectives and underlying value commitments of the people who were involved in the research were conflicting, creating an impasse. If they had not been attended to adequately, the situations that we describe could have undermined the progress of the entire project and even brought it to a halt. The members of the project team might have felt disempowered by certain developments or behaviour, which could have induced them to leave the team. We felt these situations were in need of critical reflection by the entire team, and we hoped each of these situations had a learning potential which, if applied in a timely manner, could in fact empower the members of the team. Critical moments can relate to a single situation or to a pattern of actions and behaviour during the various stages of the project. Our descriptions of the critical points have the same format: we present an issue, we illustrate it with examples from our project and we reflect on it, using an ethical approach within participatory research based on 'ethics work' (Abma, 2020).

3.1   Critical moment I: Is PAR for me?

The first critical moment is about the question whether and why an older volunteer should contemplate becoming a member of a PAR team. The reasoning that, due to their fragility, older persons are represented in participatory projects less frequently than other groups has been addressed in the literature before (Dewar, 2005; Gilroy, 2003; Ray, 2007). The growing number of PAR projects with older persons encouraged us to question that assertion. We decided to look for a more specific explanation why certain older persons choose to take part in participatory research and others do not.

During our project, the question of eligibility to become a member of the PAR team emerged during the team-building stage, and it continued to have reverberations over the duration of the project. Eligibility is understood here in terms of an individual's capacity to fulfil the expectations that the participatory project requires: jointly taking part in the meetings/brainstorming sessions, drawing up an action plan, taking responsibility for certain tasks and taking action when necessary. We assumed that the largest barriers that older FoR volunteers could face when invited to become members of the PAR team were the volunteers' physical or mental capacity related to fragile health and the expected time investment volunteering would require.

The recruiting for the research team was conducted by the chairperson of the FoR board, whom all the volunteers knew very well. No restriction in regard to age or ability was mentioned in the recruitment letter. Moreover, a special remark was made for persons with restricted mobility, that their participation was also welcome and that transportation would be arranged by the project team. The dynamics of building the team were complex. Some volunteers who joined the group at the start left shortly afterwards. Others joined the group at later stages. The critical moments we describe below concerns (1) the members who left because their expectations of PAR did not match the state of their physical and mental health, and (2) the members with fragile health who did stay on the project for the same reason.

Examples from the project

Initially, ten older volunteers responded to the invitation. Two of them left the group soon afterwards. One of them, who had joined the project team at the start, had lost her partner shortly before. In the beginning, taking part in the project appeared to her to be a sensible way to distract herself from her painful thoughts and memories. However, the active engagement and the degree of commitment that PAR demanded, especially during the initial stages of the project, did not match her expectations. Another older volunteer left the group after the first meeting, explaining that her fragile health would not allow her to take up new responsibilities within the project. All the same, both women continued doing voluntary work for FoR, thus staying in contact with their network.

During the following months, after the project had officially commenced, three new volunteers joined the project team. One of them, Elisabeth[1] (seventy-six), had also lost her partner a couple years before. She felt the loss acutely and could not talk about her late husband without becoming emotional. She also had a serious heart condition and talked openly about the fragile state of her health with the team. In contrast to the experience of the volunteer who had left the group, she saw her involvement in the project as a way to stay in control of her emotions. She resisted the idea that her health condition would define what she could or could not do. Being actively engaged in a meaningful way was exactly what empowered her and gave her strength to go on with her life.

Reflection on the critical point

These examples demonstrate that taking part in participatory research is not always associated with empowerment where older persons are concerned. The personal circumstances, health and the level of fragility varied among our potential partners. Some of them were better off refraining from new activities. When the first two women left the group, the researcher considered approaching them individually to try to convince them to stay on board. She would have been driven by two incentives: first, her own conviction that PAR was good for older participants and would have a positive impact on their lives; second, without enough team members, the project would fail. Whereas both incentives had empowerment at the basis of her reasoning, the result could have been disappointing for all parties involved. Besides, keeping people from leaving the team on the grounds of saving the project would be what we can call a lack of ethical sensitivity. Furthermore, the two women in question could have left the project at a later stage after all, and the negative impact of their departure would then have been felt much more strongly, both within and outside the team.

All this means that what we as researchers experience as a practice of empowerment during PAR can have a very different meaning for the participants. The example with Elisabeth illustrates this point. In her case, the impulse of the researcher could have been to protect her from harm by excluding her from certain project activities. But as the conversations with Elisabeth at later stages of the project showed, such a condescending attitude could well have resulted in undermining Elisabeth's good will and her being in control of her own decisions.

From the first critical moment, we learn that empowerment and disempowerment in PAR are embedded in practices of inclusion and exclusion and that the impact of participation of older persons cannot be assessed without taking into account their autonomous and relational choices. Fragile physical and mental health does not necessarily lead to disempowerment, as long as the persons themselves are well in charge of their decisions, including the decision to not participate in research. This critical issue also makes us aware of our normative ideals as participatory researchers (PAR is empowering for older people) and how these ideals can become disempowering when implemented in a paternalistic or dogmatic way.

3.2   Critical moment II: Am I worthy?

The second critical moment relates to the societal imaginary of ageing and the self-perception of older persons (Levy, 2009; Lindenberg, 2019). When older persons are invited to participate as co-researchers in PAR, they – as well as the researchers – have certain expectations in regard to their involvement in the research activities. The societal perception of ageing, however, can be experienced as disempowering at the moment when an older person considers joining a research team. The predominant image of older persons as fragile, infirm or needy, which is often conveyed in the media and political discourses, can lead to self-stigmatisation and impede older persons from participating in research (Schuurman et al., 2020).

Examples from the project

Martha (eighty-seven) joined our project later than most of the other volunteers. She had just started as a volunteer at FoR and did not feel confident enough for that work, as she explained later. She was curious though, and that was the reason why she had joined the PAR team, albeit provisionally at first. It was much later, when she became one of the most active team members, that she explained how she felt about herself at the beginning of the project:

> I have always done voluntary work, also when I was working. However, eventually, especially when you have passed eighty, they think that you don't want to anymore, don't they? Or that you are not able to do it anymore.

Anyway, they don't invite you any longer. And that is a pity. And then I heard about the Festival of Recognition and I thought, I could do that, and I am going to apply. Because I think that you also do it for yourself. It goes in both directions, doesn't it?

Reflection on the critical point

Martha's experience shows us how the societal division on the basis of chronological age can have a double negative influence on an older person. First, the person feels excluded from activities on the grounds of perceived fragility. Such a protective behaviour, which can also be called paternalistic, does not take into account the opinion of the individual person. Second, the older person can internalise this imaginary of old age, which disempowers the individual even further, because she or he would tend to comply with these images and behave accordingly. Martha's example was different. PAR offered her an opportunity to do meaningful work, irrespective of her age and health condition. With the support of the team, she managed to turn the disempowering image of her own old age into an example that repeatedly inspired the entire team. For instance, she openly voiced her dissatisfaction with the 'societal ado about loneliness', stressing that 'talking without taking action would not help people who feel lonely'. To show how it could be done, she placed an announcement in the local Catholic Union newspaper just before Christmas, inviting people who felt lonely on Christmas day to join her for a cup of tea. That Christmas day, she received eleven guests who had responded to her invitation. As Martha put it herself, empowerment goes both ways: you give and you receive something in return; it is reciprocal.

Martha's example entails another important lesson of how practices of empowerment and disempowerment can interact. An important condition for Martha to turn away from self-stigmatising thoughts about her age towards active participation was the communicative space that had been created within the PAR project. That space was based on equality of all the group members, irrespective of their chronological age or former experience, and was characterised by mutual trust and a feeling of belonging. The creation of such a space involved a lot of ethics work on the part of the researcher and the rest of the team (see also the next critical moment). 'We want to hear what everybody's thoughts are on the matter, and we do not interrupt each other' was the ground rule of the team, to which everybody agreed at the very beginning. The application of this rule was not self-evident, though. For instance, it took some time before the members of the team started to present their opinion openly, and even more time before they actually started listening to each other.

In the beginning, the researcher and the local leader of the project addressed Martha directly, asking for her opinion and by doing this offering her the floor to speak. Soon, it became the norm within the group to ask somebody who had kept silent to give an opinion on the matter. Martha had kept quiet when she first joined the team. Only when she saw that the opinions that were given did not have a hierarchy of power, that her life experience as the oldest member of the team was an advantage and not an obstacle in the eyes of the others, did she find her voice, literally and figuratively. The respect and genuine interest with which her co-researchers listened to her was empowering for Martha as well as for the rest of the team. Martha became one of the focal points of the end conference organised by the project team, where the co-researchers and the researcher presented the results of the project.

3.3   Critical moment III: Who is in charge?

The third critical moment touches upon gender and power sensitivity in PAR projects with older persons. It demonstrates the importance of the methodological and ethical principles of PAR regarding the practices of empowerment and disempowerment (Abma et al., 2019; Banks & Brydon-Miller, 2018; Groot-Sluijsmans, 2021). It also shows what can happen to a project and its team if those principles are violated.

PAR is based on a democratic process of decision-making. From the first meeting when a new team comes together, it is important to 'set the rules', like mutual respect for the opinion of others, equal opportunity to voice points of view and distribution of responsibilities among the team members and others. The principles of PAR, while clear and attractive on paper, are not always easy to apply in practice (Jacobs, 2006). The older co-researchers, for instance, could belong to a generation that was brought up in times when authoritative power and fixed gender roles were still in place (Groot & Abma, 2019). Most of the female members of our PAR team belonged to the Silent Generation who were used to a one-breadwinner family model. They were supposed to be good housewives and mothers and often were obliged to quit their jobs, if they had one at all, after they got married. They were silent doers, informal caregivers in the broadest sense of the word, who also shouldered an impressive volume of voluntary work in their neighbourhoods during their entire lives.

Examples from the project

The initial group of volunteers who were interested in the project consisted of eight women and two men. Both men were retired managers with long careers.

They were sincerely interested in the goals of the project and eager to invest their time and skills in the project activities, just like the rest of the group. The first meetings of the group were chaotic, which is not unusual for such projects. After all, the members of the team needed time to get to know each other and at the same time to adjust to the principles of participatory research. The researcher's challenging role was to explain how an inclusive discussion can be conducted and to facilitate the egalitarian process of interaction.

However, the first meetings demonstrated that there wasn't any room yet for an inclusive conversation. The team agreed that each issue on the agenda would be discussed by making rounds, so that every member of the team could voice her or his opinion. In practice, however, the procedure was often thwarted by one of the male members, who dominated the entire conversation. This happened so frequently that one of the team members, who was a FoR board member as well, felt the need to address him directly and ask him not to interrupt the others. He consented to the request but soon afterwards resumed his previous behaviour. The tension within the group increased and the meetings became strained. Then one initially enthusiastic female member left the group without providing a clear explanation, so the researcher feared that the others could soon follow her example. Then, after a disagreement about the wordings in one of the project documents, that same male team member left the group. The second one stayed on for a couple months but, in the end, he left the group as well. Both male members explained that the difference between the researcher's approach to the project and their own views on how the project should be run was the main reason for leaving the team.

Reflection on the critical point

Losing a team member is always a loss. In this case, the two male members felt disempowered by the participatory approach, which did not match their experience and expectations. Their background had taught them that making plans top-down and following the chosen strategy was the only way to be successful. PAR employs a very different approach to planning and action. In PAR, plans and actions are in fact the result of a research process and not its starting points. The messiness that can accompany the process of coming to a conclusion together is also a part of the team-building process (Cook, 2009). It is a way of conducting research that has little in common with the traditional managerial approach.

Looking back, it is difficult to say whether there could have been a way to keep those men on board. The situation was complex, time sensitive and emotionally charged. At that point, open reflection on the situation within the team was not possible because a communicative space of trust and mutual respect had not been created yet. Only after the first male member had left the group, four months after the start of the project, did an open conversation between the rest of the team take place for the first time. The female members of the team began to speak up and give their opinion on the project planning. They expressed their joy about the fact that they finally understood what participatory approach stood for. As one of them put it: 'oh, now I understand! We may decide ourselves!' They felt empowered by the discussions in the new communicative space, where they felt safe and listened to. These women carried this project all the way to its successful conclusion. Eventually, they took charge of all project activities, leaving to the researcher the role of observer and facilitator. Both male ex-members followed the development from a distance, and the team was grateful when one of them became involved in the preparations for the end conference of the project.

Much can be learned from this critical moment. First, the practices of empowerment and disempowerment are gender-sensitive, especially where older persons are involved. The historical and cultural background of the people involved, their life courses and careers are all important during the team-building process. During this process, the emotional aspects can become extreme for the participants and researchers alike, which can even derail the entire project. An open discussion is helpful but not always possible at a given moment. Finally, the empowerment of one person can lead to disempowerment of another one. This is not always a choice we make; it is the process that we go through during PAR. As researchers, we could not always interfere, but we always share responsibility for what takes place within the project.

3.4   Critical moment IV: Dead after the deadline?

The fourth critical moment refers to the complex organisational dynamics of the entire project, based on the expectations of the participating older volunteers and the donor organisation, which expects certain deliverables and sets deadlines for the project. The ultimate goal of the research team involved in any PAR is successful continuation of the activities after the project has officially come to an end. If this is the case, then one can talk about sustainable change that PAR has brought about, including the empowerment of the participants, who were able to plan, take action and reflect on their activities on their own. That also means that the learning process that the PAR team underwent collectively during the project has been successful and that there has been enough time for the co-researchers to claim and assume ownership of the current and future project activities.

Examples from the project

Two organisational aspects of our project can be described as disempowering: the time limitations and the binding condition of the charity fund to specify certain deliverables for the project. The project duration was limited to sixteen months and extension was not negotiable. The project was financed from the last round of a national programme called 'More resilience – longer independent at home'. From experience, we know that in order for it to produce sustainable change, participatory research requires time. The description of the third critical point already demonstrated how slow a team-building process can unfold and how long it can take before the PAR principles sink in. In our case, it took about six months before our group of older volunteers began to act as a team. By then one third of the project time had already been spent. The team members discussed the time issue many times over the course of the project. They voiced their frustration about what they experienced as 'making no sense'. They kept asking why the project could not continue for another six more months if the general goal of the charity fund's programme was to empower older persons living at home? Our older volunteers were convinced that certain actions could be planned differently, less hastily and that more people could have been involved in FoR activities if the project had been allowed extra time. Their dissatisfaction with the time frame was so strong that two team members addressed the researcher personally more than once, requesting her to transmit their opinion to the fund authorities. The fund's representative responded respectfully to this, showing an understanding for the request but nevertheless stuck to the deadlines, which could not be altered.

Another issue that put pressure on the project was the deliverables that had been included in the research documentation. They had to be tangible and measurable. Therefore, the planning had to contain a number of targets. The PAR team was expected to have attracted at least fifty new volunteers for FoR by the end of the project, as well as at least one hundred community-dwelling older persons as participants in FoR reminiscence sessions throughout the province. In fact, FoR had much more than fifty new volunteers by the end of the project and had also managed to organise reminiscence sessions for more than five hundred community-dwelling older people in Zeeland. Whereas the final figures were very inspiring, the process that led to those achievements has been far from linear. The details of that process are described elsewhere (Bendien et al., 2020). Moreover, these measurable outcomes did not reflect the important intangible outcomes and impact of the PAR project, such as the individual empowerment of the co-researchers. At the end of the project, at least two of the co-researchers took the position of leadership within this voluntary organisation, one co-researcher became engaged in a large voluntary project abroad, and two other team members established a new foundation that publishes a free-of-charge reminiscence newspaper in the province of Zeeland. The research team felt that narratives would have given a much better picture of what this project brought about.

Reflection on the critical point

For participatory research the ethical sensitivity of planning based on figures is high. PAR is not just a methodology; it is a process of personal, interpersonal and community-based change based on learning. There are many unknown factors that cannot be forecast with certainty at the moment a project proposal is submitted, such as the personal features of the team members, their group dynamics and the commitment to the project goals of all parties involved. When the proposal for our project was being written, neither the researchers nor the representatives of FoR could lean on any statistical or other data that could predict the outcome of the project. Therefore, the commitment of the team was to a large extent based on their good intentions only. The planned deliverables of the project were under a lot of pressure when, after the first six months, the team had come to the conclusion that various professional organisations in Zeeland were not prepared to respond quickly and cooperate with our voluntary organisation as we had hoped they would.

The time pressure and the pressure to deliver did not derail the project in the end. The solution came from the team itself, showing how the framework of organisational disempowerment that had been imposed could be neutralised by a creative process and joint action. The team came up with the idea to publish a free-of-charge reminiscence newspaper, which would be of direct interest for the older inhabitants of Zeeland and also contain invitations to FoR's reminiscence sessions.

One of the most important elements that helped the co-researchers to overcome the effects of disempowerment caused by the pressure of time and deliverables was that they acted as a team, which we call *relational empowerment* (VanderPlaat, 1999). This meant sharing responsibilities and openly discussing all the failures of the first stages of the project. During those discussions, the language was almost rough at times, and some of the volunteers became quite emotional. Their pride and honour stimulated the feeling that they should deliver what they had promised to do. The challenge that they faced was to show to all parties involved that older volunteers, in fact seven older women, could, with the support from the other FoR volunteers, indeed effectuate substantial change.

The researcher felt the same kind of pressure as the rest of the team, but the feeling was not new to her. As researchers, we are often expected to work within a time frame that is too short to achieve our goals, working overtime and sometimes promising to deliver more than we know is reasonable – all this to secure funding for the project. In participatory research, you share part of this kind of pressure with the volunteers who, if paid at all, are compensated on a very basic level only. The financial accountability, while important in itself, can therefore also have a disempowering effect on participatory research with older persons. Such thoughts can become disempowering to the researchers themselves as well. At such moments, the support of colleagues and critical friends is invaluable.

The main lesson here is that in order to overcome the disempowering effects of organisational issues, you need to trust your team and take responsibility for any outcomes the project can have. For traditional projects, this is the task of the researchers only, but PAR is about sharing successes and also failures of research with the co-researchers. Doing PAR is challenging but, when employed the right way, PAR will never feel like a solitary process. A key issue is that PAR is time sensitive and often requires time. When the time is right, which means when the PAR team starts acting as a team, an iterative exchange between situations of disempowerment and empowerment can be observed. Without proper ethics and personal involvement, empowerment can turn into disempowerment, but when proper attention is paid to that, the situations of disempowerment can be turned into an empowering process of learning and co-creation. During those moments, the researcher, too, can often learn a lot from the team, especially from the older volunteers with a life worth of experience.

4. Discussion: Lessons learned

The analysis of the four critical moments shows that empowerment or disempowerment that occurs during PAR is a moral-relational process that requires continuous reflection from all parties involved. PAR can foster relational empowerment of a mutually supportive process, mobilising the strengths of people. Relational empowerment emerges through interaction with others (VanderPlaat, 1999; Sprague & Hayes, 2000). Yet, in this process, disempowerment can also occur, and this will challenge the researcher to continuously engage with ethics work and emotion work at all stages of the research (Woelders-Peters, 2020; Groot-Sluijsmans, 2021).

The first lesson learned is that empowerment or disempowerment can be connected with practices of inclusion and exclusion. This means that the introduction of PAR on an individual or community level must be followed by explanation and fine-tuning in regard to the wishes and assumptions of all interested parties. The researchers as well as the potential participants can be influenced by societal clichés about who may or may not participate in research. An open conversation about PAR before the start of the project can reduce these barriers, but that takes time, which can become an issue because of the project's limited time frame. If, however, the participants have sufficient information and time in advance to make their decisions, then there is more chance that, whatever decision they take in regard to their participation in the project, they will feel empowered by it. Not participation itself but the possibility to make their own decisions and express what they need to participate in a manner that is meaningful to them empowers older people. This implies that researchers need to be open to the expectations and ideas of older people about what makes participation meaningful for them. As we saw in the first critical moment, researchers can overestimate or underestimate the capacities of older people. They should always be aware of their own normative assumptions regarding what older people can and want to contribute to the research.

The second lesson is that the practices of disempowerment, as in the case with the volunteer who felt excluded from the voluntary work because of her age, can be internalised; to address that, we need to have an open and safe space, or enabling niches, where people can experiment and where each opinion and each team member matters. Participation and empowerment are not static phenomena that develop in a linear fashion (Van Regenmortel, 2008). Participation and empowerment cannot be 'given' to people; that would be a paternalistic move, introducing a hierarchy and power asymmetry. Giving power would imply that one can also take that power away again. Empowerment needs to grow from 'within', and that process cannot be steered or quickly fixed by an overambitious researcher or policymaker. On the contrary, an overambitious professional may lack the sensitivity and empathy to tune into people's deeply held, and often unconscious, ideas about older people's capacities. When older people feel isolated, cut off from the rest of society, lacking a role and without perspective or control, one cannot just expect them to be willing to participate. What one can do is create a welcoming, social and safe environment. Through interaction, people can strengthen their 'power from within' and develop confidence in themselves and the group (Baur & Abma, 2012). To paraphrase Paulo Freire: people cannot empower themselves, nor can others. It is through communal experiences that people, who experience a lack of influence or the burdening of stereotypes that marginalise their position in society, can become empowered. Empowerment understood as growth and not as an external activity which is directed at fixing a person can be an answer to the paternalistic ageist approaches where older persons are turned into subjects to protect or activate.

The third lesson is related to the principles of PAR (ICPHR, 2013), which, generally speaking, have to be observed, even if it means that some of the team members could feel disempowered on a specific moment. The implementation of ethical principles in PAR is closely linked to the personal moral compass and intuition of the researcher. Blindly following the principles can result in 'thinning out' the good ethical foundation on which the relationships are built in the first place (Abma, 2020). Besides, as we have seen, power and ownership within PAR can turn into gender-sensitive matters. They entail a lot of emotion work on the part of the researcher as well as the co-researchers. Emotion work includes the efforts to show the 'right' emotions in a particular situation, according to Arlie Hochshield (Abma, 2020). In PAR it is expected that the researchers are empathic and caring, yet there are limits to what PAR researchers can do, and there are occasions when researchers may cross their own personal boundaries. The first author of this piece reflects how this work can be emotionally intensive. This is a direct result of the relational and ethical dimensions of participatory research in relation to people who find themselves in marginalised positions. The PAR researcher is not neutral and may encounter situations of injustice that make an appeal on the responsibilities of the researcher. Think of the situation when the co-researchers requested the researcher to renegotiate the time frame with the funding agency. The researcher sees the irrationality of the situation and tries to change the situation but is not able to do so. A way out of such emotionally charged situations is an open conversation about the issue at hand, which, again, is difficult to carry out if the communicative space of trust has not yet been created.

The final lesson is that almost any practice of disempowerment can be turned into empowerment after all. We can identify several conditions that facilitate such a turnaround. First, the team must act as a team, including the researcher. The teamwork means that emotions can be showed openly, and frustrations, too, can be aired. Second, the openness about mistakes and failures must be as welcome as sharing a success. Once again, this would require a safe space, where the team members can trust each other. Third, any project team needs critical friends, within or outside academia, so that complex situations involving difficult decisions and emotional work can be held against a new, refreshing, critical and constructive perspective.

5. Conclusion

In our vision, PAR is not only a technical endeavour but a practice in need of reflection on normative and ethically challenging situations. We have shown how, in the context of involving older people as co-researchers, PAR can stimulate empowerment but at the same time can create situations of disempowerment. This indicates that, in practice, normative ideals of social inclusion and justice may be hard to realise, for example, because we as researchers and the older people themselves, too, have internalised notions regarding ageism, which can lead to an underestimation of their capacities and desire to participate. Therefore, PAR researchers have a moral responsibility for 'ethics work' (Abma, 2020). This is more than just following ethical principles and codes of conduct. Ethics work entails the work and effort one puts into recognising ethically salient aspects of situations, developing oneself as a reflexive practitioner, paying attention to emotions and relationships, working out the right course of action together and reflecting on it in the company of critical friends (Abma, 2020). Ethics work is practical because it is always situated and attuned to the particulars of a situation.

Working in this way, PAR with older people extends instrumental and proportional knowledge about their lives, and it yields knowledge related to morally and relationally challenging situations that they encounter, living a meaningful life where one is still valued as an older person. The co-creation of this kind of knowledge is empowering for everybody involved if deliberate attention is paid to a communicative space where each participant can share experiences and mutually create and nurture an 'empowering society' (Van Regenmortel, 2002; Van Regenmortel & Fret, 2000). As Tine Van Regenmortel pointed out, an empowering society is a society that responds creatively to the capacities of individuals, including older people, organisations, groups and communities, leaving room for autonomy, stimulating partnerships, and providing reinforcement and silent support where necessary. In a society like this, attention is paid to structural mechanisms of social exclusion, including ageism, whereas opportunities for everyone are promoted through active participation.

Notes

1.   All names here are pseudonyms.

References

Abma, T. (2020). Ethics work for good participatory action research. *Beleidsonderzoek Online*, 1. https://doi.org/10.5553/BO/221335502020000006001

Abma, T. A., & Baur, V. E. (2014). User involvement in long-term care. Towards a relational care-ethics approach. *Health Expectations*, *18*(6), 2328–2339. https://doi.org/10.1111/hex.12202

Abma, T., Banks, S., Cook, T., Dias, S., Madsen, W., Springett, J., & Wright, M. T. (2019). *Participatory Research for Health and Social Well-Being*. Springer.

Abma, T. A., Visse, M., Hanberger, A., Simons, H., & Greene, J. C. (2020). Enriching evaluation practice through care ethics. *Evaluation*, *26*(2), 131–146. https://doi.org/10.1177/1356389019893402

Backhouse, T., Kenkmann, A., Lane, K., Penhale, B., Poland, F., & Killett, A. (2016). Older care-home residents as collaborators or advisors in research: a systematic review. *Age and Ageing*, *45*(3), 337–345. https://doi.org/10.1093/ageing/afv201

Banks, S., & Brydon-Miller, M. (2018). *Ethics in Participatory Research for Health and Social Well-Being: Cases and Commentaries* (1st ed.). Routledge.

Baur, V., & Abma, T. (2012). 'The Taste Buddies': participation and empowerment in a residential home for older people. *Ageing and Society*, *32*(6), 1055–1078. https://doi.org/10.1017/s0144686x11000766

Bendien, E., Groot, B., & Abma, T. (2020). Circles of impacts within and beyond participatory action research with older people. *Ageing and Society*, *42*(5), 1014–1034. https://doi.org/10.1017/s0144686x20001336

Cook, T. (2009). The purpose of mess in action research: building rigour though a messy turn. *Educational Action Research*, *17*(2), 277–291. https://doi.org/10.1080/09650790902914241

Dewar, B. J. (2005). Beyond tokenistic involvement of older people in research – a framework for future development and understanding. *Journal of Clinical Nursing*, *14*, 48–53. https://doi.org/10.1111/j.1365-2702.2005.01162.x

Duijs, S. E., Baur, V. E., & Abma, T. A. (2019). Why action needs compassion: Creating space for experiences of powerlessness and suffering in participatory action research. *Action Research*, *19*(3), 498–517. https://doi.org/10.1177/1476750319844577

Gilroy, R. (2003). Why can't more people have a say? Learning to work with older people. *Ageing and Society*, *23*(5), 659–674. https://doi.org/10.1017/s0144686x03001351

Groot-Sluijsmans, B. C. (2021). *Ethics of Participatory Health Research: Insights from a reflective journey* [Doctoral dissertation, VU University Amsterdam]. Ridderprint. https://research.vu.nl/ws/portalfiles/portal/123135037/B+C++Groot-Sluijsmans+-+thesis.pdf

Groot, B. C., & Abma, T. A. (2019). Participatory health research with older people in the Netherlands: navigating power imbalances towards mutually transforming power. In M. Wright & K. Kongrats (Eds.), *Participatory Health Research: Voices from around the world* (pp. 165–178). Springer.

Groot, B., & Abma, T. (2020). Participatory health research with mothers living in poverty in the Netherlands: pathways and challenges to strengthen empowerment. *Forum: Qualitative Social Research*, *21*(1). https://doi.org/10.17169/fqs-21.1.3302

International Collaboration for Participatory Health Research (ICPHR) (2020). Position Paper 3: Impact in Participatory Health Research (Version: March 2020). http://www.icphr.org/position-papers--discussion-papers/position-paper-3-impact-in-participatory-health-research

Jacobs, G. (2006). Imagining the flowers, but working the rich and heavy clay: participation and empowerment in action research for health. *Educational Action Research*, *14*(4), 569–581. https://doi.org/10.1080/09650790600975809

Levy, B. (2009). Stereotype Embodiment. *Current Directions in Psychological Science*, *18*(6), 332–336. https://doi.org/10.1111/j.1467-8721.2009.01662.x

Lindenberg, J. (2019). *Beeldvorming van ouderen*. Leyden Academy on Vitality and Ageing. https://www.leydenacademy.nl/wp-content/uploads/2019/10/Rapportbeeldvorming-vanouderen2019.pdf

Ray, M. (2007). Redressing the balance? The participation of older people in research. In M. Bernard & T. Scharf (Eds.), *Critical perspectives on ageing societies* (pp. 73–87). Policy Press.

Reason, P., & Bradbury-Huang, H. (2007). *The SAGE Handbook of Action Research: Participative Inquiry and Practice* (2nd ed.). SAGE.

Schuurman, B., Lindenberg, J., Huijg, J. M., Achterberg, W. P., & Slaets, J. P. J. (2020). Expressions of self-ageism in four European countries: a comparative analysis of predictors across cultural contexts. *Ageing and Society*, 1–18. https://doi.org/10.1017/s0144686x20001622

Sprague, J., & Hayes, J. (2000). Self-Determination and Empowerment: A Feminist Standpoint Analysis of Talk about Disability. *American Journal of Community Psychology*, *28*(5), 671–695. https://doi.org/10.1023/a:1005197704441

VanderPlaat, M. (1999). Locating the Feminist Scholar: Relational Empowerment and Social Activism. *Qualitative Health Research*, *9*(6), 773–785. https://doi.org/10.1177/104973299129122270

Van Regenmortel, T. (2002). *Empowerment en maatzorg. Een krachtgerichte, psychologische kijk op armoede* [Empowerment and tailored care. A strength-oriented psychological view on poverty]. Acco.

Van Regenmortel T. (2008). *Zwanger van empowerment. Een uitdagend kader voor sociale inclusie en moderne zorg* [Pregnant with empowerment. A challenging framework for social inclusion and modern care]. Fontys Hogescholen.

Van Regenmortel, T. (2009). Empowerment als uitdagend kader voor sociale inclusie en moderne zorg. [Empowerment als a challenging framework for social inclusion and modern care] *Journal of Social Intervention: Theory and Practice*, *18*(4), 22. https://doi.org/10.18352/jsi.186

Van Regenmortel, T. (2020). Bouwen aan een wetenschappelijke basis voor sterk sociaal werk. Onderzoek dat er toe doet! [Building a scientific foundation for a strong social work. Research that matters!]. Tilburg University. https://www.tilburguniversity.edu/sites/default/files/download/TiU_200173_Oratie%20Tine%20Van%20Regenmortel-digitaal.pdf

Van Regenmortel, T., & Fret, L. (2000). Van moralisme tot empowerment als ethisch perspectief binnen het welzijnswerk en van armoedebestrijding. [From moralism to empowerment as an ethical perspective within welfare work and from poverty reduction]. In J. Vranken, D. Geldof & G. Van Menxel (Eds.), *Armoede en sociale uitsluiting* [Poverty and social exclusion] (pp. 291–313). Acco.

Wallerstein, N. (1992). Powerlessness, Empowerment, and Health: Implications for Health Promotion Programs. *American Journal of Health Promotion*, *6*(3), 197–205. https://doi.org/10.4278/0890-1171-6.3.197

Woelders-Peters, S. (2020). *Power-full patient participation: Opening spaces for silenced knowledge* [Doctoral dissertation, VU University Amsterdam]. Ridderprint. https://research.vu.nl/ws/portalfiles/portal/96812547/186845.pdf

ENHANCING PERSON-CENTRED CARE TO ENABLE OLDER PERSONS TO BE INVOLVED IN LONG-TERM CARE

M.M. Janssen[1], K.G. Luijkx[1], A. Scheffelaar[1], A. Stoop[1]

The prevalence of chronic conditions and limitations across all domains of health increases with age. Not all older persons are confronted with complex health and social care needs but, compared to other age groups, a large proportion of older persons do. Although this may lead to reduced self-reliance and increased dependence, older persons prefer to live their lives as they desire by making their own choices regarding different aspects of daily life. Over the last few decades, long-term care for older persons has been shifting from a biomedical model (aiming for safety and risk reduction) towards a broader concept of health that recognises the individual personhood of each older person. In this chapter, we make a plea to put the perspective of older persons at the centre in both research and care practice in order to contribute to person-centered care for older persons. After an introduction on person-centred care, our Academic Collaborative Center Older Adults (ACC) is described, in which we aim to create both scientific and societal impact to facilitate and stimulate professionals to involve older persons in their own care and support and to empower older persons to do so. As a new development in the ACC, the active participation – which is currently designed together with older persons – of older persons is described. Then, three examples of our research are discussed in which the perspectives of older persons are placed central to realise person-centred care: sexuality and intimacy, autonomy, and the story as a quality instrument. The chapter ends with some implications for care practice, policy and research, leading to a number of directions for the future.

1.   Person-centred care

As people age, they often suffer from multiple chronic conditions and disabilities. These can challenge older persons' social participation and independent
living and can require mobilisation of health and social care services (Fried et
al., 2004; Verver et al., 2019; Vos et al., 2020). For some older persons, it is not
possible to continue living independently in their homes and communities
because care and support at home are unable to address increasing deteriora-
tions in their health (Fried, Ferrucci et al., 2004; Fried, Tangen et al., 2001;
Markle-Reid & Browne, 2003). To receive care and support that meet their
complex care needs, older people move into residential care facilities when
their health or cognitive status deteriorates. In 2019, 115,000 older persons
lived in a residential care facility in the Netherlands (CBS, 2020).

The perspective on and, subsequently, the organisation of care and support for older persons has changed over the past few decades. For years,
the traditional biomedical model of medicine was predominant, but the
biopsychosocial model has become increasingly prevalent in the provision
of care and support for older persons. The biomedical model focuses on
biological (somatic) processes in human bodies, in which diseases were
conceptualised as deviations from normal biological functioning (Engel,
1977). The doctor-patient relationship was paternalistic and predominantly
doctor-centred. The patient's role was limited to reporting illnesses, signs
and symptoms after which a doctor started a standardised investigation,
diagnosis and treatment in order to restore the disease processes to 'normal'
(Mead & Bower, 2000). In the movement towards a more biopsychosocial
model of care, increasing attention is paid to approach the person as a whole
to understand and promote older persons' health, including a combined
biological (somatic), psychological and social perspective (Mead & Bower,
2000). As such, the biopsychosocial model can be considered an attempt to
challenge and broaden the traditional biomedical model.

In line with this broader approach, several new definitions and conceptualisations of health have been developed over the years. The concepts
of resilience and empowerment of older persons have received increasing
attention. Common elements of empowerment include, among others, feelings
of control over life or health, self-efficacy, development of personal abilities
and partnership as a means or as a goal contributing to people's quality of life
(Tengland, 2008; Shearer et al., 2012; Tsubouchi et al., 2021). According to
Van Corven et al. (2021b), empowerment may be different for older persons
with dementia because of cognitive impairments and behavioural changes.
Important themes for people living with dementia include sense of personal

identity, usefulness, choice and control, and self-worth (van Corven et al., 2021a, 2021b). The development towards empowerment is widely supported and shifts focus from people's disabilities to their abilities, also when they face problems and limitations (Books, 2009; Huber et al., 2011). In addition to medical conditions such as physical ailments and disabilities, aspects such as meaningfulness, social participation and well-being are covered (Huber et al., 2016). Such new health concepts change thinking about care and support for older persons. Based on what is important to the person, empowerment shifts the focus: it is no longer exclusively on medical treatment but also using people's abilities to cope, adapt and self-manage to improve their situation and thus on empowerment of the individual (Huber et al., 2016).

Furthermore, this broader approach includes recognition of the individual personhood of each older person. This means that older persons are regarded as unique persons. As is essential for all people, an older person wants to be seen, heard and respected as a unique human being. Although chronic conditions and disabilities can cause considerable changes in the way older persons used to live, they prefer to be in control of their lives by making their own choices regarding different aspects of their life, such as the care and support they receive (Lette et al., 2017).

Person-centred care, as the term suggests, places older persons at the centre of their own care and support. Older persons, and if preferred their informal caregivers, are actively involved in decision-making and planning their care process in order to tailor the delivery of care and support to their individual needs and preferences across all domains of health, including meaningful-ness, social participation and well-being, in order to empower them and give them control over their lives (Coulter et al., 2013; Langberg et al., 2019). The term *person-centred care* is widely used, and many different definitions and frameworks of person-centredness have been proposed over the years (Bechtel & Ness, 2010; Leplege et al., 2007; Mead & Bower, 2000). Empowerment and person-centredness show several similarities in which individual needs and preferences and partnership between care recipients and care providers play an important role (Holmström & Röing, 2010; Kitwood & Kitwood, 1997).

Although more insights of how to design and implement a person-centred care approach and an understanding of how to measure its outcomes and experiences are still needed (Rathert et al., 2013; Santana et al., 2018), person-centred care is expected to have a positive impact on older persons, informal caregivers and staff members. A recent systematic review of the literature found positive relationships between person-centred care processes and patient satisfaction and well-being (Rathert et al., 2013). Also on the staff level, several studies showed that person-centred care has beneficial impacts,

Figure 7.1: Person-centred nursing framework. Retrieved from T. McCance, B. McCormack, & J. Dewing (2011), 'An exploration of person-centredness in practice', *Online Journal of Issues in Nursing 16*(2), 1. Reuse with permission from the authors.

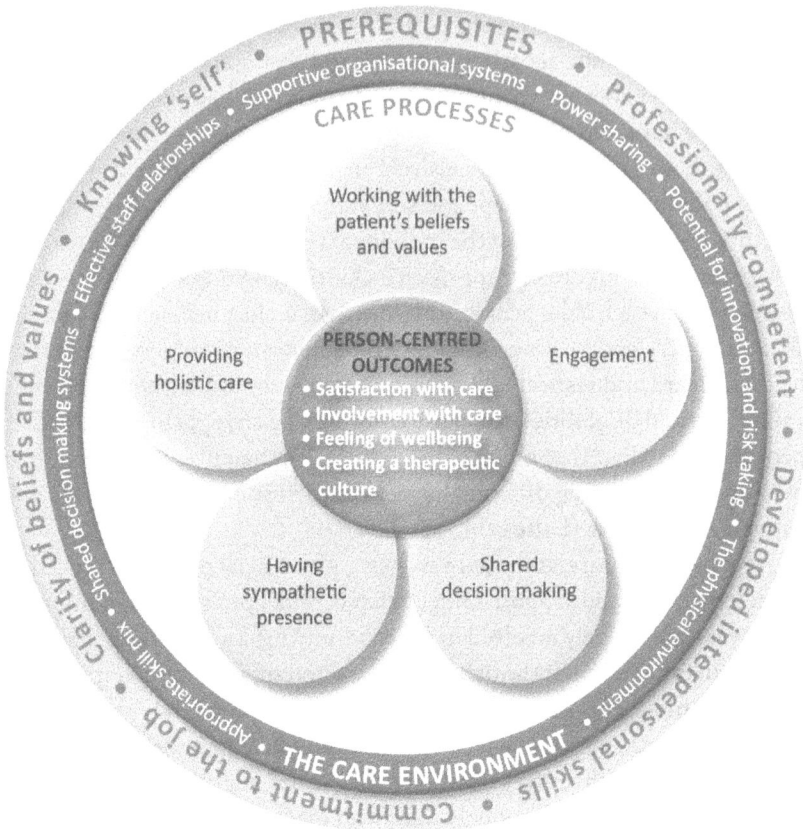

including higher levels of staff satisfaction and lower levels of job strain (Sjögren et al., 2015; van Diepen et al., 2020).

One of the theoretical frameworks that has been developed is the person-centred nursing framework by McCormack and McCance (McCormack & McCance, 2016, 2006). Person-centred practice focuses on 'the formation and fostering of healthful relationships between all care providers, service users and others significant to them in their lives' (McCormack & McCance, 2016), and 'is underpinned by values of respect for persons, individual right to self-determination, mutual respect, and understanding' (Brendan et al., 2010).

The framework comprises four key constructs that are closely related to each other. First, prerequisites for person-centred practice: the attributes of the nurses, such as being professionally competent. Second, the care environment: the context in which care is delivered, such as an appropriate skill mix in the nursing team. Third, person-centred processes: delivering care to the person through a range of activities, such as working with persons' beliefs and values. Finally, person-centred outcomes: the results of effective person-centred nursing, such as satisfaction with care (McCormack & McCance, 2016).

Although the framework has been developed as part of a large-scale project evaluating the effectiveness of person-centred nursing in a hospital setting (McCormack & McCance, 2016), it has been used widely across several countries in multiple contexts, including long-term care for older persons. Several studies describe how the framework has been used in many different ways in long-term care. The framework provides a basis for evaluating existing practices, determining changes needed and guiding the implementation and evaluation of developments in practice (McCance et al., 2011). For instance, a qualitative study explored nursing assessments and care plans of residents in long-term care for evidence of person-centred care using the person-centred nursing framework (Broderick & Coffey, 2013). In addition, a recent systematic literature review applied the framework to identify facilitators and barriers to autonomy of older persons with physical impairments living in residential care facilities (van Loon et al., 2019).

Although the framework has received much attention on an international stage and has been validated as an intervention to implement person-centred nursing (McCormack & McCance, 2016, 2006), the framework has also been critically evaluated. One potential limitation of the framework is the restricted role older persons play. Older persons (or 'patients', as the framework suggests) appear as subjects or passive recipients of care in the different constructs in the model rather than as active participants. In addition, two specific issues will be mentioned here.

First, the model has been developed, tested and refined in collaboration with co-researchers and practitioners from a range of clinical settings (McCormack & McCance, 2016). However, engagement of those whom person-centred care concerns mostly – in other words, older persons themselves – is vital to make sure that it reflects and respects what is important to them. Since older persons or their representatives (e.g. informal caregivers or representative organisations) were not explicitly engaged in the development of the framework, older persons' perspectives remain under-represented while their active participation is essential to refine and improve the concept of person-centred nursing.

Second, the framework appears to be used as a tool for practice which particularly covers the attributes of staff, the context in which they provide care and a wide range of nursing activities (McCormack & McCance, 2016). Person-centred care as well as empowerment emphasise establishing an accommodating, ongoing partnership and collaboration between the older person receiving care (and the informal caregiver) and professionals as equal partners (Mead & Bower, 2000). Unfortunately, the framework provides no central role for the key players – the older persons as active, empowered participants in person-centred care.

These two issues illustrate the challenges to appreciate older persons as key actors in person-centred care. Many steps still have to be taken. Also, academia has an important role to place older persons at the heart of person-centred care and make sure they have an equal and active role in adopting and promoting a truly person-centred approach.

2. The Academic Collaborative Center Older Adults

Tranzo, a department within the Tilburg School of Social and Behavioral Sciences of Tilburg University (the Netherlands), strives to connect science and practice in the field of care and well-being. In co-creation between scientists, professionals and citizens/clients, knowledge is developed and exchanged, with the aim to promote evidence-based practice. Collaboration takes place in so-called Academic Collaborative Centers (ACCs), which are long-term and structural collaborations between science and practice and in which scientists and professionals from practice define a research programme in an equivalent way (Tranzo, n.d.).

An ACC within Tranzo that aims to contribute to person-centred care for older persons and to empower older persons is the ACC Older Adults. As person-centred care for older persons requires a different position of older persons than has been common up to this point; it is essential to understand their perspectives in several respects, including their needs and preferences for care and support. Scientific research can help understand the different experiences, preferences and capabilities of older persons as unique individuals as well as a heterogeneous group. These insights are essential to facilitate and stimulate professional caregivers to involve older persons in their own care and support. Traditionally, scientific research is *about* older persons (not including them) and focuses on care professionals or their relatives as a proxy. However, scientific research can give voice to older persons who are receiving care and support by gathering data about their lifeworld. Older persons themselves should be the most important and primary source in research because the perspectives of older persons differ from the estimation of proxies, such as loved ones and care professionals, as is shown by research (Dröes et al., 2006; Gerritsen et al., 2007; Kane et al., 1997; Larsson et al., 2019). These differences in perspective, although sometimes nuanced, may affect the older persons' experience of the genuine experience of person-centred care. Moreover, although physical or cognitive limitations – including dementia – may complicate older persons' position as the primary source in scientific research, it is possible and worthwhile (Roelofs et al., 2017).

Within person-centred care for older persons as the main theme of research in the ACC Older Adults, the following research lines have been developed: autonomy, informal care, quality of care, participatory research, technological innovation, palliative care and dementia care. The ACC Older Adults is a cooperation between Tilburg University (Tranzo department), ten organisations that provide long-term care for older persons and the CZ zorgkantoor (Luijkx et al., 2020). Of the ten care organisations, eight are located in the province Noord-Brabant in the south of the Netherlands, one is located in the province Zeeland in the south-west of the Netherlands, and one is located in the province Gelderland in the east of the Netherlands. All ten organisations provide long-term extramural and intramural care, of which eight also provide short-term rehabilitation care. The organisations differ in size. Six organisations provide intramural care in ten to twenty locations, three in twenty to thirty-five locations and one in more than sixty-five locations. The CZ zorgkantoor also participates within the ACC Older Adults. A *zorgkantoor* works on behalf of the Dutch government and makes agreements with care providers on cost and quality of long-term (residential) care. Moreover, a *zorgkantoor* advices persons who need long-term care about possible options regarding their unique personal care needs and preferences (Luijkx et al., 2020).

The slogan of the ACC Older Adults is 'science in practice to contribute to person-centred care for older adults' (Luijkx et al., 2020). We strive to create scientific knowledge and societal impact by conducting scientific research and creating products for practice in order to facilitate care professionals to involve older persons in their own care and support. We create scientific and societal impact in co-creation with older persons, care professionals providing long-term care to older persons, and researchers, in an equivalent way (Luijkx et al., 2020). The process of creating scientific knowledge and societal impact to contribute to person-centred care for older persons starts with a PhD study. In four to six years, a main research topic is studied through multiple sub-questions resulting in theoretical scientific knowledge. This knowledge is of value for scientists, managers and highly educated professionals (e.g. policy workers, elderly care physicians, psychologists) working in research or long-term care practice. However, this theoretical knowledge is often too abstract to be used in daily care practice. Therefore, after a PhD study, a 'science-to-practice project' is started. A science-to-practice project is a scientific study in which the theoretical results of a PhD study are translated into a practical tool or working method. Intensive co-creation between the researcher, older persons and care professionals is key to ensure that the tool or working method suits daily care practice well and is feasible to implement and leads to involving older persons in their own care and support. During and after a PhD study and a science-to-practice project, a communication expert, an education expert and an implementation expert employed by the ACC are continuously involved to think along with the researcher to share the research findings in a comprehensible and attractive way and make scientific knowledge directly applicable for practice. In this way, they enable the use in daily care practice and thus contribute to the societal impact (Luijkx et al., 2020).

To be able to contribute to person-centred care for older persons and create scientific knowledge and societal impact, it is necessary to ensure that research questions arise from daily care practice, and thus from care professionals and older persons. In the ACC Older Adults, so-called science practitioners and research brokers play an important role. A science practitioner combines working in daily care practice – for instance, as a psychologist, policymaker, nurse specialist, or an elderly care physician – with a PhD study. A science practitioner formulates a research question starting from a question or problem in her or his daily care practice, which also fits within the main research theme of the ACC Older Adults (i.e. person-centred care) and one of the subthemes of study (i.e. autonomy, informal care, quality of care, participatory research, technological innovation, palliative care and dementia care). PhD studies are, for example, about intimacy and sexuality of older persons with dementia living in a nursing home (Roelofs et al., 2019a, 2019b), autonomy (Van Loon, Janssen et al., n.d.; Van Loon, Luijkx et al., 2019), access to care (Schipper et al., 2015a, 2015b), and the use of tobacco and alcohol by residents who live in a nursing home (de Graaf et al., 2021). Care organisations contribute to conducting the PhD studies of the science practitioners by enabling them to work on the research during contract hours. In the ACC Older Adults, science practitioners conduct about two thirds of the current PhD studies.

Moreover, five research brokers, who also work as senior researchers, work within the ACC Older Adults. In their role as senior researchers, they conduct scientific activities at the university like submitting grant proposals and supervising PhD students and science practitioners. In their role as research brokers, each research broker connects closely with two or three partnership organisations to foster and strengthen the collaboration and knowledge exchange between science and care practice. They get to know care practice from within by participating in relevant committees, for instance a science committee, by meeting and talking with older persons and care professionals in daily care and by meeting regularly with professionals who are enthusiastic about scientific knowledge exchange and implementing research findings into practice work. Moreover, they are able to discover topics that are relevant to formulate new research questions on and to detect possibilities to implement or share our knowledge. As such, research brokers contribute to improving care practice by using scientific knowledge (Luijkx et al., 2020).

As explained above, in the ACC Older Adults, we aim to create new scientific knowledge about person-centred care for older persons to stimulate and facilitate professional caregivers to involve older persons in their own care and support to empower older persons. We strive to do so with, for and by older persons. Until now, older persons have mostly been included in our research in less active roles as research participants. Although their perspectives are the main focus of our research, older persons are usually not yet actively involved as co-designers of new studies or as co-researchers during execution of the study.

There are several motivations for actively involving older persons in research as research partners, including substantive, normative and instrumental reasons. The involvement of older persons is likely to improve the quality of research, as it better fits their knowledge, ideas, needs and priorities. Involvement of older persons in the dissemination and implementation of research products is likely to increase the fit and usefulness of products especially designed for these target group. Furthermore, older persons have the democratic right to be involved in the issues that matter to them ('nothing about us without us') (Baldwin et al., 2018; Scheffelaar, 2020). Inviting and encouraging them to participate as active and equal partners may contribute to feelings of empowerment, as they have more choice and control over the research which is performed with them, which also is likely to make them feel useful and significant.

Moreover, there are many different ways in which participation of older persons can be realised. Older persons can be involved in a more structural way by providing their ideas and feedback, on a regular basis and transcending individual. Several examples exist in the Netherlands using terms such as expert panel, older persons' council and pool of client representatives. Additionally, there are examples in which older persons are involved in a specific research. In the role of co-researcher, older persons can be involved in the definition of the research question or topic, the development of a study design, and in data collection; for example, they can conduct interviews, analyse data, present the study findings, or help translate study findings into practical tools (Baldwin et al., 2018; Bindels et al., 2014; De Graaff et al., 2019; Scheffelaar et al., 2020).

Doing research with and by older persons in participatory research designs has high priority in the ACC Older Adults. To realise meaningful involvement of older persons, we decided to directly ask older persons themselves which contributions and roles they find important to make the ACC inclusive in the long term. In this way, we ensure that the cooperation and involvement of older persons does not remain instrumental or incidental, in other words, that older persons are only involved if researchers decide so. Instead, the participatory structure is co-designed together with older persons so that older persons can consider themselves when and how their contribution can be useful. By thinking along and making decisions together, a joint vision is created on the roles and tasks of older persons in our research and on the more abstract level of the ACC in general.

To start engaging older persons in the ACC Older Adults, a preparatory group was set up in 2021. The preparatory group consisted of three older persons, one postdoctoral researcher and one implementation expert. The older persons differed in age (from sixty-seven to seventy-seven years old), sex (two male, one female), relations with care provision, and personal and professional background. The group met once or twice a month for one and a half hours to gradually draft a proposal on the participatory structure.

The preparatory group developed a proposal for a Platform of Older Adults, in which eight to ten older persons would meet four times a year to give their requested advice and opinions on research issues of the ACC Older Adults as well as spontaneous advice. The proposal describes that the Platform of Older Adults should consist of older persons (sixty-five years and older) who receive care themselves or have experience with care in their close environment as relatives or volunteers. The preparatory group presented their proposal to the different stakeholders involved in the ACC Older Adults (including representatives of care organisations and researchers) and, after some minor adaptations, the proposal was formalised into a plan of action.

The preparatory group thereafter helped set up the Platform of Older Adults by developing 'job' profiles for the future older persons who would become involved. Moreover, they proactively developed a handbook with regulations to define the assignment of the platform, to name the formal status and position within the ACC, and to establish a number of practical agreements with regard to the composition, communication and meetings of the platform. The preparatory group thereafter developed recruitment material and participated in the recruitment and selection of new candidates. A financial budget was made available for paying older persons an allowance for their participation and for their travel expenses. The Platform of Older Adults was launched in January 2022. In 2022, they are further concretising their role in the ACC, while they also start being involved in research taking place within the ACC.

3. Placing the perspective of older persons central

In the ACC Older Adults, the perspective of older persons is placed central in the research. This way of working might empower the older persons themselves. Moreover, these insights help facilitate and stimulate professional caregivers to involve older persons in their own care and support. By giving voice to older persons who are receiving care and support, care professionals are supported to place older persons at the centre of their care and support. Therefore, in most of the research projects in the ACC, the first empirical research question studies the perspective of older persons to maximise the impact of understanding the perspective of older persons. Qualitative methods of data gathering prove to be the most helpful to understand perspectives, meanings and experiences of older persons as a heterogeneous group regarding their capacities, limitations, goals, preferences and habits (Luijkx et al., 2020).

To illustrate the value of studying the perspective of older persons, three examples of studies in the ACC Older Adults are provided below: two about living in a nursing home and one about the usefulness of narratives of older persons for quality improvement in care for older persons. These examples show how the perspectives of older persons are placed at the centre in both research and care practice to contribute to person-centred care for older persons.

3.1 Sexuality and intimacy

The shift from the biomedical model towards the person-centred care model in nursing home care (Koren, 2010; White-Chu et al., 2009) implies that nursing home residents, also those with dementia, are valued as unique individuals and are able to live their lives as they desire. Intimacy and sexuality, in a broad sense, are essential for all human beings during the whole life course, including nursing home residents with dementia (WHO, 2006). It is therefore important to enable experiences with intimacy and sexuality in nursing homes, despite the fact that it is often still a taboo.

Older persons with a more advanced stage of dementia live in nursing homes because they need daily care and support. Enabling residents to experience intimacy and sexuality in the way they prefer should be a natural part of person-centred caregiving. According to a psychologist working within one of the partnership organisations of the ACC Older Adults, staff in nursing homes often experience and label sexual behaviour as problematic behaviour and do not feel equipped to enable residents in this life domain. This insight from daily care practice motivated a psychologist to conduct a PhD study about intimacy and sexuality of older persons with dementia living in a nursing home (Roelofs, 2018).

The conducted study aimed to give voice to nursing home residents and their spouses (if relevant) and to make professional caregivers aware of these needs and to challenge them to act accordingly. Therefore, the study addressed the following overarching research question: 'in what way can nursing home residents with dementia, and possibly their partners, be best supported in their wishes and needs with regard to intimacy and sexuality?' (Roelofs, 2018). To discover the perspective of nursing home residents and their spouses, couple interviews have been held, but also individual interviews with residents and individual interviews with spouses (Roelofs et al., 2019a, 2019b). Although it was not easy to interview residents with dementia, it was possible and worthwhile (Roelofs et al., 2017, 2019a). The eight interviews with either individual residents or couples revealed that sexuality and intimacy is an individual matter that is interwoven with the whole life course. Different types of stories were shared by interviewees. Some stories started with the way spouses fell in love a long time ago, while other stories started with the onset of dementia. All interviews revealed that intimacy and sexuality are still important in their lives, despite the fact that dementia and the move to a nursing home had a great impact on these important aspects of life. However, residents and their spouses did not feel that the nursing home is a place where intimacy and sexuality can be experienced satisfactorily. This is prevented by practical, emotional and communicational issues, like the absence of a double bed, the lack of a secure feeling of privacy and the difficulty to talk about this topic with caregivers (Roelofs et al., 2019a). For example, although all participants found it important to be intimate within their relationship, only one couple experienced physical sexuality in the nursing home. Interviews with nine spouses of nursing home residents revealed similar experiences (Roelofs et al., 2019b). This knowledge challenges care professionals to think about how they can involve older persons and their partners in care and support to ensure that they can have such important experiences, also in nursing homes.

3.2 Autonomy

The second example about strengthening person-centred care and giving voice to older persons by placing their perspective central is about autonomy of older persons who live in a nursing home due to physical impairments. Based on a systematic literature review, autonomy can be described as the 'capacity to influence the environment and make decisions irrespective of having executional autonomy, to live the kind of life someone desires to live in the face of diminishing social, physical and/or cognitive resources and dependency' (Van Loon et al., 2019). Two polarities of autonomy – decisional and executional autonomy (Collopy, 1988) – are taken into account in this description. Older persons who live in a nursing home might be able to decide how they prefer something without being able to execute this decision themselves due to their physical impairments. Autonomy in a nursing home is an example of relational autonomy because it is not about being independent in daily life but about being in relation with others.

To be able to provide person-centred care, caregivers must establish and maintain a care relationship with older persons and get to know the core values of each resident. Autonomy needs to be seen as an interactive process, requiring the help and support of others (Abma et al., 2012). To find out how older persons with physical impairments living in a nursing home prefer to live their lives and maintain autonomy, one of the science practitioners conducted a PhD study about autonomy and has shadowed older persons. Shadowing is a non-participatory observational method in which the researcher, the shadower, observes the respondent, the shadowee, like a fly on the wall which comes close to experience, see, feel, hear and smell whatever the shadowee experiences (Van der Meide et al., 2013).

The method of shadowing gives the opportunity to include all older persons, also those who are not able to verbally express themselves well due to frailty, dementia or aphasia. Seventeen older persons with physical impairments who live in two nursing homes have been shadowed during several hours on one day during morning care, meal times and activities. During the shadowing, six elements were seen that older persons use to maintain their autonomy: 'being able to decide and/or execute decisions', 'active involvement', 'transferring autonomy to others like family members or other informal care givers', 'using preferred spaces', 'continuing the life you like to live' and 'deciding about important topics', e.g. about medical decisions, treatment in a hospital, or access to the elderly care physician (Van Loon et al., n.d.).

To enable older persons to be not only subject of research but also actively involved in care, the perspective of staff members has also been studied. Staff members have been shadowed to find out which actions they take to enhance the autonomy of older persons with physical impairments. Moreover, an action research has been conducted in which older persons and staff members formulated concrete actions with the aim to strengthen the autonomy of older persons (Van Loon et al., 2022). By studying both perspectives of older persons and of staff members, and by facilitating a dialogue between older persons and staff members about the study insights, older persons become more empowered and actively involved in care; in this way, care and autonomy can be provided in a more person-centred way.

Another way to involve older persons in their own care and support is listening to the story of an older person for quality improvement, as is discussed in the third example.

3.3   The story as a quality instrument

A transition related to realising person-centred care concerns the approach chosen in quality research. Quality of care is assessed traditionally by means of quantitative survey instruments, such as the Consumer Quality Index (CQ index) (Triemstra et al., 2010). With the use of a quantitative instrument, a reliable and valid measurement can be achieved on relevant quality indicators including safety, physical body care, provision of meals and hygiene. As a standard for quality, the CQ index was used for a number of years as an obligatory measure for external accountability in the care provision for older persons (Triemstra et al., 2010). However, it is not always sure whether the indicators measured are relevant from the perspective of older persons or only from the perspective of care organisations and health insurers (Van Campen et al., 1998). Although such quantitative findings provide a general view on the experiences of older persons, they do not provide insight into individual levels of expectations, needs and wishes of care provision. Furthermore, the mean scores do not adequately represent the lifeworld of each unique older persons.

In response to these observations, the ACC Older Adults has developed 'The Story as a Quality Instrument'. This is a quality instrument that primarily focuses on the experiences of each individual older person (Scheffelaar et al., 2021). The quality instrument is based on narrative research principles, in which narratives or stories are obtained by avoiding a question-answer structure and simply encouraging older persons to tell their story (Rosenthal, 2018). A rich description in a narrative helps to understand experiences of quality of care from each older person's point of view, combined with other experiences such as social ties and life history (Rosenthal, 2018; Wang & Geale, 2015). Rather than structuring the relevant topics for them by posing standardised questions, older persons prioritise themselves by talking about the topics that matter to them.

To allow the older person to talk about their experiences freely, the interview is based on one simple open invitation: 'you have been receiving care at organization X for a while. Please tell me about this'. After this open invitation, the flow of a natural conversation is followed. The interviewer does not introduce any further themes, but keeps the conversation going by using non-verbal body language, such as nodding and verbal cues, like repeating the last sentence or using affirmative statements. When the older person seems to have finished a story, the interview moves on to the second stage. In the second part of the interview, probing questions can be posed using the wording of the older person to supplement information that is shared by the older person. Interviews are audio recorded and transcribed verbatim afterwards, and they are used to create a holistic portrait of each interviewed older person. A reliable representation of the respondent's story is achieved by staying close to the respondent's words. The holistic portraits can be used for a variety of purposes, including team reflection to achieve improvement in quality towards person-centred care (Scheffelaar et al., 2021).

Care professionals play a special role in the execution of the quality instrument. After a training, they perform the role of interviewer and analyst as 'insider researcher' (Leslie & McAllister, 2002; Unluer, 2012). In contrast to academics, care professionals benefit from their contextual knowledge of the care environment when relating to each older person and interpreting the interview content. Furthermore, listening to client experiences first-hand stimulates care professionals towards learning, increases their understanding of the client perspective, and supports their plans for improvement emerging from quality research. Care professionals interview older persons with whom they do not have a care relationship to ensure that older persons feel free to talk about anything that is important to them (Scheffelaar et al., 2021).

A follow-up study has started to develop a structured approach for care professionals to jointly translate the narrative portraits into actions targeting quality improvement in the long-term care of older persons (Scheffelaar et al., 2021). In this way, the rich stories of older persons including their experiences, needs and views become the key towards quality improvement of care.

4.   Future directions

In the ACC Older Adults, we strive to empower older persons and involve them in their own care and support by creating scientific knowledge and societal impact about person-centred long-term care for older persons, in co-creation with older persons, care professionals and researchers, in an equivalent way. We aim to place the perspectives of older persons central in each first empirical study of a PhD study. When older persons have a voice and can share insights into how they prefer to live their lives, they are empowered to share their needs and wishes.

However, getting insight into the perspectives of older persons is not enough for empowering older persons and will not evidently lead to involvement of older persons in their own care and support. Therefore, care professionals working in long-term care for older persons are as important as older persons themselves. For this reason, the perspectives of care professionals in addition to the perspectives of older persons are studied in the research of the ACC Older Adults (Roelofs et al., 2018; Waterschoot et al., 2022). These different yet complementary perspectives contribute to get insight into what is needed and can be done to empower older persons and involve them in their own care and support. Moreover, scientific knowledge is often not immediately applicable into care practice. Therefore, we started and will continue to translate our knowledge in co-creation with older persons, care professionals and researchers into practical tools and working methods that can be implemented in care practice (Haufe et al., 2019; Janssen et al., 2019).

An additional benefit of discussing and implementing the study results about the perspective of older persons and about person-centred care on different levels in a care organisation is that evidence-based practice is stimulated throughout the whole organisation. Hopefully, this fruitful approach will inspire others to do the same.

To benefit from the involvement of older persons in our ACC, we want to move beyond studying the perspectives of older persons and strive to involve older persons structurally, for example, by having them provide input about research topics that are important to them. The Platform of Older Adults was installed with a preparatory group of four older persons, a postdoctoral researcher and an implementation expert to set up structural participation of older persons in the ACC Older Adults.

The study results of the ACC Older Adults contribute to science as well as to policy and daily care practice. We recommend that the new insights from our studies are spread and implemented within care organisations at different levels. Most of the organisations providing care to older persons strive to provide care in a person-centred way. However, in daily practice, regulations and rules of care for older persons (e.g. time schedules for morning care or meal times, pragmatic habits and routines constraining, for example, sexuality and intimacy with a spouse) dominate daily care practice at the expense of person-centred care. Therefore, a recommendation for policymakers and managers is to enable and stimulate professional caregivers to balance the perspective – in other words, the living world of each older person should be constricted only by rules and regulations that are essential. This would make it easier for care professionals to realise person-centred care in practice and might contribute to the empowerment of older persons. Limiting rules and regulations to the essential ones should provide care professionals liberty in being creative to involve older persons in their own care and support and to provide person-centred care. Moreover, is it recommended to share best practices of how to place the perspective of the older person central and how to care in a person-centred way within and between care organisations and preferably worldwide to encourage learning and improvement.

Research that is characterised by scientific and practical relevance and practical tools and working methods that are actually used by care organisations legitimise the existence and continuations of the ACC Older Adults. This motivates us to continue to develop new scientific knowledge and practical products based on this knowledge that fit care practice. Despite the realised results of the ACC, a thorough understanding of the impact and the implementation of practical tools and working methods is lacking. Whether and to what extent the ACC Older Adults is successful in contributing to person-centred care for older persons is still unknown. Therefore, to gain more insight into our impact on person-centred care in daily practice, three lines of development are valuable. First, at the scientific level, the way the ACC works needs to be scientifically substantiated; every step, including the development and implementation of different practical tools or working methods, based on our scientific insights, should be thoroughly evaluated. Second, an approach to evaluate and, if necessary, adapt the process of making scientific knowledge applicable for practice could bring the ACC a step further. Third, when the tools and working methods are implemented on a large enough scale, the impact and implementation should be evaluated in co-creation with older persons and care professionals to learn how, when and why our approach works and how it can be improved.

Notes

1.   Each author contributed equally to this chapter

References

Abma, T., Bruijn, A., Kardol, T., Schols, J. M. G. A., & Widdershoven, G. (2012). Responsibilities in elderly care: Mr Powell's narrative of duty and relations. *Bioethics, 26*(1), 22–31. https://doi.org/10.1111/j.1467–8519.2011.01898.x

Baldwin, J. N., Napier, S., Neville, S., & Wright-St Clair, V. A. (2018). Impacts of older people's patient and public involvement in health and social care research: a systematic review. *Age and ageing, 47*(6), 801–809. https://doi.org/10.1093/ageing/afy092

Bechtel, C., & Ness, D. L. (2010). If you build it, will they come? Designing truly patient-centred health care. *Health Affairs, 29*(5), 914–920. https://doi.org/10.1377/hlthaff.2010.0305

Bindels J, B. V., Cox K, Heijing S, Abma T. (2014). Older people as co-researchers: a collaborative journey. *Ageing Society, 34*(6): 951–973. https://doi.org/10.1017/S0144686X12001298

Books, Z. (2009). What is health? The ability to adapt. *The Lancet, 373*(9666), 781. https://doi.org/10.1016/S0140-6736(09)60456-6

Brendan, M., Breslin, E., Dewing, J., Tobin, C., Manning, M., Coyne-Nevin, A., Kennedy, K., & Peelo-Kilroe, L. (2010). The implementation of a model of person-centred practice in older person settings final report.

Broderick, M. C., & Coffey, A. (2013). Person-centred care in nursing documentation. *International journal of older people nursing, 8*(4), 309–318. https://doi.org/10.1111/opn.12012

CBS. (2020). *115 duizend mensen in verzorgings- of verpleeghuis.* [115 thousand people in care or nusing homes] https://www.cbs.nl/nl-nl/achtergrond/2020/13/115-duizend-mensen-in-verzorgings-of-verpleeghuis

Collopy, B. J. (1988). Autonomy in Long Term Care: Some Crucial Distinctions. *The Gerontologist, 28*, 10–17. https://doi.org/https://doi.org/10.1093/geront/28.Suppl.10

Coulter, A., Roberts, S., & Dixon, A. (2013). Delivering better services for people with long-term conditions. *Building the house of care. London: The King's Fund,* 1–28.

De Graaf, L., Janssen, M., Roelofs, T., & Luijkx, K. (2021). Substance use and misuse of older adults living in residential care facilities: a scoping review from a person-centred care approach. *Ageing & Society,* 1–27. https://doi.org/10.1017/S0144686X21001215

De Graaff M, S. A., & Leistikow I. (2019). Transforming clients into experts-by-experience: a pilot in client participation in Dutch long-term elderly care homes inspectorate supervision. *Health Policy, 123*(3), 275–280. https://doi.org/10.1016/j.healthpol.2018.11.006

Dröes, R., Boelens-Van Der Knoop, E. C. C., Bos, J., Meihuizen, L., Ettema, T. P., Gerritsen, D. L., Hoogeveen, F., De Lange, J., & Schölzel-Dorenbos, C. J. M. (2006). Quality of life in dementia in perspective: An explorative study of variations in opinions among people with dementia and their professional caregivers, and in literature. *Dementia, 5*(4), 533–558. https://doi.org/10.1177/1471301206069929

Engel, G. L. (1977). The need for a new medical model: a challenge for biomedicine. *Science, 196*(4286), 129–136. https://doi.org/10.1126/science.847460

Fried, L. P., Ferrucci, L., Darer, J., Williamson, J. D., & Anderson, G. (2004). Untangling the concepts of disability, frailty, and comorbidity: implications for improved targeting and care. *The Journals of Gerontology Series A: Biological Sciences and Medical Sciences, 59*(3), M255–M263. https://doi.org/10.1093/gerona/59.3.M255

Fried, L. P., Tangen, C. M., Walston, J., Newman, A. B., Hirsch, C., Gottdiener, J., Seeman, T., Tracy, R., Kop, W. J., & Burke, G. (2001). Frailty in older adults: evidence for a phenotype. *The Journals of Gerontology Series A: Biological Sciences and Medical Sciences, 56*(3), M146–M157. https://doi.org/10.1093/gerona/56.3.M146

Gerritsen, D. L., Ettema, T. P., Boelens, E., Bos, J., Hoogeveen, F., Lange, J. d., Meihuizen, L., Schölzel-Dorenbos, C. J., & Dröes, R. M. (2007). Quality of life in dementia: do professional caregivers focus on the significant domains? *American Journal of Alzheimer's Disease and Other Dementias, 22*(3), 176–183. https://doi.org/10.1177/1533317507299771

Haufe, M., Peek, S. T. M., & Luijkx, K. G. (2019). Matching gerontechnologies to independent-living seniors' individual needs: Development of the GTM tool. *BMC health services research, 19*(1), 1–13. https://doi.org/10.1186/s12913-018-3848-5

Holmström, I., & Röing, M. (2010). The relation between patient-centeredness and patient empowerment: a discussion on concepts. *Patient education and counseling, 79*(2), 167–172. https://doi.org/10.1016/j.pec.2009.08.008

Huber, M., Knottnerus, J. A., Green, L., van der Horst, H., Jadad, A. R., Kromhout, D., Leonard, B., Lorig, K., Loureiro, M. I., & van der Meer, J. W. (2011). How should we define health? *BMJ, 343*. https://doi.org/10.1136/bmj.d4163

Huber, M., Vliet, V., Giezenberg M., Winkens, B., Heerkens, Y., Dagnelie, P. C., & Knottnerus, J. A. (2016). Towards a 'patient-centred' operationalisation of the new dynamic concept of health: a mixed methods study. *BMJ Open 6:e010091*. doi:10.1136/bmjopen-2015-010091

Janssen, M. M., Vos, W., & Luijkx, K. G. (2019). Development of an evaluation tool for geriatric rehabilitation care. *BMC geriatrics, 19*(1), 1–10. https://doi.org/10.1186/s12877-019-1213-0

Kane, R. A., Caplan, A. L., Urv-Wong, E. K., Freeman, I. C., Aroskar, M. A., & Finch, M. (1997). Everyday matters in the lives of nursing home residents: wish for and perception of choice and control. *Journal of the American Geriatrics Society, 45*(9), 1086–1093. https://doi.org/10.1111/j.1532-5415.1997.tb05971.x

Kitwood, T. M., & Kitwood, T. M. (1997). *Dementia reconsidered: The person comes first*. Open University Press.

Koren, M. J. (2010). Person-centred care for nursing home residents: The culture-change movement. *Health Affairs, 29*(2), 1–6. https://doi.org/10.1377/hlthaff.2009.0966

Langberg, E. M., Dyhr, L., & Davidsen, A. S. (2019). Development of the concept of patient-centredness–A systematic review. *Patient education and counseling, 102*(7), 1228–1236. https://doi.org/10.1016/j.pec.2019.02.023

Larsson, H., Edberg, A.-K., Bolmsjö, I., & Rämgård, M. (2019). Contrasts in older persons' experiences and significant others' perceptions of existential loneliness. *Nursing ethics, 26*(6), 1623–1637. https://doi.org/10.1177%2F0969733018774828

Leplege, A., Gzil, F., Cammelli, M., Lefeve, C., Pachoud, B., & Ville, I. (2007). Person-centredness: conceptual and historical perspectives. *Disability and rehabilitation, 29*(20–21), 1555–1565. https://doi.org/10.1080/09638280701618661

Leslie, H., & McAllister, M. (2002). The benefits of being a nurse in critical social research practice. *Qualitative Health Research, 12*(5), 700–712. https://doi.org/10.1177%2F104973202129120098

Lette, M., Stoop, A., Lemmens, L. C., Buist, Y., Baan, C. A., & De Bruin, S. R. (2017). Improving early detection initiatives: a qualitative study exploring perspectives of older people and professionals. *BMC geriatrics, 17*(1), 1–13. https://doi.org/10.1186/s12877-017-0521-5

Luijkx, K., van Boekel, L., Janssen, M., Verbiest, M., & Stoop, A. (2020). The academic collaborative center older adults: A description of co-creation between science, care practice and education with the aim to contribute to person-centred care for older adults. *International Journal of Environmental Research and Public Health, 17*(23), 9014. https://doi.org/10.3390/ijerph17239014

Markle-Reid, M., & Browne, G. (2003). Conceptualizations of frailty in relation to older adults. *Journal of advanced nursing, 44*(1), 58–68. https://doi.org/10.1046/j.1365-2648.2003.02767.x

McCance, T., McCormack, B., & Dewing, J. (2011). An exploration of person-centredness in practice. http://dx.doi.org/10.3912/OJIN.Vol16No02Man01

McCormack, B., & McCance, T. (2016). *Person-centred practice in nursing and health care: theory and practice.* John Wiley & Sons.

McCormack, B., & McCance, T. V. (2006). Development of a framework for person-centred nursing. *Journal of advanced nursing, 56*(5), 472–479. https://doi.org/10.1111/j.1365-2648.2006.04042.x

Mead, N., & Bower, P. (2000). Patient-centredness: a conceptual framework and review of the empirical literature. *Social science & medicine, 51*(7), 1087–1110. https://doi.org/10.1016/S0277-9536(00)00098-8

Rathert, C., Wyrwich, M. D., & Boren, S. A. (2013). Patient-centred care and outcomes: a systematic review of the literature. *Medical Care Research and Review, 70*(4), 351–379. https://doi.org/10.1177%2F1077558712465774

Roelofs, T. (2018). *Love, intimacy and sexuality in nursing home residents with dementia: An exploration from multiple perspectives.* [Doctoral dissertation, Tilburg University].

Roelofs, T., Embregts, P., & Luijkx, K. (2017). A person-centred approach to study intimacy and sexuality in residential care facility (RCF) clients with dementia: Methodological considerations and a guide to study design. *Neuropsychological Rehabilitation, 41*(2), 359–373. https://doi.org/https://doi.org/10.3233/NRE-172205

Roelofs, T., Luijkx, K., & Embregts, P. (2018). The attitudes of residential care staff toward the sexuality of residents with dementia: Organizational factors. *Innovation in Aging, 2*(Suppl. 1), 340. https://dx.doi.org/10.1093%2Fgeroni%2Figy023.1249

Roelofs, T. S., Luijkx, K. G., & Embregts, P. J. (2019a). Love, intimacy and sexuality in residential dementia care: A client perspective. *Clinical gerontologist,* 1–11. https://doi.org/10.1080/07317115.2019.1667468

Roelofs, T. S., Luijkx, K. G., & Embregts, P. J. (2019b). Love, intimacy and sexuality in residential dementia care: a spousal perspective. *Dementia, 18*(3), 936–950. https://doi.org/10.1177%2F1471301217697467

Rosenthal, G. (2018). *Interpretive social research: An introduction.* Universitätsverlag Göttingen.

Santana, M. J., Manalili, K., Jolley, R. J., Zelinsky, S., Quan, H., & Lu, M. (2018). How to practice person-centred care: A conceptual framework. *Health Expectations, 21*(2), 429–440. https://doi.org/10.1111/hex.12640

Scheffelaar, A. (2020). *About the client perspective. A participatory study evaluating the quality of long-term care relationships* [Doctoral dissertation, Utrecht University].

Scheffelaar, A., Bos, N., de Jong, M., Triemstra, M., van Dulmen, S., & Luijkx, K. (2020). Lessons learned from participatory research to enhance client participation in long-term care research: a multiple case study. *Research Involvement and Engagement, 6, 1–17.* https://doi.org/10.1186/s40900-020-00187-5

Scheffelaar, A., Janssen, M., & Luijkx, K. (2021). The story as a quality instrument: Developing an instrument for quality improvement based on narratives of older adults receiving long-term care. *International Journal of Environmental Research and Public Health, 18*(5), 2773. https://doi.org/10.3390/ijerph18052773

Schipper, L., Luijkx, K., Meijboom, B., Schalk, R., & Schols, J. (2015a). Access to long-term care: Perceptions and experiences of older Dutch people. *Qual. Ageing Older Adults, 16,* 83–93. https://doi.org/10.1108/QAOA-12-2014-0046

Schipper, L., Luijkx, K. G., Meijboom, B. R., & Schols, J. M. G. A. (2015b). 'It is a completely new world you step into.' How older clients and their representatives experience the operational access to Dutch long-term institutional care. *Journal of Aging Studies, 35,* 211–220. https://doi.org/10.1016/j.jaging.2015.09.002

Shearer, N. B., Fleury, J., Ward, K. A., & O'Brien, A. M. (2012). Empowerment interventions for older adults. *Western journal of nursing research*, *34*(1), 24–51. https://doi.org/10.1177/0193945910377887

Sjögren, K., Lindkvist, M., Sandman, P. O., Zingmark, K., & Edvardsson, D. (2015). To what extent is the work environment of staff related to person-centred care? A cross-sectional study of residential aged care. *Journal of Clinical Nursing, 24*(9–10), 1310–1319. https://doi.org/10.1111/jocn.12734

Tengland, P. A. (2008) Empowerment: A Conceptual Discussion. *Health Care Analysis, 16*(2), 77–96. https://doi-org.tilburguniversity.idm.oclc.org/10.1007/s10728-007-0067-3

Tranzo. n.d. Tilburg University. https://www.tilburguniversity.edu/research/institutes-and-research-groups/tranzo

Triemstra, M., Winters, S., Kool, R. B., & Wiegers, T. A. (2010). Measuring client experiences in long-term care in the Netherlands: a pilot study with the Consumer Quality Index Long-term Care. *BMC health services research, 10*(1), 1–11. http://www.biomedcentral.com/1472–6963/10/95

Tsubouchi, Y., Yorozuya, K., Tainosyo, A., & Naito, Y. (2021). A conceptual analysis of older adults' empowerment in contemporary japanese culture. BMC geriatrics, 21(1), 672. https://doi.org/10.1186/s12877-021-02631-x

Unluer, S. (2012). Being an insider researcher while conducting case study research. *Qualitative Report, 17*, 58. http://www.nova.edu/ssss/QR/QR17/unluer.pdf

Van Campen, C., Sixma, H., Kerssens, J., Peters, L., & Rasker, J. J. (1998). Assessing patients' priorities and perceptions of the quality of health care: the development of the QUOTE-Rheumatic-Patients instrument. *British journal of rheumatology, 37*(4), 362–368. https://doi.org/10.1093/rheumatology/37.4.362

van Corven, C., Bielderman, A., Wijnen, M., Leontjevas, R., Lucassen, P., Graff, M., & Gerritsen, D. L. (2021a). Defining empowerment for older people living with dementia from multiple perspectives: A qualitative study. *International journal of nursing studies, 114*, 103823. https://doi.org/10.1016/j.ijnurstu.2020.103823

van Corven, C., Bielderman, A., Wijnen, M., Leontjevas, R., Lucassen, P., Graff, M., & Gerritsen, D. L. (2021b). Empowerment for people living with dementia: An integrative literature review. *International journal of nursing studies, 124*, 104098. https://doi.org/10.1016/j.ijnurstu.2021.104098

Van der Meide, H., Leget, C., & Olthuis, G. (2013). Giving voice to vulnerable people: the value of shadowing for phenomenological healthcare research. *Medicine, Health Care and Philosophy, 16*(4), 731–737. https://doi.org/10.1007/s11019-012-9456-y

van Diepen, C., Fors, A., Ekman, I., & Hensing, G. (2020). Association between person-centred care and healthcare providers' job satisfaction and work-related health: a scoping review. *BMJ open, 10*(12), e042658. http://dx.doi.org/10.1136/bmjopen-2020–042658

Van Loon, J., Janssen, M., Janssen, B., De Rooij, I. & Luijkx, K. (2022). How staff act and what they experience in relation to the autonomy of older adults with physical impairments living in nursing homes. Nordic Journal of Nursing Research. https://doi.org/10.1177/20571585221126890

Van Loon, J., Janssen, M., Janssen, B., De Rooij, I., & Luijkx, K. (accepted for publication). How older adults with physical impairments maintain their autonomy in nursing homes. *Ageing & Society.*

Van Loon, J., Luijkx, K., Janssen, M., de Rooij, I., & Janssen, B. (2019). Facilitators and barriers to autonomy: A systematic literature review for older adults with physical impairments, living in residential care facilities. *Ageing & Society, 41*(5), 1–30. https://doi.org/10.1017/S0144686X19001557

Verver, D., Merten, H., de Blok, C., & Wagner, C. (2019). A cross sectional study on the different domains of frailty for independent living older adults. *BMC geriatrics, 19*(1), 1–12. https://doi.org/10.1186/s12877-019-1077-3

Vos, W. H., van Boekel, L. C., Janssen, M. M., Leenders, R. T., & Luijkx, K. G. (2020). Exploring the impact of social network change: Experiences of older adults ageing in place. *Health & social care in the community, 28*(1), 116–126. https://doi.org/10.1111/hsc.12846

Wang, C. C., & Geale, S. K. (2015). The power of story: Narrative inquiry as a methodology in nursing research. *International journal of nursing sciences, 2*(2), 195–198. https://doi.org/10.1016/j.ijnss.2015.04.014

Waterschoot, K., Roelofs, T. S., van Boekel, L. C., & Luijkx, K. G. (2022). Care Staff's Sense-making of Intimate and Sexual Expressions of People with Dementia in Dutch Nursing Homes. *Clinical Gerontologist, 45*(4), 1–11. https://doi.org/10.1080/07317115.2021.1928357

White-Chu, E. F., Graves, W. J., Godfrey, S. M., Bonner, A., & Sloane, P. (2009). Beyond the medical model: The culture change revolution in long-term care. *Journal of the American Medical Directors Association, 10*(6), 370–378. https://doi.org/http://dx.doi.org/10.1016/j.jamda.2009.04.004

WHO (2006). *Sexual and Reproductive Health and Research (SRH).* https://www.who.int/teams/sexual-and-reproductive-health-and-research/key-areas-of-work/sexual-health/defining-sexual-health

CHAPTER 8
SILVER EMPOWERMENT: TOWARDS EMPOWERING POLICY, PRACTICE AND RESEARCH

Katrien Steenssens, Tine Van Regenmortel & Jasper De Witte

1.   To expand the meaningful choices for all older people

At its core, the paradigm of empowerment consists of a strengths-based perspective within a relational perspective (see Chapter 1). The strengths-based perspective stands for the acknowledgement and development of the sources of strength within the involved individuals, their personal network (containing individuals and organisations) and their community. Because of their preconditional character (as in their necessary requirements), particular attention is paid to resilience and experiential knowledge as sources of strength. The relational perspective brings to the fore the shared responsibility for empowerment on and among all levels of society, with its accompanying duty to create those conditions that enable empowerment of the target group at hand (see Chapter 1 on 'enabling niches').

The concept of Silver Empowerment expresses an empowerment approach to older people. As such, it counteracts the dominant discourse of 'ageism' that narrowly stresses unproductivity, vulnerability, decline, loss and dependency in the lives of older people. At the same time, it breaks open the widely used concept of 'active ageing', with its tendency to overlook realities of social vulnerabilities, disadvantages and marginalisation. In doing so, Silver Empowerment does not seek to impose a new singular ideal of how older people should live or what their lives should look like. On the contrary, it seeks to expand the meaningful choices on the basis of which all older people are able to maximally gain mastery over their own life. Two intertwined notions here deserve some digression: 'meaningful choices' and 'all older people'.

The notion of 'meaningful choices' here can be a tricky one, as determining a preferred choice depends not only on the choice that is expressed. Indeed, this choice in turn is influenced by many tools consciously or subconsciously used to present a choice, for example, the number and wording of the choices offered (Johnson et al., 2012; Johnson, 2020). A relevant example of a discussion of the influence of 'choice architecture' can be found in a recent study on ageing at the Flemish countryside, more precisely in its critical approach of the often empirically identified, policy influencing preference for 'Ageing In Place' among older people (De Decker et al., 2018). In the context of, among others, the observation that not all neighbourhoods are suitable to age in place (see also Chapter 4), the authors argue that the so-called overall wish of older people to stay put and age in place often is not a matter of 'wanting' but a matter of 'having to' because of a lack of appropriate, affordable and appealing (in other words, meaningful) alternatives. There is no real choice, it is concluded, because for many older persons there is only one (undesirable) alternative: the residential care centre. De Decker et al. (2018) suggest to at least complement measures focused on 'Aging In Place' with measures geared at its counterpart 'Moving In Time' through the creation of a variety of types of neighbourhoods and residences meaningful for *all* older people.

Even more than referring to the inclusive quality of empowerment, the notion of 'all older people', stresses the specific attention that should be paid to vulnerable and 'at-risk' groups among the group of older people as a whole. These groups are identifiable along the lines of personal, social and community characteristics, such as deprivation, migration background, age (younger versus older old), type of personal network and neighbourhood characteristics (see Chapters 3 and 4). Not only do these groups suffer more from the problem at hand (i.e. loneliness and inappropriate housing); at the same time, they tend to be under-represented in (large-scale and long-term) research and many types of policy and practice consultations. Hence, unless specific attention in terms of means and methods is paid to vulnerable groups, the people that suffer the most risk being met with choices that least fit their circumstances, needs and preferences.

2.   Principles to shape empowering policy, practice and research

Through applied research based on the empowerment paradigm and its accompanying theoretical framework (see Chapter 1), a number of guiding principles to develop individual empowering policy, practice and research has started to emerge (Steenssens & Van Regenmortel, 2007a; Steenssens et al., 2009). Using these principles as touchstones during the process of development and implementation of an intervention offers feedback about the extent to which the intervention, in the light of its purpose and execution, can be expected to actually lead to empowerment.

These principles can also be used as quality criteria to evaluate interventions that aim to realise empowerment. This makes sense, as the more one invests in the formative stage (the empowering process), the higher the likelihood of results in the summative stage (empowerment as an outcome or product).

The visual representation of these principles has become known as 'the empowerment flower' (Van Regenmortel, 2015). The heart of this empowerment flower contains the core principles.

Figure 8.1: The core principles of empowerment

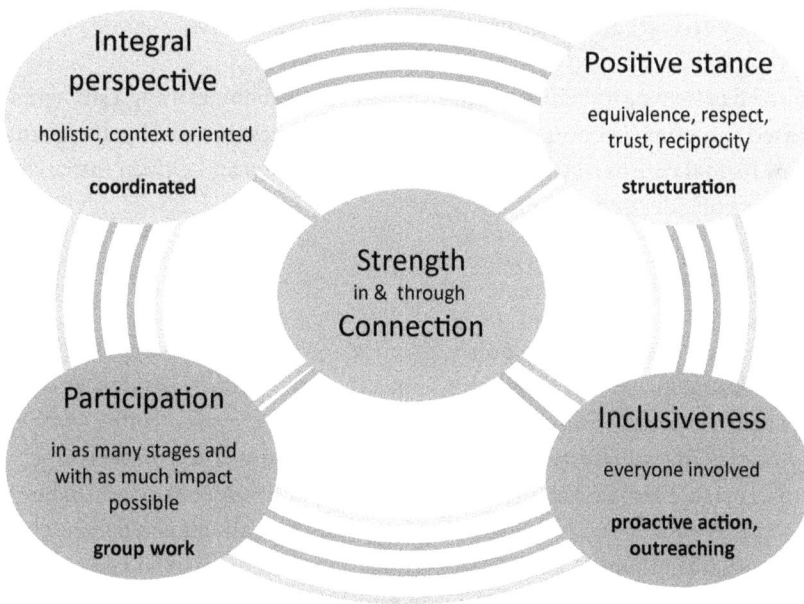

Its visual representation expresses the following:
- The centrality of the dual principle of 'strength in and through connection'.
- The cornerstone principles that contribute to the central principle: a positive stance, participation, inclusiveness and an integral perspective. Each of these principles is accompanied by a specific method of action that can support the empowering implementation of the principle: structuration, proactive action and outreaching, groupwork and coordination.
- The interdependency of all five core principles: they reinforce one another. Hence, respecting all five principles maximises the aimed for strengthening process of empowerment.

2.1. Strengths in and through connection

The first principle of any silver empowering policy, practice or research intervention is characterised by is the central 'strength in and through connection' principle. Chapter 3, on the loneliness among older people, highlights this central principle with its focus on the development of resilience and the importance of social connections.

This principle stems from the basic empowerment assumption that the strengths of any target group (e.g. older persons) can be unlocked, developed and maintained in and through fostering
– the psychological connection of the individuals with themselves and
– the social connection of these individuals with others, the communities they are part of and, ultimately, society at large.

Instead of striving for independence, this process is about realising a strengths-based autonomy in connection. Chapter 5 illustrates this goal by discussing how formal care can strenghten informal caregivers and citizen initiatives for care of older people.

2.2. A positive stance

Second, silver empowering policy, practice and research presuppose a basic attitude and a basic way of working with all stakeholders involved that can be termed as 'a positive attitude'. This positive attitude feeds into all other working principles and is characterised by acknowledging equivalence, mutual respect, trust (presupposing reliability and transparency) and reciprocity (see Chapter 1 on 'the power of giving'). Hereby, it is important that all stakeholders respect each other's autonomy, also (or especially) the autonomy of older persons and their groups at risk: experiencing autonomy motivates, gives support, amplifies the belief in one's own possibilities and stimulates a feeling of belonging.

Depending on the topic at stake – or, in the case of interventions, involving multiple groups, organisations or policy areas – this principle can be reinforced through applying structuration to the intervention (e.g. Van Regenmortel, 2015). Structuration stresses the importance of jointly creating a tailored plan in which the possibilities of the individual and his or her environment are described, goals are put forward and priorities on the short and long term determined. Such a plan not only enhances the understanding of the problem at stake and its solutions, but it also gives those persons a voice and offers structure and insight into what works. Hence, structuration clearly results in more transparency. At the same time, it offers footholds for participation.

2.3. Inclusiveness

A third hallmark of silver empowering policy, practice and research is an inclusive approach: they are geared towards all different identifiable subgroups among older people and all stakeholders involved in realising the intervention. Chapter 4 discusses this principle in the context of neighbourhood-oriented care, which offers a starting point to counteract discrimination or stereotyping of older people; at the same time, however, questions arise concerning the feasibility of neighbourhood-oriented care in deprived neighbourhoods or remote areas.

To include all subgroups and especially those that are most at risk, special attention can be paid to 'outreaching' (Van Doorn et al., 2008; Van Regenmortel, 2008). Outreaching implies going out into the open and contacting people at risk in their own living environment, such as welfare and community centres, public parks or even pubs or tea rooms. The essence lies in making contact and establishing a dialogue, that in turn and over time can become the starting point of psychological and social involvement. For vulnerable citizens, outreaching offers opportunities to reconnect.

Outreaching fits in the broader approach of 'proactive action', a concept referring to solution-oriented measures and initiatives in which the initiating responsibility to take up social rights and services shifts from the beneficiary or recipient to the supply side (Goedemé & Janssens, 2020; Van Gestel et al., 2022).

2.4. Participation

Fourth, empowering policy, practice and research are participatory. The aim is to achieve maximum input and influence, at least from the most directly concerned parties. For Silver Empowerment, this means that older persons should be able to influence an intervention (relating to 'control') based on information and insight (relating to 'critical awareness'). As in any participatory process, the breadth and depth of the actual influence can vary considerably. The breadth of participation relates to the following question: to which stages (ranging from putting a topic on the agenda to the evaluation and adjustment of an intervention) will the participation relate? The depth of participation relates to the following question: how will the participation occur (ranging from consultation for improvement to co-creation) and what impact will it have? Two different examples of participation in research can be found in Chapter 6 concerning empowerment in participatory action research and in Chapter 7 describing the initiation of structural participation of older persons in the Academic Collaborative Center Older Adults.

From an empowerment perspective, the maximum breadth and depth of participation is, of course, preferable, but context and the available time and means often pose challenges to find a balance between the desirable and the attainable level of participation. Without 'reasonable' participation, however, no policy, practice or research intervention can be empowering for the ultimate target group.

With this principle, the notion of 'perceived control' in the definition of empowerment comes into play. It should be clear that this notion relates both to a psychological *sense* of personal control as well as a concern with *actual* social influence, political power and legal rights (Steenssens & Van Regenmortel, 2013). Hence, it integrates perceptions of personal control with behaviours (e.g. participation) to exercise that control.

The empowerment framework and research furthermore suggest that attention should be given to the use of empowering techniques in the participative creation and execution of interventions, such as collaboration and group work (Steenssens & Van Regenmortel, 2007b; Paes, 2010). Through discussion and consideration, these techniques offer participants the chance

- to give and receive a more accurate view on the nature of the subject and possible solutions, which in turn offers starting points for
  - an increase of knowledge,
  - a sharpened critical awareness,
  - the development of self-awareness and an enhanced self-image,
  - the development and use of skills;
- to create more mutual commitment and more involvement with the subject, which in turn offers starting points for
  - the development of mutual understanding and a sense of belonging,
  - the development of collective strengths and qualities,
  - stimulating the motivation and the desire to exert influence.

2.5. Integral perspective

Last but not least, for Silver Empowerment to arise in policy, practice and research, it is equally crucial to take the unique needs of older persons into account based on an integral – meaning holistic and multidisciplinary – perspective. Topics need to be approached with respect to various (physical, psychological, social, financial, etc.) domains, and in a way that the past, present and future are taken into account. This principle clearly comes to the fore in the description of the intervention 'Bras dessus Bras dessous' in Chapter 3.

By listening to older persons and by focusing on the 'insider perspective', researchers can gain insight into the personal meaning older persons attribute to the topic at hand. Such 'experiential knowledge' allows for the creation, adjustment or evaluation of interventions to their specific needs and hence enhances their participation (Gobbens, 2017). Furthermore, an integral perspective also pays attention to important social, structural and physical barriers in the environment, such as the accessibility of services, initiatives and public transportation (see Chapter 1).

This principle of an integral perspective will often necessitate the involvement of multiple (domain-specific) stakeholders. It is then recommended to pay attention to the coordination of the intervention, meaning that one actor manages and coordinates all aspects of the intervention. In this regard, it is important to jointly formulate goals and work in partnership to realise a collective strategy.

3.   Going the extra mile

The discussion of the interrelated core principles to develop, implement and evaluate empowering interventions – be it in policy, practice or research – makes it clear that good intentions alone will not suffice to accomplish the aimed for strengthening process of Silver Empowerment. One will have to be willing to go the extra mile to maximally reach and involve all older people, pay attention to and develop all their strengths, stimulate their mutual connections and guarantee their impact. This 'extra mile' consists of applying the necessary means and methods to assure that no one is left behind and that meaningful choices are available for everyone. As such, Silver Empowerment invites policymakers, caregivers and researchers to combine a strong belief in democratic values with a sustained effort to uncover and involve everyone's strengths.

References

De Decker, P., Vandekerckhove, B., Volckaert, E., Wellens, C., Schillebeeckx, E., & De Luyck, N. (2018). *Ouder worden op het Vlaamse platteland. Over wonen, zorg en ruimtelijk ordenen in dun bevolkte gebieden* [Growing older in the Flemish rural areas. About living, care and spatial planning in scarsely populated areas]. Garant.

Gobbens, R. (2017). *Health and Well-Being of Frail Elderly. Towards Interventions that Really Count!* Inholland University of Applied Sciences.

Goedemé, T., & Janssens, J. (2020). The concept and measurement of non-take-up: An overview, with a focus on the non-take-up of social benefits. http://dx.doi.org/10.13140/RG.2.2.24515.43048

Johnson, E. J. (2020). *The elements of choice. Why the way we decide matters.* Riverhead Books.

Johnson, E. J., Shu, S. B., Dellaert, B. G. C., Fox, C., Goldstein, D., Häubl, G., Larrick, R., Payne, J., Peters, E., Schkade, D., Wansink, B., & Weber, E. (2012). Beyond nudges: Tools of a choice architecture. *Marketing Letters* 23(2), pp. 487–504. https://doi.org/10.1007/s11002-012-9186-1

Paes, M. (2010). Steun voor processen van onderop. Over beleid en participatie van kwetsbare burgers [Support for bottom-up processes. About policy and participation of vulnerable citizens]. In T. Van Regenmortel (Ed.), *Empowerment en participatie van kwetsbare burgers. Ervaringskennis als kracht* [Empowerment and participation of vulnerable citizens. Expertise by experience as strength] (pp. 135–150). SWP Publishers.

Steenssens, K., & Van Regenmortel, T. (2007a). *Empowerment Barometer. Process evaluation of empowerment in neighbourhood-based activation projects.* HIVA – KU Leuven.

Steenssens, K., & Van Regenmortel, T. (2007b). *De Wissel-Werking verbeteren. Verbeteronderzoek met peer research in de bijzondere jeugdzorg* [Ameliorating the Wissel-practice. Research for improvement with peer research in youth care]. HIVA – KU Leuven.

Steenssens, K., & Van Regenmortel, T. (2013). *Grondslagen en uitdagingen voor het meten van empowerment* [Foundations and challenges for measuring empowerment]. Vlaams Armoedesteunpunt.

Steenssens, K., Demeyer, B., & Van Regenmortel, T., (2009). *Conceptnota empowerment en activering in armoedesituaties* [Concept note empowerment and activation in situations of poverty]. HIVA – KU Leuven.

van Doorn L., van Etten Y., & Gademan M. (2008). *Outreachend werken. Handboek voor werkers in de eerste lijn.* [Outreach work. Manual for workers in the first line] Coutinho.

Van Gestel, R., Goedemé, T., Janssens, J., Lefevere, E., & Lemkens, R. (2022). Improving Take-Up by Reaching Out to Potential Beneficiaries. Insights from a Large-Scale Field Experiment in Belgium. *Journal of Social Policy*, 1–21. https://doi.org/10.1017/S004727942100088X

Van Regenmortel T. (2008). *Zwanger van empowerment. Een uitdagend kader voor sociale inclusie en moderne zorg* [Pregnant with empowerment. A challenging framework for social inclusion and modern care. Inaugural lecture]. Fontys Hogescholen.

Van Regenmortel, T. (2015). Empowerment en (maatschappelijk) opvoeden [Empowerment and (social) education)]. In C. Gravesteijn & M. Aartsma (Eds.), *Meer dan opvoeden. Perspectieven op het werken met ouders* [More than educating. Perspectives on working with parents] (pp. 51–64). Coutinho.

AFTERWORD

Tine Van Regenmortel & Jasper De Witte

Empowerment is the overarching perspective of this book. On the one hand, this paradigm challenges the stereotypical image that older people are, by definition, vulnerable and fragile; on the other hand, there is ample recognition of vulnerability and the need for care. Therefore, we do not go along with a discourse of successful ageing versus non-successful ageing in which older people who need less care are considered more successful than those who need more care. Silver Empowerment aims to include older people and give them a clear voice and say in their care process and in policy, and it simultaneously addresses existing structures that disempower older persons. Silver Empowerment appeals to the strengths and competences of older persons but does not imply a call for further individualisation and self-responsibility whereby the cost of care has to be kept as low as possible and every citizen has to maximise their economic return. It avoids one-sidedly blaming the victim or the system, and it instead emphasises a shared responsibility for exclusion, whereby individuals, organisations and the system all have agency to counteract exclusion within certain boundaries. For this, connections to others and to society, based on relationships of trust, are of the utmost importance.

Every older person deserves to age in dignity and with a high quality of life. Unfortunately, the way the care and support system for older persons is structured insufficiently values their strengths and respects their dignity. It is crucial to take on a person-centered, inclusive and holistic approach with regard to the care and support system for older persons, and in regard to their lives in general. In large-scale institutions, things are, for example, too often done *for* older persons instead of *with* or *by* them. Further, the dominant negative image of ageing also reinforces ageism, discrimination based on old age. For a long time, psychological support in Belgium was, for example, reimbursed for all age groups except for older persons, although many older persons would also benefit from such support. This example demonstrates that society and policymakers too often interpret older persons as unproductive and passive, and they focus too much on the medical side of the story and forget to sufficiently consider psychosocial needs.

Empowerment concurs with various current ubiquitous policy ideas such as deinstitutionalisation, person-centered care, ageing in place, caring neighbourhoods and active ageing. However, in contrast to some of these concepts, empowerment specifically emphasises the importance of having sufficient attention for social inequality, vulnerability and disadvantage and not imposing a singular ideal of how older people should live (e.g. 'active'). Rather, empowerment focuses on expanding meaningful choices through which older people can gain more mastery over their own lives. This framework emphasises the importance of participation, reciprocity in relations and inclusiveness, and it can be used to guide a wide variety of empowering interventions on the individual, relational and structural levels. The lifeworld of community-dwelling older persons who are confronted with age-related adversities (e.g. health and mobility limitations, decreased social networks) increasingly revolves around their own home and neighbourhood. In this respect, empowerment stresses the importance to adapt individual and environmental characteristics to their individual needs, so that they can fully participate in society, sustain a satisfying social network and safeguard their quality of life. Indeed, the place where older persons live matters and can hinder or stimulate their mobility, participation and general well-being. It is, for example, important to provide sufficient psychological support (to learn to accept vulnerabilities that cannot be overcome) and to take away the structural barriers that impede older persons to participate, for example, by adjusting pavements and public transportation so that they are wheelchair friendly or by providing accessible and affordable individual transportation for older persons who are unable to use public transportation. Further, it is equally crucial to provide sufficient meeting places, green spaces, local shops and public services in the local neighbourhood or, in some cases, to stimulate 'moving in time' in order to age in place.

Further, this book shows that loneliness is one of the most important indicators for well-being and that it is accompanied by enormous economic and opportunity costs for individuals, families and society in general (e.g. related to health and care expenditure). Therefore, this subject merits necessary attention from policymakers, social organisations, individuals and society in large. However, although loneliness is a complex phenomenon that needs a wide range of interventions on the micro, meso and macro levels, often an all-encompassing vision is lacking, and too little emphasis is in particular placed on preventive measures. In this respect, empowerment is useful to improve loneliness interventions because it starts from a strengths-based perspective that focuses on resilience, strengths and connections. This is especially important for older persons who are too often unjustly considered to be vulnerable and fragile, which negatively affects their possibilities to create and maintain social relations. Based on the empowering principles (i.e. strength and connection, integral perspective, positive stance, participation and inclusiveness), loneliness interventions can be developed that reinforce the strengths and connections of older persons: health promotion, stimulating general resilience, reimbursing psychological support, taking away structural and financial barriers to participation, stimulating 'the power of giving' and 'moving in time'.

The empowerment framework is also useful to guide 'caring neighbourhood' initiatives, since the place where people live matters in old age and can both stimulate empowerment and disempowerment. In this respect, the inclusive view behind neighbourhood-oriented care implies that caring neighbourhoods should not start from a deficit view but rather seek transversality and mutual support in the community by focusing on the strengths and connections of people. Such a strengths-based approach not only counteracts ageism, but it also stimulates social cohesion and weak ties in a neighbourhood. Moreover, empowerment considers the vulnerabilities of individuals and neighbourhoods (e.g. limits to mutual support by neighbours, not all neighbourhoods are good places to age well), which is crucial to avoid reinforcing existing inequalities or establishing new ones with those 'caring neighbourhood' initiatives. Further, with respect to the triadic care between client, professional and informal caregiver, professionals can use empowering principles to create enabling conditions that enhance collaboration and mutual support. Indeed, stable connections between this care triad that are based on trust are prerequisites for a positive outcome. For this, policy should be directed at supporting and empowering informal caregivers and consider them as co-experts 'with their own specific needs'. Hereby, it is again important to take some pitfalls into account. Such initiatives could reinforce inequalities or establish new ones because both neighbourly support and citizen initiatives are often reserved for those who are better off, and vulnerable citizens often have more difficulties appealing to informal care networks. Also, policymakers and professionals should not take over these bottom-up, informal initiatives but rather respect their informal, often organic nature (which is often their actual power) by acting on the basis of equity as an empowering method of action.

Further, participatory action research with older persons can both lead to empowerment and disempowerment. Therefore, it is crucial to reflect on normative and ethically challenging situations and to consider the specific situation of the older person (experiences, desires, capacities) to avoid disempowerment. For this, one has to develop oneself as a reflexive practitioner and consider individual emotions and hardships when collaboratively working out the right course of action. By creating enabling conditions during such research, more instrumental and proportional knowledge can be co-created, which is empowering for all actors involved. Similarly, in academic collaborative centres where scientific knowledge and societal impact is co-created by older persons, professionals and researchers, it is crucial to give voice to older persons and professionals and involve both actors in an equitable way during this process as empowering methods of action.

Silver Empowerment is based on five core principles: strengthening in and through connecting, an integral perspective, a positive stance, participation and inclusiveness. These principles form a useful guide to develop, implement, evaluate and improve the care and support system for older persons – be it in policy, practice or research. Therefore, it is not just another rhetoric but, on the contrary, it requires a different way of thinking and acting and a different design for care and policy. Not only words but also actions are needed to put Silver Empowerment into practice. Let us start together to deal with this challenge and strive for a warm, inclusive and age-friendly society.

ABOUT THE AUTHORS

Jasper De Witte has a PhD in sociology (KU Leuven), and he works as a research expert on inclusion and care for socially vulnerable groups at HIVA – KU Leuven, where he is active in the group Social and Economic Policy & Social Inclusion. His research focuses on socially vulnerable groups such as persons with limitations, minors who receive youth care, homeless persons and people who live in poverty. Between 2018 and 2022, he conducted research on vulnerable older persons for the be.Source University Chair Empowerment of Underprivileged Elderly. Currently, he is coordinator of the Strategic Basic Research (SBO) project of the Research Foundation – Flanders (FWO) about the impact of the neighbourhood where people live on feelings of loneliness in Flanders, Belgium.

Professor **Tine Van Regenmortel**, doctor in psychology, is head of the Social and Economic Policy & Social Inclusion Research Group at HIVA – KU Leuven. She is an international expert on empowerment and inclusion of vulnerable groups. She teaches about 'Empowerment: theory, practice and (evaluation) research' in the Master of Social Work and Social Policy at the KU Leuven Faculty of Social Sciences. She is also Professor of Social Work at Tranzo at the Tilburg University, Tilburg School of Social and Behavioral Sciences (the Netherlands), where she leads the Academic Collaborative Centre Social Work. She supervises several PhDs on inclusion and vulnerability, and she is holder of the KU Leuven be.source Chair Empowerment of Underprivileged Elderly. Finally, she is Promotor of the Strategic Basic Research (SBO) project of the Research Foundation – Flanders (FWO) about loneliness and the influence of neighbourhood and environment.

Leen Heylen is a sociologist. She earned her PhD in 2011 with a dissertation on the risk factors for social and emotional loneliness in old age. Since 2011, she works as a senior researcher at Thomas More University of Applied Sciences (Flanders, Belgium). At Thomas More, she conducts evidence- and practice-based research. She works on the topics of loneliness, informal care, neighbourhood-oriented care and caring neighbourhoods.

Benedicte De Koker has a degree in sociology and a PhD in social sciences, specifically in social work. Benedicte is head of the research centre 360° Care and Well-being at HOGENT. The centre focuses on practice-oriented multidisciplinary research to enhance quality and sustainability of care. Benedicte also works as a lecturer in the programme of occupational therapy, where she teaches research methods, political reasoning and occupational therapy from international perspectives. Benedicte has extensive expertise on the topic of informal caregiving. Her dissertation, defended at the University of Antwerp in 2018, examines the role and experiences of informal caregivers in Flanders in the context of community care.

Dimitri Mortelmans is Professor in Sociology at the Faculty of Social Sciences of the University of Antwerp (Belgium). He is head of the Centre for Population, Family and Health. His research concentrates on family sociology and the sociology of labour. He has published on divorce, new constituted families, gendered labour careers and work-life balance. In 2022, he acquired an Employee Retention Credit Advanced Grant on singleness in the life course (Singleton project). He is also the main author of the *Step in Statistics* book series (in Dutch) (Acco, since 2010). On qualitative methodology, he has published the *Handbook of Qualitative Research Methods* (Acco, 2020) and *Qualitative Analysis* with NVivo (Acco, 2017). In demography, he co-edited *Changing Family Dynamics and Demographic Evolution. The Family Kaleidoscope* (Edward Elgar, 2016), *Lone Parenthood in the Life Course* (Springer, 2017), *Divorce in Europe* (Springer, 2020) and *Shared Physical Custody* (Springer, 2021).

Anja Declercq studied applied economics and sociology, and she has a PhD in sociology. She is a Professor at KU Leuven, Faculty of Social Sciences (sociological research unit), the promotor-coordinator of the Policy Research Centre for Well-being, Public Health and the Family and a project leader (director from 1 October 2022 on) at LUCAS – Centre for Care Research and Consultancy. Her research interests include the organisation of care, quality of care and the quality of life of people who need or give care and support, and the analysis of societal changes that have an impact on care and care systems.

Tineke Abma is Professor 'Participation of older people' at Leiden University Medical Center, and she is Executive Director of Leyden Academy on Vitality and Ageing in Leiden. In 2010, she was appointed as an Endowed Chair in the field of client participation in elderly care. She is a member of the International Collaboration for Participatory Health Research (ICPHR) and Director of the International Longevity Centre (ILC) NL that is part of ILC Global Alliance. Abma has published extensively in the fields of patient participation, participatory action research and responsive evaluation. Her work has been awarded for its social value impact. New books include *Evaluation for a Caring Society* (JAI Press, 2018) and *Participatory Research for Health and Social Well-Being* (Springer, 2019).

Elena Bendien is a social scientist, social and cultural gerontologist, senior researcher and lecturer at Leyden Academy on Vitality and Ageing (the Netherlands). Her expertise lies in the transdisciplinary field of ageing studies, with a focus on life course perspective, life review, ageism and the intersection between gender and ageing. She specialises in intersectional analysis and participatory action research with older co-researchers. Dr. Bendien is a representative of the International Longevity Centres (ILC) the Netherlands in the working group of ILC Women and Ageing.

Susan Woelders is senior researcher at Leyden Academy on Vitality and Ageing in Leiden, the Netherlands. She has an MSc degree in Organizational Science (Culture, Organization and Management). Woelders finished her PhD, entitled *Power-full Patient Participation*, at the Department of Medical Humanities, VU University Medical Center in Amsterdam. Her research focuses on the participation of diverse patient and client groups, including older people, through dialogue in long-term care organisations and research approaches.

Meriam Janssen is employed as research broker and senior researcher at the Academic Collaborative Center Older Adults of Tranzo, Tilburg University. She has an educational background in Health Sciences. Until 2017, she worked in the area of public health, including active ageing. She has experience in combining working in practice of public health and conducting scientific research, and her areas of expertise are qualitative research and autonomy for older adults.

Katrien Luijkx is employed as professor to the Academic Collaborative Centre Older Adults of Tranzo, Tilburg University. She has an educational background in interdisciplinary social sciences and aims to contribute to person-centred care for older adults using science. Therefore, it is important to study the perspective of frail older adults themselves. Characteristic for her work is co-creation with different stakeholders during the process of knowledge creation and translation of research findings into care practice. The research of Luijkx and her PhD students is related to care practice.

Aukelien Scheffelaar is employed as research broker and senior researcher at the Academic Collaborative Center Older Adults of Tranzo, Tilburg University. Dr Scheffelaar has an educational background in interdisciplinary social sciences. Her areas of expertise concern participatory research and qualitative methods for quality research in long-term care.

Annerieke Stoop is employed as research broker and senior researcher at the Academic Collaborative Center Older Adults of Tranzo, Tilburg University. Her PhD project focused on integrated care for older people. She has an educational background in International Development Studies and Health Sciences. Her areas of interest are qualitative research and family caregiving.

Jozef Pacolet has a PhD in Economics, and he is Emeritus Professor with formal duties in the group Social and Economic Policy & Social Inclusion at HIVA – KU Leuven, of which he was head from 1983 until 2017. Since 1983, he has conducted research on the relation between the economy and the welfare state, focusing on the relation between the economy, ageing and social protection and the financing of the social security in Belgium and on the European level. In his research, special attention is given to the system of pensions, healthcare and long-term care.

Gregorio Rodríguez Cabrero has a PhD in economics, and he is Emeritus Professor at the University of Alcalá, where he was Dean of the Faculty of Economics. He has been a national expert of the European Commission of independent experts on social inclusion (2008–2014) and European Social Policy Network (ESPN) (2014–2022). His main fields of research are social protection and social inclusion, welfare state comparative analysis, non-profit sector and social economy, and longevity and long-term care. He coordinated in 2011 and 2022 the evaluation of the Spanish long-term care system.

Simón Sosvilla-Rivero has a BA in Economics from Universidad de La Laguna (1984), an MSc in Economics from Universitat Autònoma de Barcelona (1986), an MSc in Economics from London School of Economics (1987) and a PhD in Economics from the University of Birmingham (1990). He is currently a Professor of Economic Analysis at Universidad Complutense de Madrid, a Senior Research Fellow at the Complutense Institute for Economic Analysis (ICAE) and a Research Fellow at the Riskcenter (IREA – Universitat de Barcelona). His research interests include time-series analysis, macroeconometric modelling, international finance, the welfare state and European integration.

Katrien Steenssens is a sociological research expert at the research group Social and Economic Policy & Social Inclusion of HIVA – KU Leuven. In her research, she focuses on social exclusion and integration, mainly through the use of qualitative research methods. Within the empowerment framework, she has been researching poverty and activation towards the labour market, proactive action to reduce non-take-up of social benefits, homelessness in Flanders, residential youth care and the development and use of empowerment evaluation instruments.

www.ingramcontent.com/pod-product-compliance
Lightning Source LLC
Chambersburg PA
CBHW071103280326

41928CB00051B/2767